MARXIST GOVERNMENTS

A World Survey

Volume 1   Albania – The Congo

Also edited by Bogdan Szajkowski

MARXIST GOVERNMENTS

DOCUMENTS IN COMMUNIST AFFAIRS – 1977

DOCUMENTS IN COMMUNIST AFFAIRS – 1979

DOCUMENTS IN COMMUNIST AFFAIRS – 1980

MARXIST GOVERNMENTS

A World Survey

Volume 1   Albania – The Congo

Edited by

BOGDAN SZAJKOWSKI
Lecturer in Politics and Comparative Communism
University College, Cardiff

St. Martin's Press   New York

All rights reserved. For information write:
St. Martin's Press, Inc., 175 Fifth Avenue, New York, N.Y. 10010
Printed in Hong Kong
First published in the United States of America in 1981

Volume 1   Albania – The Congo   ISBN 0–312–51857–9
Volume 2   Cuba – Mongolia   ISBN 0–312–51858–7
Volume 3   Mozambique – Yugoslavia   ISBN 0–312–51859–5

Library of Congress Cataloging in Publication Data

Main entry under title:

Marxist governments.

    Includes indexes.
    CONTENTS: v. 1.   Albania – The Congo.
– v. 2.   Cuba – Mongolia. – v. 3.   Mozambique – Yugoslavia.
    1.   Communist state.   2.   Communist countries –
Politics and government.   I.   Szajkowski, Bogdan.
JC474.M3512   1980   320.9′171′7   79–25471

FOR MARTHA

Contents

List of Maps

List of Figures

List of Tables

Preface

The growth in the number, global significance and ideological and political impact of countries ruled by parties which subscribe to the principles of Marxism-Leninism has presented students of politics with an increasing challenge. In meeting this challenge, Western commentators have put forward a dazzling profusion of terms, models, programmes and varieties of interpretation. It is against the background of this profusion that the present comprehensive survey of the Marxist-Leninist regimes is offered.

This collection, in three volumes, is envisaged as a textbook and to some extent reference book on the governments and politics of these states. Each of the monographs in these volumes was prepared by a specialist on the country concerned. Thus, twenty-five scholars from all over the world have contributed monographs which are based on first-hand knowledge. The geographical diversity of the authors, combined with the fact that as a group they represent many disciplines of social science, gives their individual analyses, and the collection as a whole, an additional and unique dimension. Each volume contains short biographical notes on the relevant authors.

The collection, which is organised alphabetically by country, is preceded by two theoretical chapters. The first, 'The Communist Movement: from Monolith to Polymorph', by outlining the history and development of the study of the Marxist-Leninist regimes, suggests that a radically new approach be taken to the study of the politics of communism. The second chapter, on the meaning of a Marxist regime, examines the theoretical parameters of the collection.

Three regimes have had to be omitted. In the case of the Democratic Republic of Afghanistan and the Democratic Republic of Madagascar, this was more for reasons of insufficient data than because their Marxist-Leninist orthodoxy was in dispute. Also excluded from the analysis is the communist government of San Marino, which was voted into office when the preparation of this collection was in its final stages.

It is hoped in subsequent editions to include chapters on the communist-led state governments in India, the communist parties' experiences in post-war West European governments, and the communist-led local councils in Italy, France, the Federal Republic of Germany and Portugal.

Each of the twenty-five scholars who contributed to this collection was asked to analyse such topics as the governmental structure, including the constitutional framework, the system of elections, the ruling party – variously called communist, labour, socialist or workers' – other mass organisations, party–state relations, the economy, domestic policies and foreign relations, as well as any features peculiar to the country and/or party under discussion. The exceptions to the pattern are the chapters on the USSR and China, where the wealth of material available could not be satisfactorily presented within the available space, and the article on Ethiopia, where the Marxist-Leninist experiment is still very new and does not yet permit extensive analysis.

Every effort has been made by the contributors to compile and present data on party and mass-organisation membership, electoral returns and multiple office-holding, except in the few cases where no such data exist.

Perhaps a word should be added about the chapter on China, a country which during the writing of this collection has been in considerable turmoil. In this case it was thought that the format and approach adopted by Dr Bill Brugger would prove most useful not only as a background to, but also as an explanation of, the on-going changes in China. His chapter was written in 1978 but includes some economic material issued in 1979, which he found able to insert at proof stage. While the collection was being printed, China's State Council decided to use the Chinese phonetic *Pinyin* alphabet, to standardise the romanisation of Chinese names of persons and places. This decision was announced at the beginning of December 1978 with effect from January 1979. Unfortunately it has not proved possible to incorporate these changes in this edition, and throughout the collection the Wade–Giles system is used for names of persons and places.

In the preparation of this collection I have been given help by many people, some of whom should be singled out for special acknowledgement.

I am most grateful for the help afforded me by the Hon. Dr Abdulai Conteh, Minister for Foreign Affairs, Sierra Leone; Dr Thomas G. Hart of the Swedish Institute of International Affairs; Dr Tom Keenoy of University College, Cardiff; Dr Gary Troeller of the United Nations High Commission for Refugees; and Mr Richard Hodder-Williams of the University of Bristol.

I am grateful to all the contributors. Special thanks are due to Mr

Michael Waller, Dr Ronald Hill, Ms Laura Summers, Professor Peter Schwab, Mr Fred Singleton and Dr Leslie Holmes.

Very special thanks are also due to Mrs Val Dobie for her help with the manuscripts, to Mr Tom Dawkes for his help in compiling the indexes, and to Mr Michael Breaks, the Social Science Librarian at University College, Cardiff, for his advice. I would also like to thank Miss Valery Brooks and her colleagues at Macmillan for their help in seeing these books through the press.

I am also very grateful to Mrs Jeanne Moorsom, whose house, The Coppice, proved to be the perfect place in which to write and was a most welcome refuge from the noise of my otherwise lovable children.

All the maps in this collection have been superbly drawn by Mrs Margaret Millen of the Department of Geology of University College, Cardiff; her patience and endeavour were very much appreciated.

Above all, my very special gratitude goes to my wife, Martha, whose encouragement and help have been invaluable throughout the many months of work on these volumes.

4 January 1979   BOGDAN SZAJKOWSKI
Dinas Powis

List of Abbreviations

Note: Owing to their great familiarity, abbreviations such as km., vol., EEC, US and USSR are omitted from this list.

ASEAN   Association of South-east Asian States
BAU   Bulgarian Agrarian Union
BCP   Bulgarian Communist Party
BWSDP   Bulgarian Workers' Social Democratic Party
CCR   Conseil Communale de la Revolution [Commune Revolutionary Council] (Benin)
CEAP   Comité d'État d'Administration de la Province [State Committee for Provincial Administration] (Benin)
CFA   Communauté Financière Africaine [African Monetary Community]
CIA   Central Intelligence Agency (USA)
CMP   Comité Militaire du Parti [Party Military Committee] (Congo)
Comecon   Council for Mutual Economic Assistance
Cominform   Communist Information Bureau
Comintern   Communist International
CPC   Communist Party of China
CPPCC   Chinese People's Political Consultative Conference
CPR   Conseil Provincial de la Révolution [Provincial Revolutionary Council] (Benin)
CPSU   Communist Party of the Soviet Union
CRAD   Comité Révolutionnaire d'Administration du District [Revolutionary Committee for District Administration] (Benin)
CRD   Conseil Révolutionnaire de District [District Revolutionary Council] (Benin)
CRL   Conseil Révolutionnaire Local [Local Revolutionary Council] (Benin)
CSC   Confédération Syndicale Congolaise [Congolese Confederation of Labour]

CUS	Comité de l'Unité Syndicale [Labour Unity Committee] (Benin)
DISA	Directorate of Information and Security of Angola
EPLA	[People's Army for the Liberation of Angola]
FAPLA	[People's Armed Forces for the Liberation of Angola]
FDRCO	[Democratic Front for Congolese Resistance]
FNLA	[National Front for the Liberation of Angola]
FRG	Federal Republic of Germany
GDR	German Democratic Republic
JMNR	Jeunesse du Mouvement National de la Révolution [Youth of the National Revolutionary Movement] (Congo)
KONARE	[Committee for National Liberation] (Albania)
MNR	[National Revolutionary Movement] (Congo)
MPLA	Movimento Popular de Libertação de Angola [Popular Movement for the Liberation of Angola]
OAU	Organisation of African Unity
OCAM	Organisation Commune Africaine et Malgache [Mutual Organisation of Africa and Madagascar]
OMA	[Organisation of the Angolan Woman]
OPA	[Organisation of the Angolan Pioneer]
PCT	Parti Congolais du Travail (Congolese Labour Party)
PIDE	[International Police for the Defence of the State] (Angola)
PLA	Party of Labour of Albania
PLUA	[Party for the United Struggle of the Africans of Angola]
PRPB	Parti de la Révolution Populaire du Benin [People's Revolutionary Party of Benin]
SDR	Special drawing rights (International Monetary Fund)
SECCR	Sécrétariat Exécutif du Conseil Communal de la Revolution [Executive Secretariat for the Commune Revolutionary Council] (Benin)
UDEAC	Union Douanière et Économique de l'Afrique Centrale [Central African Customs and Economic Union]
UDI	Unilateral declaration of independence
UGEEC	Union Génèrale des Élèves et Étudiants Congolaise [General Union of Congolese Pupils and Students]
UJSC	Union de la Jeunesse Socialiste Congolaise [Congolese Young Socialists' Union]
UNITA	[National Union for the Total Independence of Angola]
UNTA	[National Union of Angolan Workers]

URFC	Union Révolutionnaire des Femmes Congolaises [Congolese Women's Revolutionary Union]
WTO	Warsaw Treaty Organisation

Notes on the Editor
and Contributors

BOGDAN SZAJKOWSKI was educated in Eastern Europe and the Centre for Russian and East European Studies at Birmingham University. He conducted his postgraduate research at King's College, Cambridge, and St Antony's College, Oxford. Subsequently he was appointed to a lectureship in Comparative Communism at the Australian National University in Canberra. He has also taught at University College, Dublin, and is now Lecturer in Politics and Comparative Communism at University College, Cardiff. His writings on contemporary communist affairs have appeared in professional journals and the press, and he has extensive broadcasting experience. He is the editor of the annual volume *Documents in Communist Affairs*.

BILL BRUGGER received his undergraduate and postgraduate education at the School of Oriental and African Studies, University of London. From 1964 he taught for two years at the Peking Second Foreign Languages Institute. Later he worked with the Contemporary China Institute, University of London. In 1972 Dr Brugger was appointed lecturer at the Flinders University of South Australia. He is the author of *Democracy and Organization in the Chinese Industrial Enterprise 1948–53* (Cambridge: Cambridge University Press, 1975) and *Contemporary China* (London: Croom Helm, 1977), and editor of *China: The Impact of the Cultural Revolution* (London: Croom Helm, 1978). Dr Brugger is at present Reader in Politics at the Flinders University of South Australia.

SAMUEL DECALO obtained his BA in 1961 from the University of Ottawa, and MA and PhD (1970) from the University of Pennsylvania, all in political science. He has taught at several American universities and is currently Professor and Head of the Department of Politics and Administration at the University College of Botswana. He has written extensively on the politics and international relations of Africa and the

Middle East. Among these publications the most recent is *Coups and Army Rule in Africa* (New Haven, Conn.: Yale University Press, 1976).

NEIL HARDING was educated at University College, Swansea, and the London School of Economics. Since 1965 he has taught in the Department of Politics and the Centre for Russian and East European Studies at University College, Swansea. He has written articles on socialist thought and on Lenin and is the author of *Lenin's Political Thought*, 2 vols (London: Macmillan, 1977 and 1979) and *Marxism in Russia* (London: Macmillan, 1979).

LESLIE HOLMES was educated at the Universities of Hull and Essex, where he obtained his MA and PhD in political science. He spent most of the period between 1974 and 1976 conducting research at the Free University of Berlin and the Universities of Moscow and Leningrad. In 1976 he was appointed to a lectureship at the University College of Wales, Aberystwyth. Articles by him have appeared in the *Times Literary Supplement, Interstate* and elsewhere. Dr Holmes is the author of *The Politics of Industrial Association Development in the USSR and GDR*, to be published shortly by Cambridge University Press, and is currently writing a book on comparative communism. He is at present Lecturer in Politics and Governments of Eastern Europe at the University of Kent at Canterbury.

MICHAEL WALLER read Literae Humaniores at Corpus Christi College, Oxford, and followed this with a further Honours degree, this time in Russian. Thereafter he spent a year at the State University of Leningrad studying the impact of revolution on the Russian language. His interest in the rhetoric of the communist movement as a whole led to the publication of his *Language of Communism* (London: Bodley Head) in 1972. A further book, *The Leaders and the Led: the Idea of Democratic Centralism in its Origins and Evolution* is soon to be published. Articles by him have appeared in *Soviet Studies* and *Government and Opposition*. He was responsible for planning the Department of Russian and Soviet Studies at the University of Lancaster, before taking up a post in the Government Department of Manchester University where he now teaches.

   He serves on the Editorial Board of *Documents in Communist Affairs* and on the Committee of the National Association for Soviet and East European Studies.

MICHAEL WALLER read Literae Humaniores at Corpus Christi College, seven years on the editorial staff of *The Times* of London, latterly as

Africa correspondent. From November 1975 to February 1978 he worked in Angola with the Government of the People's Republic of Angola and in radio and television services. His publications include *Black Man's Burden Revisited* (London: Allison and Busby, 1974), *Politics in the Organisation of African Unity* (London: Methuen, 1976), and translations of Angolan literature in Portuguese for the Heinemann's African Writers series. He is at present writing a political study of the first years of independence of Angola.

1 The Communist Movement: from Monolith to Polymorph

MICHAEL WALLER and BOGDAN SZAJKOWSKI

If spirits can be assigned geographic or cultural characteristics, the spectre of communism which, for Marx, was haunting Europe in 1848 was itself European. It was an emanation of the circumstances of early industrialism in that part of the world where the industrial revolution was taking place. It spoke (or got a variety of mortal voices to speak for it) in European languages about a European predicament.

By the turn of the century the spectre had learned Russian, and, at the periphery of Europe, it was speaking through the mouth and pen of the Russian Lenin about a double predicament: still about that of European industrialism, but also now about the predicament of another world, which was being economically and politically penetrated by the advanced industrial nations, whose military resources were now not only overwhelming, but also more mobile in effecting and ensuring this penetration.

Yet another three-quarters of a century and the spectre is no longer only European, nor is it haunting only Europe. It is, however, despite its linguistic virtuosity and cultural adaptability, Marxist, in a fundamental sense which is spelled out in the second chapter of this volume. Though it speaks still about the same double predicament, the balance has clearly shifted. It was in Chinese that the spectre first spoke unequivocally of the encirclement of the world's cities by the world's countryside.

The imagery of the preceding paragraphs may not appeal to pragmatic readers. It has, however, a certain value for understanding what communism has been about for the last 150 years and also quite simply for understanding what has been happening in the world in the twentieth century. For Marxism has been a *movement*, and movements are like spectres in important ways. They can adopt different guises in different places at one and the same time. In a sense they escape the constraints of time and space. A movement carries its past with it into the present, and can perform the apparently mysterious feat of gathering wide cultural divergences into a single stream. Since, however, the age is not one of mysticism (or, in so far as it is, it is so in reaction against a prevailing pragmatism), we must oblige by clothing the spectre in the more acceptable garb of concrete events, concrete social forces, and the pronouncements of real live men and women.

Seen from the vantage point of the present day, the fulcrum around which the history of Marxism as a movement turns is the revolution in Russia in 1917. The discussion which preceded that revolution and the events which succeeded it are worth examining in some detail.

When the Russian Lenin wrote *What is to be Done?* in 1902, he was taking part, and saw himself as taking part, in a debate within the European Marxist parties of the day. This was a debate about the way in which the pursuit of radical change in Europe should be conducted, and it was one which set English Fabians, French 'ministerialists' and German 'revisionists' against those who condemned a gradualist strategy and an obsession with immediate economic goals on the grounds that such concerns distracted the working class from the political goal of a radical reordering of society. Lenin saw this 'revisionist' debate as of relevance to the strategy of a Marxist party operating in Russian circumstances. The practical conclusions which he drew, however, centred on the impediments which were imposed by tsarist absolutism on political organisation *of any kind at all* in Russia. If the view of party organisation which he put forward in 1902 has been seen as Jacobin, this is entirely owing to the fact that he could see that 'broad democracy' and full publicity were ruled out for a Russian party.

The oppressive circumstances of tsarism were somewhat eased as a result of the revolutionary upsurge of 1905. Though the concessions which the Tsar made at the end of that year were shortly to be severely whittled down, the sense of euphoria was sufficient to cause Lenin to acclaim the arrival of an era in which his earlier call for organisation and cohesion could be matched by an appeal for democratic procedures in the Party. It was in those circumstances that the idea of democratic centralism was born, the idea of a dialectical balance between organisational cohesion and democratic procedures. They were circumstances which appeared to draw the situation of the Russian Marxists closer to that of the Western European Marxists. Still, however, Lenin maintained his earlier insistence on the goal of a revolutionary reordering of society.

No political organisation of the day could claim responsibility for the collapse of the tsarist system when that event took place in March 1917. When the Bolsheviks came to power in November of that year, it was at the head of social forces which had imposed themselves autonomously on the scene under the double pressures of external war and internal frustration. The *consolidation of the Bolsheviks in power*, however, in the ensuing period of civil war and economic collapse was a different matter. For whilst the Bolsheviks were soon brought to outlaw even their rival revolutionary organisations, democratic centralism, as it had been conceived in 1905, succumbed to the ban on factional activity at the Bolsheviks' Tenth Congress in 1921. It was to start a new life, however, as a formula which validated the highly authoritarian pattern of politics which was in the making.

It was thus not the Bolsheviks who dissolved the tsarist order; but it *was* the Bolsheviks who reconstructed Russia. If the consolidation of the revolution had brought about the authoritarianism which a situation of social dislocation invites, the ensuing task of economic construction from a starting point of economic and cultural disadvantage produced, in fact if not necessarily, a continuation of authoritarian rule. And if to the historian Stalin must appear as a reincarnation of Peter the Great, dragging a backward nation into modernity, it is no less important that this more recent attempt was seen as involving the creation of the material base for the construction of a socialist society.

When, in 1928–9, this drive for economic construction was begun in earnest, with the first five-year plan and the collectivisation of the peasantry, Lenin was already in his mausoleum, and his close comrades of the revolutionary period, in most cases intellectually highly gifted people who had been brought up in the general European discourse on Marxist socialism, were soon to be cut down in the Stalinist purges. The men of the construction drive were people of a different sort: the vast army of cadres, home-grown, the produce of revolution in a country marked by a low level of literacy and of economic and cultural development; the thousand and one Khrushchevs who saw their own image in Stalin.

Before Lenin died, however, two important events had occurred; or, rather, one of them had occurred, whilst the other was an expected event which *failed* to occur. First, the enunciation of the twenty-one principles for acceptance of a party into the Third (Communist) International in 1920 split the socialist Left in Western Europe. The distinction drawn in 1920 between communist parties which adhered to the Comintern and the social-democratic parties which did not do so; the identification of the first set with Soviet policies and indeed with the Bolsheviks' organisational norms; and the concomitant association of the latter set of parties with the reformist views against which Lenin had inveighed in *What is to be Done?* – all these things lived on to become what is still now a familiar part of the furniture of the political life of Western Europe. But the implications of the splitting of the Left in 1920, and, likewise, the implications of affiliation to the Comintern, only became clear when an expected development failed to materialise: the spread of revolution to the nations of Western Europe.

For both Lenin and Trotsky, and for others too, the success of a socialist revolution in Russia was predicated upon the occurrence of revolution in Western Europe; only such an eventuality would enable the Bolsheviks to realise their socialist goals in a way which made sense within the discourse on Marxist socialism as it had been conducted up to that time. The political revolution had been achieved and socialist policies instituted. Russia alone, however, appeared to lack the economic and cultural resources to make the carrying through of those policies practicable.

By 1924 these internationalist hopes were dead. In their place arose the doctrine of socialism in one country. The Bolsheviks were left with the phrase, and the aspiration, of proletarian internationalism and a reality cruelly discrepant with both the phrase and the aspiration, at least in the short term. The phrase, of course, was retained, and the aspiration, in formal terms, upheld. But the pressures, internal and external, which the construction of socialism in one country *and in that particular country* imposed, led to the promotion of national goals, and to an emphasis on economic achievement at the expense of a deepening of democracy. It was a process from which the capitalist West benefited through the creation of a visible bogy named communism, through the association of the more radical Western political parties with this bogy, and with the resultant tendency of the less radical socialist parties to steer yet further away from a phenomenon which could easily be presented as involving the redistribution of poverty through strong-arm methods. The process can be seen now to have benefited the Soviet population considerably in material terms, and to have benefited the Soviet Union as a nation state quite massively. But it benefited not at all those who continued to present Marxist goals in terms of the growing-over of a mature capitalist society into socialism, and in terms of the end of alienation and of the control of the producer over his own product.

One thing which the Soviet Union of the Stalinist years had shown the world was a successful method of bringing development to an economically retarded country, of restoring national pride to a disfavoured nation, and of keeping the penetration of the industrialised world at bay. If it was Lenin, relying on the ideas of Hilferding and others, who had given Marxism its theory of imperialism, his Soviet heirs provided at least one set of tools for combating imperialism and for undertaking the task of untying the colonial knot. It is in this sense that the Russian revolution was a major fulcrum in twentieth-century history. It was in its inspiration an outgrowth of European Marxism, but became in its effects a catalyst in the struggle of oppressed nations against their oppressors.

If we exclude the Mongolian People's Republic, which came into being in 1924 and from the start allied itself with the Soviet Union in order to escape Chinese domination, the Soviet Union remained the single bastion of established Marxist socialism until the closing stages of the Second World War. The Comintern parties were pressed into service to support this bastion through all the tergiversations of Soviet foreign policy in the inter-war years. They also adopted the organisational norms of the Communist Party of the Soviet Union, norms which were shaped by the pressures of the period during which the Bolsheviks were securing themselves in power and addressing themselves to the tasks of economic development in a backward country. The West European communist parties thus became doubly estranged from their cultural environment: on the one hand their policies were shaped with primary reference to a foreign nation, whilst on the other hand their procedural norms conflicted with their home political cultures. Soviet influence made itself felt even more directly in the accession to power of a number of communist parties in Central and Eastern Europe in the immediate aftermath of the Second World War – in Poland, in Czechoslovakia, in Hungary, in the Soviet part of occupied Germany, in Romania and in Bulgaria.

In the same period, however, communist parties had come to power *without* overt Soviet support in Yugoslavia and Albania. Both these parties set about forming the economic and political structures of the societies over which they now ruled in conformity with the Soviet model, but the fact that these revolutions had taken place autonomously had important implications for the future configuration of what at that time was known as the socialist camp.

Meanwhile, since 1936 the Communist Party of China had been engaged in a contest with both the Chinese Nationalists (the Kuomintang) and Japanese occupying forces. The interest of this long struggle is twofold. First, Mao Tse-tung based his strategy on the *rural* areas of China. The social policies of the communists were applied first in microcosm in the peasant countryside. Spreading thus from the countryside to the cities, the revolution had a populist flavour. Secondly, this populist flavour was strengthened by Mao's concept of the people, the *renmin*, which included the national bourgeoisie but excluded the 'comprador capitalists', whose interests were associated with those of the Japanese and other foreign powers. Thus to the liberation of the peasant from the landlord was joined the liberation of the nation from foreign penetration.

As had the Yugoslavs, the Chinese communists initially set up economic and political structures which were modelled on those of the Soviet Union. Ironically, however, in 1948, the year before the Chinese revolution culminated, the Yugoslav party had been expelled from the Cominform – the international body which between 1947 and 1956 was the organisational expression of the notional socialist camp. This cardinal event, which with the hindsight of history must be seen as marking the logical development from the idea of socialism in one country to that of different national roads to socialism, was offset by the Chinese success and by the fact that the Chinese and Soviet leaderships were united at that time in their condemnation of Yugoslav 'revisionism'. Nevertheless, expansion of the 'socialist camp' had been accompanied by diversification, and it was this novel element of diversity which was most significant for later developments.

Ten years later the situation was to recur, this time Castro's success in Cuba being followed by the definitive rift between the Soviet and the Chinese communists. Both events were highly significant. In the case of the Cuban revolution, this was because the revolution was spearheaded not by the communist Popular Socialist Party but by Castro's personal following – the Movement of 26 July. The redistributive and cultural policies which Castro instituted on achieving power were indeed revolutionary, and early on a bridge was formed between the Popular Socialist Party and Castro's organisation, but this was first and foremost a nationalist revolution directed against the penetration of Cuba by the 'colossus of the North'. It was not until after the revolution that Castro embraced Marxism-Leninism.

The Sino-Soviet split was important in that it made it clear that the days of monolithic communism were over. The Cominform had been dissolved in 1956, to be replaced by *ad hoc* conferences. Soon, in fact after 1969, *ad hoc* was to become *ad numquam*.

Once again the universe of communist systems had expanded, and once again this expansion had been accompanied by diversification, but this time the resonance of the latter element was far greater than it had been ten years earlier. The Soviet Union was now but one of an increasingly diverse set of communist systems. It continued to benefit from an authority conferred by the 'October' of 1917. It had been the first in the field and it had been established longest. It was, moreover, able to dominate, by force or by blandishments, the majority of the other Marxist-Leninist ruling parties. But it was no longer *the* model of a society ruled by a Marxist-Leninist party. If it was still an emperor, from now on it was open to any Marxist-Leninist child to claim that the emperor's clothing was deficient.

Up to this point, the occurrence of revolutions involving Marxist-Leninist parties, espousing redistributive policies derived from the tenets of Marxism, and throwing up political and economic structures which seemed to form an identifiable category, had taken place rather gradually, with the important exception of the Eastern European 'revolutions'. The failure of the American involvement in Vietnam, however, was to prove exactly what American strategists had assumed; and the dominoes have since tumbled with bewildering rapidity, not only in South-east Asia, but also in South Yemen and, most recently and strikingly, in Central Africa. The phenomenon is bewildering in particular for those who have to deal with the concepts of socialism, communism, Marxism and Marxism-Leninism. From studying, in the inter-war period, a single example of a Marxist-Leninist party in power, the student of the communist movement now has to deal with the wide spectrum, in terms of culture and economic development, of established regimes on four continents. Nor is this all. The West European communist parties have at last begun to retrace the steps which they have taken since the splitting of the Left in 1920, and have in certain cases gone so far as to expunge the 'Leninism' from Marxism-Leninism. They have, however, been outflanked by the reinvigoration of the radical Marxist Left in the Western industrial societies, and the European debate is in a sense back where it was at the beginning of the century, when revolutionaries confronted reformists in that first re-visionist debate. What is new in the present situation is that the world is well populated with Marxist-Leninist parties in power, which owe their inspiration to the success of the Bolshevik revolution. It is these parties, and the political systems which they have created, which form the material of these volumes.

We shall shortly be turning to the nature of Western comment which the evolution of the communist movement has elicited, and a statement will be made as to what, in the present circumstances, it may mean to call a regime 'Marxist'. First, however, it is worth drawing attention to some of the implications, from the vantage point of the present day, of the evolution of the communist movement as it has been described above. The first of these implications concerns the way in which the term 'ideology' has been used and the way in which it must now be understood.

It should be clear from the foregoing that the fundamental conflict of values in the world as a whole today – a conflict which is older than our century but which was given its present configuration by the revolution in Russia in 1917 – is no longer simply a conflict within the world of West European culture between bourgeois liberal and socialist values.[1] It has become a conflict between the developing world and the West, and the developing world has brought onto the battlefield where it has confronted the technological superiority of the West a number of prominent values deriving from the political modalities of cultures which have for centuries been regarded as alien to West European culture, and remain so in their post-revolutionary guise, whatever the debt which they owe to the West European Marx.

The result is that the earlier problem of ideology, in which ideology was seen as a simple conflict between liberal democracy and Marxist socialism, is now beginning to be seen as a much more complex affair. In fact, it comprises a tight knot of problems concerning ideology, culture and language. This lesson is now being learned both by practical political figures and by commentators on communism. For the first, the Euro-communist parties are coming to realise that Soviet political practices are separable from Marxist socialism; for the second, scholars such as Tucker and Meyer have pointed out that the communist systems derive their values, including their political values, as much from their cultural past as from the tenets of Marxism.[2] These advances in our understanding of what has been happening under the label of socialism are valuable; but they also serve to increase our perplexity. For the phenomenon with which we have to deal turns out to be composed of a number of intersecting dimensions. To the two dimensions suggested above – on the one hand the class conflict of industrialising Europe and the ideas which that conflict generated, and on the other the conflict between the West and the developing nations – must be added a third: that provided by cultural dissonance between the various societies of the world, a dissonance which may seem to present us with a series of totally disparate cultures, but which does not in fact do so, since these various conflicts of interest and ideas reinforce each other. There emerges a world of liberal democracy, comprising distinct cultures which, none the less, at a certain level, coalesce; and there is also a world of communism, made up of societies which again exhibit wide cultural variation, but which share a range of values deriving from a refraction of the tenets of Marxism through a shared historical predicament of national disadvantage.

Secondly, the story recounted above has answered the question 'How has the communist movement developed since Marx's days?' If, however, we were to pose a rather different question and ask what, in the most general terms, has been happening in the world in the twentieth century, a rather different perspective would be obtained. For the twentieth century has been one of revolution, yet not of revolution in the industrialised world. The mainstream of the century's upheavals, which have combined political with social revolution, has flowed in the economically less-developed areas of the globe. Since these revolutions have in most cases, and with increasing frequency, brought a Marxist-Leninist party to power, the process has presented the now familiar triad of revolution/national liberation/Marxism-Leninism.

It is illuminating to consider the cases of the revolutions in Mexico and Cuba within the framework which is here being presented. The 'forgotten revolution' in Mexico happened, as it were, before Lenin came along. That revolution in 1910, together with the political forms and processes which it engendered, has much in common with the experience of the communist systems. And yet it lacks an important dimension which has been almost universally shared by upheavals of a similar nature which have occurred since 1917, and which are being reproduced almost annually in Asia and Africa. Even more interesting is the case of Cuba, where the revolution owed little to the ideas of Marxism-Leninism, and indeed was carried through by a force which was independent of the Marxist-Leninist Popular Socialist Party, but then went on to adopt not only the symbols, but also the organisation characteristic of the communist systems. This has been seen as the price paid for Soviet assistance – an argument which carries some force, but which, if carried through, requires us to believe that the Soviet Union has purchased virtually the entire national-liberation movement of the twentieth century. There is no doubt an element of truth in this, but at the same time it is difficult to believe that so many shoppers did not understand the market they have been shopping in.

This view of what has been happening in the twentieth century helps us to get into perspective a series of revolutions and the political forms which emerged from them. And not merely a series of revolutions, but *the mainstream* of twentieth-century revolutions, in which considerations of national liberation and national development have been paramount. The Russian revolution, semi-industrialised though Russia was at the time, may be seen, for present purposes, as the first of these, with the series constantly augmenting itself in Angola, Mozambique, Ethiopia and Benin.

But other things have been happening in the twentieth century which are important for a perspective on the political forms and processes of the communist systems. It will have been noted that the post-war 'revolutions' in Eastern Europe do not fit the pattern outlined above. In fact they form a special case, in which extraneous factors (including such overwhelming factors as the presence of the Soviet Army and proximity to the Soviet Union itself) were present and indeed determinant. But they are special cases for another reason, relevant to the development of the Soviet Union as an industrial giant. If the revolutionary phenomenon described above has predominantly involved the developing countries, the twentieth century has seen, in the more developed parts of the globe, the growth of industrial society into the stage of high technology. This has brought with it new problems of the relationship between the individual and this new pattern of production, the new Leviathan which has preoccupied Huxley, Zamyatin, Orwell, Marcuse and so many others.

But there is no need to refer to fictional works for evidence. If the regulatory power of the state is greater in the Soviet Union than in the Western industrial nations, it is only a matter of a greater distance covered along the same path. The same can be said for the development of planning, of developments in communications and the control of them, and, indeed, all the rest of the convergence thesis, which, like the other models so far suggested to aid our understanding of the communist systems, has its failings but also an irresistible grain of truth.

Looking at the politics of the communist systems from *this* aspect of what has been happening in the twentieth century throws us into an entirely different discourse from that other revolutionary aspect; and what is interesting about communist politics is that both these strands run strong and that they interconnect – indeed, that they are in contradiction with each other.

It is in this interconnection, and in this contradiction, that lie the clues for understanding what is specific to the communist systems. Social revolutions and national liberation movements may throw up elite leaderships, but they are none the less mass affairs, involving a high degree of spontaneity. On the other hand, the organisation of post-industrial society, as we have so far seen it, seeks stability, the dominant image of social health is 'the harmonious functioning of the system', and in the Soviet Union as in the West rewards and prestige go to the technically competent. But it is òf course in China that this contradiction has most recently been visible, and it is the Chinese who have endowed the communist movement with the phrase that encapsulates it: red and expert. This phrase has no doubt served many trivial purposes, but it enshrines a basic contradiction which runs through the politics of the communist systems, and indeed, in an indirect way, through the entire communist movement, the bureaucratic tendencies within the communist systems engendering a radical reaction amongst Marxists outside them, a spectre of redness which today is haunting communism.

We can now turn to the history of Western comment on the political forms which the communist movement has presented during its evolution. This history can be usefully seen as comprising three phases. These we shall outline and shall then go on to suggest that today's circumstances of extreme variegation in the communist movement call for a substantial rethinking of the assumptions which have informed these three phases.

The first phase need not detain us long, although it lasted for the considerable period from the establishment of Bolshevik power in the Soviet Union until the 'iron curtain' descended in the aftermath of the Second World War. These were the years of the first reactions to the novel political and economic creature which had been ripped from the womb of old Russia by the Bolshevik midwife. The discussion, in so far as it went beyond memories and eye witness accounts of the revolution and its immediate sequel, was pitched, naturally enough, in terms of the presuppositions about Marxist socialism which preoccupied Western Europe and the English-speaking world at the time of the Russian revolution. The fact that it was at times naïve reflects the circumstances. The emerging economic and political forms *were*, after all, novel; they were also, for the first ten years and more, somewhat mobile. By the time they had become less mobile, information had become exceedingly difficult to obtain, and equally difficult to digest. A command of the Russian language was a scarce commodity, and, moreover, the preoccupation with constitutional formalities which marked the political science of the day made it difficult for the few scholars who did interest themselves in the Soviet Union to deal with a political system in which the political processes differed so widely from the formal constitutional structure. Two features of those days are worth noting. First, the form of Marxism in practice which the Soviet Union presented was not taken to be an example *faute de mieux*; it was taken to be the model *par excellence*. Secondly, and more obviously, comment was partisan. The importance of this point is that it suited both apologists and critics to present the Soviet Union as the model *par excellence* of Marxist socialism – the former playing down the more objectionable aspects of Soviet life in order to build up support for the single established bastion of Marxist socialism, the latter playing them up in order to discredit the whole regrettable exercise.

The beginning of a second phase in the history of studies of communism was marked by the arrival of the first really sophisticated analysis of Soviet political forms. This analysis linked the Stalinist Soviet Union with Hitler's Germany and Mussolini's Italy in a concept of 'totalitarianism'. The theme was articulated in various ways, but the 'six-point syndrome' put forward by Friedrich and Brezinski is worth citing, since discussion of the totalitarian view has tended to revolve around it. Totalitarianism, for these two scholars, comprised the following six features: (1) an official ideology; (2) a single mass party led typically by one man; (3) a terroristic police system; (4) a monopoly, in the hands of the party, of the means of communication; (5) a similar monopoly of the means of armed combat; (6) central control of the entire economy.[3]

The historical circumstances in which the totalitarian view arose should be noted. First of all, since it accompanied the onset of the Cold War, there was a strong 'know your enemy' flavour about it. Secondly, the linking of Stalin with Hitler and Mussolini illustrates a further important point: the totalitarian view was analysing a pre-war pattern of politics in a post-war situation. As far as the communist movement as a whole was concerned, the period from 1945 to the middle 1960s – that is, the period during which the totalitarian view held sway – was one of increasing differentiation. It had seen the creation of Marxist-Leninist regimes as far apart, in terms of geography, culture and level of economic development, as China, Czechoslovakia, Yugoslavia and Cuba. The result was that the totalitarian view, whilst historically valid for an earlier period, turned out to be historically vulnerable almost as soon as it had been put forward. For, with all three tyrants – Stalin, Hitler and Mussolini – gone, with the systems created by the last two dismantled, and with the abandoning of terror as a political instrument in the Soviet Union after Stalin's death, the shrunken concept had to be fleshed out *by inference* with recently created communist systems, which did indeed show similarities to the Stalinist Soviet Union, but showed important differences from it too.

A further feature of this second phase in the study of communist politics served to perpetuate the notion that the political system of the Soviet Union provided a norm to which other communist systems had to be related. This was the abrupt upsurge in Soviet and Eastern European studies in the early 1950s. In the case of Britain, it was the armed forces, through their language courses for conscripts, which were chiefly responsible for the establishment of the Russian language and of Soviet studies in the British educational curriculum, and this development was given a further impulse by the Hayter report, which led to a very substantial investment in Soviet and Eastern European studies in institutions of higher learning and research. But Britain was by no means peculiar in this respect. The rocket which launched the first sputnik also gave a powerful boost, in the whole Western world, to the idea that the Soviet Union was the model *par excellence* of a Marxist-Leninist regime. Moreover, since the political systems of Eastern Europe resembled that of the Soviet Union in most important respects, the model appeared to be a multi-member category and therefore gained in credibility. The Prague Spring was, much later, to show that behind this enforced uniformity – for such it was – lay very different notions of what Marxist socialism involved – a message which had already been made clear by the way in which Yugoslavia, free from Soviet interference, had presented to the world its own highly original contribution.

Finally, despite the association with fascism and nazism, it was a characteristic of this second phase in the history of studies of communist politics that commentators saw the communist systems as *sui generis*, as forming a category which not only used a particular language in self-description, but which also required that a special language be used in analysing them. No way had been found of integrating studies of communist politics into the discourse on comparative politics in the broad. Partisan attitudes again played an important role here: it suited the preferences both of critics and apologists of communism to emphasise the particularity of the communist phenomenon.

For a considerable period the totalitarian view overlapped with other approaches, which were beginning to register the very real diversification which had been taking place within the communist movement.

But from the middle 1960s the emergence of a third phase in the study of communist politics was discernible. This phase, which takes us up to the present day, has been marked by a considerable variety in the approaches taken to communist politics. Some of these approaches go so far as to disestablish the communist systems as a distinct subset of the world's political systems. For Kautsky, for example, they are subsumable under the general heading of the politics of development – a view for which the historical sketch presented earlier in this chapter offers considerable support.[4] Most approaches, however, retain the idea that the communist systems do form a subset of the world's political systems, though no longer a homogeneous one. It has come to be recognised that what was originally a peculiarly Soviet product has been adapted by a variety of societies with rich and distinctive political traditions of their own and that to apply to those societies an analysis based exclusively on the Soviet model is not good enough, and more attention has begun to be given to differing traditions and differing political cultures. The result has been a merging of the study of Soviet politics and comparative politics into what is now called 'comparative communism'.

This initiative in political science combines what is unique in the various communist systems with the general concepts which were originally developed in the study of Soviet politics. At the same time it is recognised that the Soviet experience gives only partial explanations of the other communist systems and that concepts and techniques developed by comparative politics are applicable to those other systems.

It might appear that, with the emergence of comparative communism, a congruence has at last been achieved between a highly variegated object of study and an appraisal which can cope with variety on a comparative basis. A number of considerations, however, make it difficult to accept so optimistic a conclusion.

First of all, if comparative communism has so far involved a vigorous methodological debate, it is one which rides on top of a literature which is *not* comprehensive in its scope. There is a wealth of studies of individual systems or groups of systems, and of symposia. But even symposia do not meet the demand for *synthesis* which the current situation in the communist world imposes. Meanwhile, single-author works which take a synoptic view of the politics of the communist systems as a whole are so rare as to be almost non-existent.

This would not matter, and the situation might be expected to correct itself in time, were it not for a second consideration: the tendency to see comparative communism in terms of an extension of the study of Soviet and Eastern European politics.[5] It is illuminating that between a third and a half of British university courses on comparative communist politics actually *limit* themselves to the Soviet Union and Eastern Europe, and many more move outwards from that 'model'.

Now, to a certain extent this is quite understandable and unexceptionable. The Soviet Union as noted above was the first in the field; it has been able to influence in one way or another the political forms of most of the other communist systems; the problems of economic and cultural underdevelopment which the majority of the communist systems faced at their inception were faced first by the Soviet Union, and newly emerging regimes usually turn to the Soviet Union not only for political and economic support, but also for an organisational model. All this is true, and must be taken into account. But other things must today be taken into account as well. Neither historical seniority nor power and blandishments necessarily confer authority or authenticity, and one of the chief features of the communist movement today is that the Soviet Union's authority is under rather substantial attack – from other ruling parties, from non-ruling parties, which traditionally have supported the Soviet Union's policies and imitated its organisational patterns, and from the Trotskyist Left. Further, even where, as in Angola, Vietnam, Cuba and Ethiopia, Soviet influence is particularly strong, the countervailing effects of cultural diversity and local circumstances make it increasingly difficult to make these societies 'fit' a political model which draws overwhelmingly on Soviet experience. Moreover, there is ample evidence from all corners of the communist movement that the majority of the regimes that compose it are themselves not looking for the import of socialist practice from abroad. They aspire to their own original socialism, a socialism that will accord with their own circumstances. Comparative communism has so far been like a boat which originally sailed well and held water. With the passing of time new planks have had to be added here and there to keep the boat seaworthy. But recent events have meant the nailing on of so many hefty new timbers that the discerning shipwright would surely prefer to be given the separate planks and told to make a new boat. And he would be well advised, even if he keeps the Soviet keel, not to use the old and battered board which carries the legend 'Made in the Soviet Union and Eastern Europe'. That can be honourably placed in a maritime museum, along with other illustrious but now equally useless boards, such as that which proclaims the industrial revolution to have been made in England. The good ship Industrial Society now sails much better without carrying the superfluous weight of that particular plank.

But comparative communism is open to an even graver charge. It has so far presented the student of communist politics with a group of the world's political systems and has invited him to see what these systems have in common in terms of structures and functions. This again is a possible and worthwhile exercise. But is it the *best* way of making sense of the politics of communism? To repeat yet again, we are dealing with a movement, with political organisations which subscribe to a shared cosmology and to a shared set of goals which derive from it. However 'petrified'[6] a given organisation may be at a given time, there is a dynamic in the movement which the scholar neglects at his peril. For one thing, the distinction which is so obvious in Western political science between a ruling party and a non-ruling one is by no means so obvious within the logic of communist politics. In terms of the structures and functions of existing political systems the distinction is capital; in terms of the shared goals and cosmology it is much less substantial. No adequate account can be given of the politics of the communist movement, without full and equal consideration not only of the ruling parties as *individual* entities operating in highly differentiated circumstances, but also of the non-ruling parties in all their phenomenal variety – because, however varied, however mutually destructive, they are an essential part of the movement, and moreover they are politically interdependent. That movement, like any other movement, has turned out to be – and annually can be seen more and more to be – Protean. It assumes different forms at different times in different places. It is *polymorphic*. And it is ultimately more important to register this fact than to assume that any single form of it is a model *par excellence*.

The politics of communism ought therefore to be studied at three levels. First, the component organisations (states and parties) ought to be analysed as part of the general discourse on comparative politics in the broad, using the very generalised language which that discourse requires (patterns of participation and elite recruitment, present interests versus future goals, and so on). Secondly, the movement as a whole ought to be analysed in terms of its goals and its cosmology (which means analysing it in its own language, its own semantic system). And, thirdly, each component organisation requires separate investigation of a kind which will reveal its particularities, either as an individual organisation or as a member of a coherent group (the Eurocommunist parties, the Eastern European states, and the like).

These are clearly separate tasks, and yet comparative communism has so far attempted to conflate them. The result is that, with rare exceptions, the first two of these tasks have not yet been satisfactorily tackled. The third, on the other hand, has produced an abundant literature, whilst being the least comparative of the three exercises.

This collection comprises specialist contributions which analyse twenty-five regimes which define themselves as Marxist-Leninist. The foregoing should make it plain that the editor regards these regimes as but a part of the universe of political organisations which make up the communist movement. The aim is to show that *even within this category of ruling parties* the communist movement is marked by variety. What these regimes have in common (and what they have in common both with non-ruling parties which style themselves Marxist-Leninist *and* with non-ruling parties, such as the Spanish, which have dropped the 'Leninist' element of the title) is that their respective elites maintain that their countries' social, political and economic development is guided by Marxism. All alike profess what they regard as the 'scientific theory' of the laws of the development of human society and human history. This scientific doctrine is claimed by the political leaderships of these countries to consist in the discovery of objective causal relationships; it is used to analyse the contradictions which arise between goals and actuality in the pursuit of a common destiny. The acceptance by the ruling parties in these twenty-five countries of this conceptual framework has been the criterion for inclusion in this collection.

At the same time, the fact that they call themselves Marxist-*Leninist* marks their subscription also to a certain view of the relationship between the party and society. It has been argued above that this does indeed make for a family resemblance between all these systems and the Soviet Union, but that this resemblance can be overemphasised, at the cost of concealing the markedly different ways in which this relationship between party and society works out in practice – a point which can be readily exemplified by noting the highly variable role of the military and of religious organisations in these societies.

We are quite aware of the problems of taking self-ascription as the basis for accepting a regime as Marxist, or Marxist-Leninist. We are aware of the important distinction between, for example, China, where a long-established communist party's accession to power was the result of an organic relationship between the party and the masses which matured over time, and Benin, where Marxism-Leninism was rather abruptly embraced by a military government in a state which holds the African record for military *coups d'état*. There is not enough space in this introductory chapter to conduct the full exercise of comparison between these extremely diverse systems. On the other hand self-ascription is not such a bad starting-point for that comparative exercise. First of all, it is clearly better than basing the exercise on models and categories formed in an earlier situation and which by that very fact may not be capable of making sense of new phenomena. Secondly, self-ascription does at least provide an initial hypothesis, even if it does nothing more. Thirdly, however, it does in fact do more than merely provide a hypothesis. A shared rhetoric is an important factor in politics, affecting in particular the legitimacy of leaderships which espouse that rhetoric. And finally, to repeat, communism must be seen as a *movement*, and movements grow by a process of diffusion which involves not only proselytisation but also self-ascription. Calvinism, for example, must be considered a strand of the Christian tradition despite the fact that its self-ascription to the tradition jarred with the views not only of Roman popes but also of those commentators on Christianity whose theoretical constructs had no place for Calvinist notions of salvation.

The novelty of this publication is that it does not assign authenticity or authority to any single Marxist-Leninist political system. It shows that, depending on a variety of historical, cultural and political factors, the pursuit of goals derived from the tenets of Marxism has produced different political forms at different times and in different places. It also illustrates the rich diversity among these societies, where attempts to achieve a synthesis between goals derived from Marxism, on the one hand, and national realities, on the other, have often meant distinctive approaches and solutions to the problems of social, political and economic development. Furthermore, in discussing these diverse societies one can learn much more about the foundations and meaning of the ideology, development, adaptations and effect of Marxism-Leninism within them. Marxism, as Roger Garaudy points out, has as its universal vocation to be rooted in the culture of every people. An Algerian, Islamic in culture, can arrive at scientific socialism by other roads than those of Hegel, Ricardo or Saint-Simon. He has his own utopian socialism in the carmathian movement, his rationalist and dialectical tradition in Averroes, his forerunner of historical materialism is Ibn Khaldun; and it is upon these traditions that he can graft scientific socialism. This in no way excludes his integrating the heritage of our culture just as we have to integrate his.[7]

The overriding aim of this collection is to show the very varied ways in which the conceptual framework of Marxism-Leninism has been taken to make possible the construction of socialism along roads proper to local conditions.

NOTES

1. The nine paragraphs which follow are reproduced from an article by Michael Waller entitled 'Problems of Comparative Communism', which is shortly to be published in *Studies in Comparative Communism*
2. See, for example, R. C. Tucker, 'Culture, Political Culture and Communist Society', *Political Science Quarterly*, June 1973; and Alfred Meyer, 'Communist Revolutions and Cultural Change', *Studies in Comparative Communism*, v, no. 4 (Winter 1972).
3. Karl J. Friedrich and Z. K. Brzezinski, *Totalitarian Dictatorship and Autocracy*, revised ed. (Cambridge, Mass.: Harvard University Press, 1965) p. 22.
4. John H. Kautsky, *Communism and the Politics of Development* (New York: Wiley, 1968).
5. To take a prominent example, one of the very few comprehensive comparative works of recent years – Patrice Gélard's *Les Systèmes Politiques des États Socialistes* (Paris: Cujas, 1975) – is presented in two volumes. The first volume is entitled 'The Soviet Model', and the second 'Transpositions and Transformations of the Soviet Model'. And yet this work, better perhaps than any other, brings out the originality of some of the less familiar communist systems.
6. See Jerry Hough's discussion 'The Soviet System: Petrification or Pluralism', *Problems of Communism*, Mar–Apr 1972.
7. Roger Garaudy, *Marxism in the Twentieth Century* (London: Collins, 1970) pp. 35–6.

2 What Does It Mean to Call a Regime Marxist? *

NEIL HARDING

There was, of course, once a time when it was comparatively easy to define a Marxist regime. From 1917 up to the mid-1950s (with the sole exception of Yugoslavia), there appeared to be no real problem. Marxist regimes were those which acknowledged the model of Soviet development as their own. The story of how the Russians captured for themselves exclusive title to the name Marxist and universalised their revolutionary experience is written in the whole history of the Communist International. With the failure of each successive revolutionary venture in the rest of the world, the prestige, authority and almost sacred aura of the Russians was augmented. The stages of development, the organisational structures, even the revolutionary calendar of the Russian revolution were universalised and made obligatory for member parties of the Comintern, as they were later for the member states of the Communist Information Bureau. It was, therefore, hardly surprising that in the first stage of expansion of Marxist regimes established in Central and Eastern Europe at the end of the Second World War, the Soviet model was rigorously applied. These regimes after all, owed their existence (with the significant exceptions of Yugoslavia and Albania) not to any popular revolution, still less to a popular vote, but were installed in the wake of the Red Army. They were regimes created and sustained by the force of Soviet arms and Stalin determined that they should be made in the image of their maker. Within the space of a few years all the Marxist regimes of Central and Eastern Europe were obliged to inaugurate a system of government based on, and dominated by, a single political party. They almost

---

* I am grateful to my friend and colleague John Rees for his comments and suggestions.

simultaneously began the forced collectivisation of agriculture and rapid industrialisation according to the dictates of their obligatory five-year plans. It was the cult of productivity and the reign of Stakhanovism. The administrative structures through which party and State operated were everywhere standardised and everywhere the power of the party's general secretary eclipsed that of the chairman of the council of ministers. The power of the police was augmented, and party-State control over the media of information and propaganda was made as complete as was possible. Each was, or appeared to be, an exact copy of the other, for all were rolled off the same Soviet stencil.

Marxist regimes at that time were synonymous with communist regimes, which were in their turn, with some justification, regarded as mere extensions of the Russian Soviet model. It was, as we saw in the previous chapter, in this milieu that the ideal type of totalitarianism was elaborated and became so influential. It is one of the nicer ironies of communist studies that at the very time at which this ideal type was first coherently formulated there occurred a series of events which undermined its credibility as a model even for the limited universe of Marxist regimes then in existence. It was, after all, in 1956 that Khrushchev, in his attempts to conciliate Yugoslavia, proclaimed the possibility and desirability of differing paths to socialism, conceding thereby that models other than the Russian Soviet one might legitimately be considered Marxist. The idea of differing roads to socialism carried with it the recognition that there could no longer be one universally valid application of the ideology of Marxism, no single obligatory pattern of institutions or ordering of priorities. Each Marxist regime was, it seemed, invited to begin afresh by moulding Marxism to the particularities of its own traditions and cultural background. Khrushchev's swingeing denunciation of Stalin and the cult of the personality, his admission that Stalin had committed gross errors in the name of Marxism, added further fuel to the fire and finally broke the spell of Soviet infallibility. There began a ferment which has continued over since – an intensely self-conscious debate among self-styled Marxist regimes and important non-ruling Marxist parties about the proper character of a Marxist social, economic and political system.

The Hungarian revolution and the Polish events of 1956 were the first immediate responses to Khrushchev's invitation to redefine Marxism, to make it compatible with its differing milieux. In Poland at least, the attempt met with considerable success. The collectivisation of agriculture was not only stopped but put rapidly into reverse. The regime, if only fleetingly, became noticeably freer and more tolerant. The Catholic

Church was given a greatly extended sphere of freedom and the powers of the secret police were much reduced. The totalitarian paradigm appeared to be cracking up almost as soon as it had been created.

By the mid-1960s the whole economic model which had been so rigorously imposed upon Eastern Europe was under vigorous attack by Marxist economists, and by 1968 a radically new definition of socialism – of the content and objectives of a Marxist regime – was being offered by Party leaders in Czechoslovakia.

The Action Programme of the Central Committee of the Communist Party of Czechoslovakia was far more than a critique of Soviet-imposed patterns of administration and economic planning. Nor was it merely a plea that the Czechs should be allowed to mould Marxism to their national environment. It was both of these things but more besides. It offered a more cohesive and positive redefinition of the sorts of objectives a Marxist regime should aspire to and the sorts of institutions necessary for their implementation. Its concern was not with cosmetics which would make the unacceptable face of Stalinism rather more comely, but with a new specification of the goals appropriate to Marxism. Above all, what the Czechs did was to dispute the simplistic view, which Stalin had sanctified, that the concern of Marxist regimes was to maximise production and equitable distribution of the product through an elaborate system of centralised planning. The Czech critique was that such a structure of centralised direction and planning not only failed even in *this* narrow objective but also was, more fundamentally, corrosive of the larger goals at which Marxist regimes should aim. The larger goals they had in mind derived, in part at least, from the resurgence of scholarship on, and interest in, the writings of the young Marx. Marx's early writings, with their stress on humanism, self-determination and an end to alienation within the productive process, set out a vision of the free, rounded personality whose concept of his needs was far more extensive than the ascetic limitation of human needs that the theorists of what he termed 'crude communism' could possibly embrace. The Czechs, by going back to Marx's original specification of the goals of socialism, and by learning from the Yugoslav experience of workers' councils and self-management, substantiated their radical claim that what had been created in Czechoslovakia (and, by obvious implication, throughout the Soviet bloc) was not the realisation of the goals of Marxist socialism but their inversion. Their project to realise socialism with a human face, to inaugurate a genuinely participatory industrial and political democracy, to re-establish the dignity and independence of the individual as worker and as citizen, was a radical new departure for Marxist regimes, for in respecifying the goals proper to Marxism it redefined the claims to legitimacy of the Party and of the regime itself.

The Czech experiment did not, alas, last long, but, like many ventures crushed by superior force, it left a legend of martyred ideas which continues to reverberate. At the least it stirred theorists of Marxism within the communist parties of Western Europe out of their slothful conservatism. What began in Czechoslovakia was taken up by the theoreticians of the French, British and especially the Italian and Spanish communist parties. Freed from the constraints of a Soviet presence, anxious, for electoral reasons, to dissociate themselves from the Soviet regime and the brutal suppression of the Czech experiment, they began to take up the watchwords of the Action Programme. Almost overnight many of the shibboleths of the Soviet-imposed interpretation of Marxism came under biting attack from Marxists. The necessity for a dictatorship of the proletariat, the desirability of a one-party regime, the intimate relationship between the party and the State, the obligation to institute rigidly centralised economic planning – all became the subject of an intensely critical debate. The debate amongst the West European Marxists, covered by the elusive umbrella term 'Eurocommunism' has, in its turn, reacted back upon the East European regimes, adding weight to the subterranean current of ideas which continues to assert that the social, economic and political systems of the Soviet bloc are the product not of any necessary entailments of Marxism, but of the suzerainty of one, distorted version of it.

To this point we have, in the broadest generality, looked only at the European debate about the character of a Marxist regime. There are, perhaps, good reasons for this emphasis. It is in Europe, after all, that Marxist regimes are most plentiful and have existed longest. There Marxist regimes and Marxist parties self-consciously feel themselves part of a continuous tradition extending back to Marx himself and confronted with broadly similar problems in terms of cultural heritage. It is certainly only in Europe that there has been such a prevalent and comparatively open debate about goals and institutions appropriate to a Marxist regime, and this can, in part at least, be attributed to the complicated symbiosis between the ruling and non-ruling Marxist parties. It is certainly true that the existence, in Western Europe, of powerful non-ruling communist parties attempting to redefine the nature of a Marxist policy to make it accord better with the liberal democratic values and expectations of the populace adds a dimension of open, articulate and accessible debate which is absent elsewhere.

This is not to say that the preoccupations and attempted redefinitions of the Europeans are more valid or have a broader universality than those which absorb Marxist regimes in Africa or Asia. It is simply to say that they have at least self-consciously posed and continue to debate the question 'What does it mean to call a regime Marxist?' We have some evidence at least with which to reconstruct their broad range of answers; we sometimes have access to the differing standpoints, can identify their spokesmen and refer to their statements.

It goes without saying that, even in the case of the European communist regimes, evidence of this sort is very far from being complete. Governments have ever and anon hidden themselves behind a protective shield of secrecy, but there is clearly a very large difference between the few regimes which guarantee the rights of opposition parties to condemn government policy and performance and freely publish and canvass their alternatives, and the many which do not. In the former case governments are at the least obliged to offer a reasoned account of their objectives and a defence of their efforts at implementing them. Divisions within the governing party are more or less open and the alternative specifications of opposition parties are equally available as evidence of the national debate of where the country should be going and what its internal and external priorities should be. In the case of Marxist regimes much of the evidence of how the agents themselves debate the project of realising a Marxist society is lamentably inaccessible. One-party states do not, definitionally, allow the opportunity for opposition parties to canvass their alternatives; thus, governments in these countries are not obliged constantly to defend their policies. Policy-making on important matters is the exclusive preserve of the single party, or, rather, of one small section of it; and, even in the best-documented available studies of the policy-making process in these regimes, a great deal is left to conjecture and speculation. There is, none the less, clearly a difference between the reliability and volume of evidence available to the historian from the European Marxist regimes and that available from the Marxist regimes of the Third World. By way of explanation we could, of course, point to a whole number of factors: lack of linguistic expertise on the part of commentators, cultural distance, revolutionary turmoil and the purposeful prohibition or annihilation of opposition groups within the party and outside it. The fact none the less remains, as many of the contributors to this collection have found, that even the most basic data about economic and social arrangements are often painfully difficult to obtain.

It seems to me that the most assiduous student of such self-styled

Marxist regimes as Cambodia, Laos, Benin, Vietnam, North Korea, South Yemen, or even Cuba and China, would therefore find himself hard-pressed to reconstruct an articulate and accessible debate on the proper character of a Marxist regime. It may be that a controversy of this sort becomes important only at a particular stage of industrial and social development and within the context of a certain intellectual tradition. It may well be the case, as Lenin argued in the early years of the Soviet Republic, that arguments about alternative goals – indeed, arguments about politics *per se* – lose their force, become almost obscene, when famine or the constant threat of it sweeps the land.

The more exotic Marxist regimes of Africa, Asia and the Middle East have none the less to be accommodated within some sort of framework. If they do not appear to be conscious participators in a debate about the goals and institutions proper to a Marxist regime, they are, from the fact of their existence, available as putative models for the future. Each has its own distinctive character, each in one way or another raises, at least implicitly, the question of the bounds of Marxism. For example, can a Marxist regime be overtly Mohammedan, can it be run by a small military clique, or can it be made viable in an almost wholly agrarian society? These and other problems raise the general issue of whether Marxism is an infinitely elastic doctrine. If it were infinitely elastic, then, clearly, it would merge with other doctrines, it would lose all its particularity. Is there not a case for arguing that there are limits beyond which any regime calling itself Marxist could not step? We are here concerned not with specifying a list of necessary institutional arrangements which every Marxist regime should incorporate, but, rather, with characterising the ethos and the goals particular to Marxist regimes.

One way of approaching this problem would be to locate and describe those features which Marxist regimes, and they alone, have in common. An examination of this sort, of the regimes dealt with in these three volumes, would, no doubt get us part of the way. We could, with some qualifications perhaps, point to such distinguishing characteristics as the existence of, or at least progress towards, a command economy, effective monopoly of political power in the hands of one political party, and so on.

The limitations of this sort of exercise are clear enough. In the first place, it is clear than many non-Marxist authoritarian regimes of the Right may, and indeed do, share these same characteristics. There is, in other words, nothing peculiarly Marxist about them at all. It could indeed be argued that such features as a command economy and monopoly of political power in the hands of one party are typical not of

Marxist regimes as such, but of Marxist regimes at a particular, and relatively primitive, stage of development. It is, for instance, quite clear that in Eastern Europe some regimes at least are moving away from the Soviet command-economy model and would have moved faster but for Russian interference. It is equally clear that Yugoslavia has been attempting (more in theory than in practice, perhaps) to disengage the Party from identification with the State – a position taken up and considerably extended by theorists of Eurocommunism.

A larger objection to this reductionist procedure would be that any list of characteristics of this sort would not tell us a great deal of the ethos which, in varying degrees, articulated in the most diverse ways, all these regimes embody. The problem with any list of essential characteristics is that it is static and necessarily procrustean. Each regime in turn would have to be measured against the paradigm and adjudged Marxist or less than Marxist according to its tally of points as each feature in turn was read off and applied to its particular formation. The element of growth, of comparative adolescence or maturity in advance towards a goal, would be quite neglected. It is, however, clear and obvious that Marxist regimes are goal-oriented. They have, or at least allege that they have, clearly specified aims in view which their long-term policies are designed to realise. It is, indeed, from these goals that the very legitimacy of these regimes derives. They form the core of their propaganda and the centre of their recurrent campaigns to mobilise their populations behind governmental policies. It is in terms of their own expressed goals that we can best characterise Marxist regimes, for all their institutional, political and economic formations are held to derive from them.

We are now led to the obvious questions, What are the goals of Marxist regimes? Are they indeed shared by all regimes professing themselves Marxist? How do they help us characterise Marxist regimes?

At the most basic level we can say that Marxist regimes have as their objectives the end of exploitation and the securing of equality and social justice both internally and externally.

The claim to legitimacy is the same for all Marxist regimes. It is the claim that social justice can be secured only by ending the exploitation of man by man, by eliminating an economic system based upon competition and individual appropriation and substituting for it one based upon co-operation and social appropriation of the product. The regimes concerned take as their principle axiom the contention that man's material and physical needs are capable of satisfaction given the present level of development of the productive forces available to him, and given, furthermore, a rational, planned use of these productive forces and an egalitarian distribution of the goods produced. The basic justification of these regimes, their claim to legitimacy, is, then, that they bring conscious order and social planning to an economic system alleged to have proceeded hitherto in an anarchic, unconscious and anti-social manner. This is the positive side to their anti-capitalism. Their claim to legitimacy, repeated tirelessly in all their programmes, constitutions and propaganda, is, at heart, the claim to plan and consciously to regulate the scarce resources of the country with a view to the continuous and broadly equal material advantage of the largest and poorest class – those who were hitherto exploited.

The question now is, How does this class articulate its interest? The answer of all Marxist regimes, as of all Marxists anywhere, is that the class expresses itself through its party. To explain the implications of this would lead us into a lengthy digression on Marxist theories of history. For our purpose it will be sufficient to note that, since Lenin at least, most Marxists have accepted that there are stages in the evolution of the development of the class which express its ascent from the particular to the general. Corresponding to the different stages of the development of its consciousness there are stages in the evolution of its organisation. Thus, at a comparatively low level of consciousness – when, for instance, workers have only ascended to the consciousness of their shared economic interest within a particular plant or trade – the appropriate organisational form would be the trade union. When, however, the workers begin to realise that their battle is with the whole class of employers, who defend themselves with the power of the State, at that point they are obliged to form an organisation which transcends the particularities of trades or regions, one which will articulate their general interests and organise them for the battle with the bourgeois State. That organisation is, of course, the Marxist party.

The party therefore articulates the general interests and the historical goals of all the exploited. This does not mean, however, that it can be identified with the class of the exploited. Again since Lenin, almost all Marxists have warned against this confusion. The party, or the Marxist regime, does not passively reflect an achieved level of consciousness and organisation, for to do so would dilute it by compelling it to bend itself to the profusion of sectional, particular interests which the prerevolutionary period had inculcated in the mass of the people. The party represents the advanced workers; it leads them and, after them, the mass of the exploited. The role of the party, its particular claim to dominate the regime, is always that it, through its study of the laws of history and economics, is able to comprehend the stage ahead. Through its prescient awareness of what is coming into being, it is able to lead the advanced workers and, through them, the mass of the exploited to higher consciousness and better organisation. The party, blessed with the predictive power of theory, is able to comprehend the general outlines of the phase that lies ahead; is able, therefore, to help the mass of the exploited to avoid pitfalls and wastage of its resources. Only in so far as it does this and proves itself the most active and dedicated section of the population in promoting the general interests of the exploited can the Marxist party claim legitimate domination of the regime.

This claim to legitimacy is, of course, fraught with the same sorts of problems as any such claim which invokes a distinction between real and felt needs. Thus, for all these regimes there is a clear distinction between what people conceive their interests to be and what their interests really are. The mass, they argue, may be, and frequently are, captive to false consciousness, sectional, merely fleeting or local, craft or ethnic particular interests, which for the time being prevent them from appreciating their general class and long-term historical interests. If these general historical interests were universally felt and acted upon, then, evidently, the party would lose its *raison d'être*.

All of these regimes bolster their claims to legitimacy by the claim that they represent the interests of social justice not only internally but also internationally. They all assert that social justice among nations cannot be secured so long as economically weak nations are subject to the economic tutelage of the economically powerful, so long as the rich and industrially developed regimes continue to exploit the poor and underdeveloped regions of the world for their own ends, as sources of cheap raw material and labour and as profitable outlets for the export of their surplus capital and finished goods. It is no accident that Marxist regimes have arisen most plentifully (excepting areas such as Eastern Europe, where they were imposed by force) in countries of the world which were, until comparatively recently, colonial dependencies. Marxism has given these countries not only a sophisticated and cohesive explanation of their own comparative poverty but also a rationale which vindicates national pride and patriotic assertiveness in terms of a larger contribution to a progressive world struggle. Anti-imperialism is the negative side of the goal of international social justice – it is arguably the single most important uniting principle and claim to legitimacy of all the regimes dealt with in these volumes.

All Marxist regimes share a broadly similar conception of the world they inhabit and the character of the epoch they are living through. They believe that international finance capitalism, expressing its domination through multinational companies and the economic hegemony of the imperialist countries over world trade and prices, reflect the fact that capitalism has become oppressive and parasitic. The epoch is that of the final degeneration and death agony of international finance capitalism and the advent of socialism on a global scale. Capitalism, it is argued, is so rent with internal contradictions that it can, in its imperialist monopolist phase, only survive by exacting tribute from the underdeveloped world and by averting attention from its internal problems by fomenting external enmities. War, and preparations for war, are therefore, conditions for its continued survival. The self-seeking anarchy of its internal relations are replicated internationally.

A major claim to legitimacy of all Marxist regimes is, then, that they are striving to free their peoples from the thrall of international finance capitalism, as a precondition for economic reconstruction and an end to internal poverty. This goal is presented in the context not of a narrow nationalism but of a common, worldwide struggle for a more peaceful, stable and equitable system of international relations. The imperative for economic planning, and the careful direction of scarce material and intellectual resources is therefore given all the more cogency by being justified in terms of repairing the imbalances and arrested development which imperialism purposefully fostered. In this way popular demands for national assertiveness, for economic improvement and international acknowledgement (if only by like-minded regimes) are fused together and used as complementary justifications for the regime's policies.

It is, of course, obvious that anti-imperialism is not exclusively a trait of Marxist regimes. Not all anti-imperialist regimes are Marxist, but all Marxist regimes are anti-imperialist. The distinctive mark of Marxist regimes is that in their own accounts of what they are about, they have successfully fused the goals of internal and international social justice as their basis of legitimacy.

The question which now arises is, Does the agents' account of the bases of legitimacy of Marxist regimes tell us much about their actual policies and organisational forms? It is clear, even from a cursory glance at the vast variety of these latter, that there is no sense in which the acceptance of very generally specified aims can be said to entail specific policies or particular organisational forms. Generalised aims of this sort never do contain the rules of their own application, so we should not be surprised to encounter in the following chapters the broadest variety of policies and institutions justified in terms of movement towards a common goal.

Justification of policies is one thing, the real political motivation for them is quite another, and in politics generally the attribution of motives is notoriously difficult to establish even in polities where politicians are obliged to be more open and forthcoming than is the case within the regimes discussed here. It is the conclusion of many of the contributors to these volumes that the rather lofty generalisations with which Marxist regimes decorate their policies are often no more than an altruistic gloss to the more mundane considerations prompting their adoption. Let us take, for instance, the development of a national economic plan. It could, of course, be maintained that the rational allocation of scarce resources to obtain an optimum return has long been regarded as a necessary means to realising the goal of satisfying the expanding needs of individuals under socialism. It also happens that State control over the economy, health and education provides any regime with a large reservoir of patronage. It creates under its direct control interlocking hierarchies of comparatively well paid jobs carrying prestige, authority and alluring prospects of promotion for those with the necessary qualifications, conscientiousness and, above all, loyalty. In this way a Marxist regime is peculiarly well placed to reward the pre-revolutionary support – often vital to its success – of the indigenous middle-class intelligentsia. After victory it is able to integrate other sections of the old middle class into the regime. This is, obviously, a major factor in ensuring the stability of any regime and it applies particularly to the growing number of Marxist regimes in the Third World. They have experienced, it would seem, little difficulty in absorbing into the regime the articulate intelligentsia and middle class, who outside it would have constituted a permanent threat to stability. These regimes have, indeed, been almost too successful, for, in the view of some of the contributors to this collection, swollen bureaucracies have been created on a scale quite disproportionate to the modest services they provide. A situation seems to have arisen reminiscent of Soviet Russia in the early 1920s,(when Lenin's constant plaint was against the proliferation and remorseless extension of bureaucratic structures, which, as far as he could see, contributed only negatively to the goal of increasing social well-being, At an even more sordid level, there seems to be evidence enough to support the contention that in the more backward Marxist regimes the elaboration of a national plan and State control over production, imports and exports has been a lucrative source of immediate advantage to particular individuals or dominant tribal or clan groups upon which the regimes depend for their support. The moral in short, is plain and obvious: there may be, and often is, a world of difference between the way in which policies are justified and legitimised, and the actual motives for their implementation.

At another level, we could distinguish between the differing strategic objectives at which economic planning aims. In the case of the Soviet Union, Eastern Europe and the more developed Marxist regimes, the objective is clearly stated: to replace the anarchic, wasteful and inequitable structure of capitalism with a planned, efficient, social mode of production and appropriation which, in terms of its productivity and the rewards it yields to everyone within society, will demonstrate its superiority. The objective in hand is to demonstrate on a global scale the superiority of the socialist mode of production over the capitalist mode. Since Khrushchev's rejection of the feasibility of resolving the antagonism between capitalism and socialism via armed conflict, the Soviet and East European regimes have nailed their colours to the masthead of increased productivity and material abundance as the principal means of winning the world to socialism. In the Third World generally, the objectives of economic planning and the motives for its introduction are quite different. There the preoccupation is not with superseding capitalism, but with transcending what are loosely termed feudal economic relations. The principal economic objective has therefore been the destruction of ancestral or colonially imposed patterns of landownership in which a small minority of large landowners disposed of a very large proportion of the arable land and exacted punitive rents from a thoroughly impoversihed peasantry. (See, for instance, the chapters on Vietnam, Ethiopia and Yemen.) Land reform rather than industrial planning has typically been the major concern of these regimes both during the struggle for power (in the base areas) and after the establishment of a Marxist regime. In this respect they have been avowedly anti-feudal rather than anti-capitalist, and for this reason they have often won the enthusiastic support of large numbers of the impoverished peasantry. Here, again, there is an obvious similarity with the early years of Soviet power in Russia and it can be argued that similar sorts of problems emerge.

There is, as Lenin observed, a logic internal to Marxism which asserts that a regime can rise no higher than the prevailing level of development of industry, education and popular culture will allow. As Lenin was painfully aware, the lower this economic and cultural level, the more difficult the realisation of socialism would be, the more the State would develop with a 'bureaucratic twist', the more significant the qualities of leading individuals would become and the greater the dangers to the regime from their dispute one with another. All of this followed from the

analysis of the phasal progress of capitalism, which was complemented
by the phasal progress of class-consciousness and political organisation,
expressing the ascent of the class from local and particularistic
grievances to an awareness of its real general and historical objectives. It
was, therefore, an essential precondition for the seizure of power that the
process of class formation should have been well developed in the course
of the pre-revolutioanry struggle with capitalism. This process would
then be consummated in the actual struggle for power during the
revolutionary period, which would itself act as an enormous accelerator
to the development of consciousness and class organisation. As an
alternative, the theorists of guerrilla war, Mao Tse-tung, Ho Chi Minh
and Che Guevara, have argued that this same process of class
formation, in terms both of consciousness and of organisation, can in
certain circumstances be forged in the course of a protracted war moving
from the rural periphery towards the urban strongholds of the *ancien
régime*, in the course of which the population as a whole is mobilised,
organised and made aware of its general interests. In both models there
is agreement that consciousness and mass organisation must precede the
conquest of power and are necessary conditions for mass participation
in decision-making, which all Marxist regimes are pledged to realise.

Let us now attempt to draw some of the threads of our argument
together. Marxists assert that certain conditions have to be fulfilled
before a bid for power can responsibly be made.

1. The productive forces of the capitalist mode of production should
   have developed to a point where the continued existence of private
   ownership and private appropriation of the product becomes a fetter
   on their further development. Only at this point, it is argued, will it be
   possible to begin to implement the slogan 'From each according to
   his ability; to each according to his needs.' Where an attempt at
   egalitarian levelling is made prior to this, all that would ensure would
   be, according to Marx, 'crude communism', which he characterised
   as an artificial restriction of human need to Spartan asceticism.

2. The class which leads the struggle overcomes its local particular
   interests and consolidates itself on a national plane in the course of its
   struggle for emancipation, articulating its interest through its
   political party. If a seizure of power takes place prior to this
   development of consciousness and organisation, then, Marx had no
   doubt, it will not be possible to realise the goal of democratic mass
   participation in decision-making and the regime will degenerate into
   a Jacobin coterie of self-styled magistrates of the public good. Politics

would, in this case, become the preserve of the few, and whatever mass organisations might arise after the revolution would have as their objective not the integration of the mass into decision-making, but the mobilisation of their support for decisions already arrived at.

The implications are fairly clear. A Marxist regime cannot simply be characterised in terms of the goals it professes. These, certainly, are necessary but by no means sufficient to an adequate characterisation. We have to add to them the appropriate means and preconditions for their realisation. These preconditions and means are not merely contingent and are not amenable therefore to infinite mutation and adaptation to local circumstances. They cannot with impunity be disregarded or ignored without seriously jeopardising any attempt at realising the Marxist project, in which means and end are bound one to the other. There is, to put it at its most extreme, something very odd about the emergence of a self-styled Marxist regime as a result of a shift of political allegiance within a small sector of an army's officer corps in a country where subsistence agriculture is the overwhelmingly preponderant mode of production. The regime might profess the goals of Marxism, but it is certain that, according to Marxism's own logic, its road towards the realisation of Marxist goals will be exceedingly rocky. In such a regime Marxism may well become merely a convenient rhetoric of legitimation for Jacobins, populists, nationalists or tyrants.

3 Socialist People's Republic of Albania

BOGDAN SZAJKOWSKI

Albania is the smallest of the socialist countries in Europe and the least economically developed. Geographically it occupies a strategically important position in Southern Europe, a fact that has played an important role in the history and development of the country. Ruled by the Ottoman Turks for almost 400 years from 1468, it gained independence in September 1912, only to become an Italian satellite after the First World War. Since the end of the Second World War the successive close relationships with Yugoslavia (1944–8), the Soviet Union (1946–60) and China (1961–78) reflect not only Albania's inherent insecurity but also its importance.

Some 70 per cent of Albania's terrain is rugged mountains, almost inaccessible in the north-east and south-east. The remaining 30 per cent consists of a coastal plain. The topography of the country hindered the development of communications, the growth of national consciousness, and modernisation. It played a major factor in creating close family ties and an attachment to the local community – which remain a strong social force and consequently were the main influences in the pre-servation of ethnic identity through the centuries of foreign domination.

The Albanians are divided into two groups: the less homogeneous Tosks, who live to the south of the Shkumbin River and in scattered communities in northern Greece; and the Gegs who account for some 67 per cent of the population and inhabit the territory to the north and also Kosovo-Metohija in Yugoslavia. Despite linguistic and ethnical differences between the Tosks and the Gegs, Albania is ethnically one of the most homogeneous countries in Europe.

Albania: provincial boundaries

THE ALBANIAN COMMUNIST MOVEMENT, 1917–41

The pre-war Albanian communist movement was both fragmented and closely linked with Albanian nationalism and its aspirations. Communism had its first appeal in Albania when in November 1917, after the Bolshevik revolution, the Soviet government revealed the text of the secret London Treaty (1915), by which Albania was to be divided among Italy, Serbia, Montenegro and Greece.[1] This action was seen by many Albanians as salvation from partition and Lenin was regarded as the saviour of their homeland. After his death, in January 1924, five minutes of silence was observed in his honour by the Albanian Constituent Assembly.

The principle of national self-determination proclaimed by the Bolsheviks attracted many of the nationalists dedicated to the restoration to Albania of the Kosovo province. In the early 1920s they opened up regular contacts with the Comintern and later with the Balkan Communist Federation.

When, in December 1924, Ahmet Beg Zogu established his authoritarian regime first as President (1925–8) and later as Zog I, King of the Albanians (1928–39), many of his opponents went into exile, where they formed two main organisations: the National Union and the Committee for National Liberation (KONARE). KONARE, based in Geneva, was the more vocal group and received financial assistance and support from the Balkan Communist Federation. It also arranged for some of the exiles to go to the Soviet Union. By 1928 KONARE was formally associated with the Comintern. Also, in August 1928, the political refugees in the USSR established an Albanian communist group. The group was dominated by the Comintern and its main function was to educate and prepare party workers for Albania, where a few communist cells had been clandestinely established by Comintern functionaries in 1927.

These cells lacked central organisation and leadership. They operated in isolation from the mass of the population and independently of each other. The oldest and most active was the Korça communist group, and prominent among its leaders was Enver Hoxha, a schoolteacher. By 1941 there were about eight communist groups operating in the major urban centres in the country.

1941–8: THE YUGOSLAV PHASE

The unification of the Albanian communist movement came about after three years of negotiations between the various communist groups and commissaries of the Yugoslav Communist Party. Miladin Popović and Dustan Mugoša convened a meeting of twenty delegates, on 8 November 1941, at which the Albanian Communist Party was founded. The meeting also elected a provisional Central Committee, headed by Enver Hoxha.[2]

The Party was instrumental in the creation of a united front of all anti-Fascist forces in Albania and the formation in September 1942 of the National Liberation Front, consisting of communist and non-communist resistance groups.[3] It was also at the suggestion of the communists that the Albanian National Liberation Army was formed on 10 July 1943.[4]

In October 1942 a rival group, the National Front, was formed. Representatives of the two Fronts, who met in Mukje in August 1943, decided to establish a joint organisation: the Committee for the Salvation of Albania. Part of the Mukje agreement called for the incorporation of Kosovo-Metohija into Albania after the war. The Albanian Communist Party, dominated by the Yugoslavs, was ordered by its advisers to repudiate the agreement. Consequently it had to wage war on two fronts: on the one hand against the Germans and on the other against its domestic opponents.

Successful on both fronts, the communists convened a national congress at Përmet on 24 May 1944, which elected an Anti-Fascist National Liberation Council under the chairmanship of Enver Hoxha, who was also appointed Commander-in-Chief of the National Liberation Army.[5] The congress also forbade the exiled King Zog and his government to return to Albania.

In October 1944, after the liberation of three-quarters of the country, the Anti-Fascist National Liberation Council, at its second session, in Berat, decided to transform itself into the Provisional Democratic Government of Albania, with Enver Hoxha as its Prime Minister.

Albania was liberated by the National Liberation Army on 29 November 1944. Yugoslavia apart, it was the only country in Europe where the communists seized power by their own efforts, without the assistance or presence of Soviet or foreign troops.[6]

After the liberation the new Albanian government followed a path of socialist development familiar to that in other people's democracies: nationalisation of all industrial plants and mines as well as all means of transport and water resources (December 1944).[7] It also nationalised all forest and pasture lands, and seized land belonging to large landowners and distributed it to landless peasants (August 1945).[8]

On 2 December 1945, Albanians held the first elections for the candidates of the Democratic Front, an umbrella organisation for a number of political, social and professional groupings, but dominated by the Communist Party, as in the case of other East European countries. The elected Constituent Assembly formally abolished the monarchy and on 11 January 1946 proclaimed Albania a People's Republic. In March of the same year it promulgated a new constitution.[9]

During this period Yugoslav influence on Albania and the Albanian Communist Party turned into domination. The two countries concluded on 9 July 1946 a Treaty of Friendship, Co-operation and Mutual Aid, which was supplemented by a series of technical and economic pacts. These provided for the establishment of an agency to co-ordinate the economic plans of Albania and Yugoslavia, and for the standardisation of their monetary systems and creation of a common price system and customs union, thus laying the ground for a merger of the two economies. Albania was not asked to participate in the organisational meeting of the Cominform in September 1947, a fact which increased Yugoslavia's grasp on her. Plans were also made by Belgrade and its supporters in the Albanian leadership, led by Koçi Xoxe, to merge the two countries' armed forces. In April 1948 he proposed that Albania should be incorporated into the Yugoslav Federal Republic.

Albanian independence was preserved by the expulsion of Yugoslavia from the Cominform in June 1948 and the Stalin–Tito split that followed.[10]

The Communist Party of Albania was renamed the Party of Labour of Albania (PLA) in September 1948 and purged of Yugoslav supporters. Enver Hoxha and Mehmet Shehu emerged victorious after a short but bitter power struggle within the Albanian leadership. Between 1948 and 1952, as a result of verification of Party cards, 8 per cent of Party members were expelled.[11]

1948–61: SOVIET PHASE

Following the Soviet–Yugoslav and Albanian–Yugoslav splits, Albania entered a period of direct Soviet influence and full integration into the socialist camp. Yugoslav advisers and credit facilities were replaced by Soviet and East European technicians and long-term grants. In February 1949 Albania was admitted to the Council for Mutual Economic Assistance (Comecon). Between 1949 and 1953 Albania adopted the essential features of the Soviet model: planned economy, development of heavy industry, electrification, rapid and forced collectivisation, mechanisation and modernisation of agricultural techniques. During this period the regimes also embarked on major anti-illiteracy, education, health and housing campaigns. The creation, on 14 May 1955, of the Warsaw Treaty Organisation (WTO), of which little Albania was a founding member, had special significance for her: it meant that her security was now guaranteed by one of the super-powers and a group of friendly countries.

Soviet–Albanian relations prospered till the Twentieth Congress of the Communist Party of the Soviet Union (CPSU) in February 1956. The strong denunciation, at the Congress, of Stalin and Stalinism disturbed the Albanian leadership and Enver Hoxha, who supported both vigorously. At about the same time, the Albanians became alarmed at the improvement of Soviet–Yugoslav relations, as they feared that Tito's price for reconciliation with the USSR would be the annexation of Albania by Yugoslavia.

Albania now began to consolidate its ties with China, which also opposed de-Stalinisation, the Khrushchev 'phoney socialism' and the 'revisionist' policies of the Yugoslavs, and granted Albania a massive loan and a technical assistance programme. The Soviet–Albanian rift came into the open at the Twenty-second Congress of the CPSU, on 17 October 1961, when in his opening speech Khrushchev bitterly attacked the Albanian leadership. The climax of the Soviet anti-Albanian campaign came in his concluding speech to the Congress, on 27 October. He accused the Albanian leaders of 'malicious, dirty attacks on Communism, such as not even our enemies, open or concealed' carried on. He described them as nothing less than 'Judases' whose slanders were preparing the way for them to be able to claim alms from the imperialists. According to Khrushchev, the leadership of the PLA did not like the decisive condemnation of the cult of Stalin and its pernicious consequences. Hoxha and Shehu, he said, supported despotism and misuse of power. In fact, it had now reached the point where they could maintain their position only by using force and despotic methods. He concluded by calling on the Albanian people to overthrow them.[12]

Albania's response was to call up all reservists up to the age of thirty-five. This was followed on 7 November by a speech by Enver Hoxha, who accused the Soviet leadership of 'sinister plans, demagogy, hypocrisy and slander'. The removal of Stalin's body from its tomb, he said, was an inhumane game. 'For us,' he said, 'Stalin was and will remain, both as a practical politician and theoretician, one of the most outstanding leaders and one of the most outstanding personalities not only in the Soviet Union but also in the whole communist and labour movement; one of the most ardent defenders and the greatest theoretician of Marxism-Leninism.'

He rejected Khrushchev's concept of peaceful co-existence, because it was 'fraudulent and anti-Marxist' and because it would end in the negation of the class struggle. The Soviet concept of the different forms of the transition to socialism by peaceful means would arouse in the workers the illusion that they could achieve power by parliamentary means.[13]

The Soviet–Albanian dispute deepened further over the next twelve months. On 3 December the USSR broke off diplomatic relations with Albania – an act without precedent in the history of the communist movement.

1961–78: CHINESE PHASE

The third period in the post-war history of Albania began with the outbreak of the Sino-Soviet dispute in 1961 and the disappearance of Soviet and Eastern European political and economic influence, which was replaced by that of China. In November 1961, in a telegram sent by Mao Tse-tung, the PLA was described as the 'glorious member of the great socialist community' which in their south-western outpost of the socialist camp had made important contributions to the defence of the security of the camp. The party remained 'true to Marxism-Leninism and to the principle of proletarian internationalism'. In this way, according to the telegram, the people of China and Albania were closely linked brothers in the great socialist community.

After the break with the Soviet Union, Albania became economically and ideologically increasingly dependent on China. According to the Sino-Albanian economic agreement signed on 25 April 1961, China agreed to supply Albania with aid amounting to £43·8 million ($123 million), between 1961 and 1965.[14] Chinese credits for Albania between 1966 and 1970 are estimated at £76·3 million ($214 million).[15]

Albania also began copying the Chinese model. In February 1966 Hoxa initiated the Albanian Cultural Revolution. Unlike its Chinese counterpart, the Albanian Cultural Revolution was not designed to mark an intra-party power struggle, but represented a unified effort by the Party leadership to reassert its authority over the regional and local Party organisations, as well as to restore its influence in all sectors of Albanian life and to rally the people behind the regime. During the first stage of the revolution, following Chinese example, military ranks were abolished and several high-ranking Party and State functionaries were assigned to work with local and regional Party and State organs. Attempts were also made to reduce the bureaucracy by transferring administrative staff to work in factories and on farms. The second period of what is now called the Ideological and Cultural Revolution was launched by Enver Hoxha on 6 February 1967, and was designed to intensify the struggle against bureaucratism and to eliminate all remaining bourgeois traits from Albanian life. Again, as in China, the red guards played a major part in it, but unlike their Chinese counterparts they remained firmly under the control of the Party. On 15 March 1973, Hoxha concluded the third phase of the revolution, designed to 'preserve Marxist-Leninist purity in all aspects of Albanian life'; this, according to Hoxha, included elimination of all traces of religion, emancipation of women and eradication of undesirable foreign influences, such as long hair, lack of respect for authority, and modern styles in clothing.

The fourth period – to date – of what is also known as a re-volutionisation movement is the anti-bureaucracy campaign, which began on 3 April 1975 and is aimed at reducing the staff of government agencies and the number of non-production employees in agriculture and industry. The main reason for this campaign is the regime's fear of the development of institutionalised opposition or competition to the Party in policy-making. The Ideological and Cultural Revolution has been an on-going process for more than a decade. In 1975 the Albanian leadership decided that it would be a permanent feature of Albanian life until the final victory of socialism had been achieved.

The Sino-Albanian alliance that developed from 1961 and proved to be mutually beneficial ended in a bitter vindication campaign. When China was isolated both within the communist movement and in the international community, Albania acted as a spokesman for China's interests. In turn, China was a vital source of sustenance and support for Tirana in an otherwise hostile world. Internally, Chinese aid allowed Albania to develop its economy, particularly its extractive industry, at a faster pace than would otherwise have been possible, while externally it helped Albania to withstand Soviet pressure and to defy the rest of the world. As long as China remained isolated, there was a natural community of interests between them. However, serious ideological and political divisions between the two countries began to develop[16] and culminated in the announcement on 7 July 1978 of the cessation by China of aid and credits to Albania.[17]

THE SINO-ALBANIAN DISPUTE AND THE 'THREE WORLDS' THEORY

The emergence of China from its diplomatic isolation and in particular its reconciliation with the United States caused Albania to suspect that, if China pursues its *Realpolitik* to its logical conclusion, Albania could become a pawn in the Peking–Washington rapprochement. Gradually the common denominator of Sino-Albanian differences became the so-called 'two-front' struggle theory, with the Albanians supporting the principle that it is impossible to use one imperialism to oppose the other. In addition to its dislike of Peking's contacts with the USA, Albania disagreed with China's favourable evaluation of NATO and the EEC, which China saw as counterweights to Soviet power. After Mao's death in September 1976, the divergence became more obvious and strains more serious. The downfall of the 'Gang of Four' and the rehabilitation of Teng Hsia-ping, who was openly criticised in the Albanian press, played an important role in freezing relations between the two countries. The relations deteriorated even further after the first-ever visit to China, in September 1977, of President Josip Tito, whom the Albanians called the 'father of modern revisionism'.

The Sino-Albanian dispute came into the open over their divergent views of the 'three worlds' theory.[18] China classifies the world's political forces into three parts that are both interconnected and in contradiction to one another. The United States and the Soviet Union make up the First World. The developing countries in Asia, Africa and Latin America make up the Third World. The developed countries, both socialist and capitalist, that are between the two make up the Second World. The two super-powers, according to the theory, are the 'common enemies of the people of the world' and, of the two, the Soviet Union is the more 'ferocious source of world war'. While the countries and people of the Third World, to which China belongs, constitute the main force combating imperialism, colonialism and hegemonism, the Second World is a force that can be united within the struggle against hegemonism. In Albania's view this new global strategy is a flagrant betrayal of Marxism-Leninism. There are only two worlds: the socialist and the non-socialist; revolutionary Marxist-Leninist states and capitalist reactionary states. The idea that one super-power is less dangerous than the other or that the Third World represents a shield against both not only ignores the contradictions between the two rival social systems but is down-right opportunistic, anti-Marxist and anti-revolutionary, as it calls upon the oppressed millions to abandon the revolution.

Albania also rejects the principle that 'the enemy of my enemy is my friend', often used by China both in its analysis of the international situation and in its relations with foreign countries. Tirana maintains that the United States and the Soviet Union are equally dangerous to all people in striving to extend their domination.

As the polemics between Tirana and Peking deepened, with neither country, however, openly attacking the other by name, China, exactly a year after Albania's public condemnation of the 'three worlds' theory, announced the ending, with immediate effect, of all aid and all civilian and military credits to Albania and the withdrawal of all Chinese specialists working in Albania. Thus, small and developing Albania, uniquely among the socialist countries, has now been economically punished, by its three former friends and allies – Yugoslavia in 1948, the Soviet Union in 1961 and China in 1978 – for aspiring to political independence and ideological purity.

INDEPENDENT ALBANIA

Always staunchly nationalist, Albania was the continuous object of invasion and occupation throughout the nineteenth and early twentieth centuries. Since its independence from Turkey in 1912, Albania has always been directly or indirectly dependent on one foreign power or another. With the end of the Chinese phase, Albania, for the first time in its history, is politically and economically totally independent of foreign patronage. The main factor in achieving this independence is self-reliance, which according to Enver Hoxha 'is correctly understood when it is implemented in every field of social activity, on a national and district scale, when it is extended to every link and cell of our life, to every enterprise and cooperative, to every institution and army unit when people work and live everywhere as in a state of siege'.[19]

The end of Chinese economic aid may slacken somewhat the rate of Albania's economic development, but it is unlikely to have the same grave economic consequences as did the cessation of Soviet aid, in the early 1960s. Economically the country is in a better position than ever before. Self-sufficient in wheat production and high octane petroleum, it now also has a larger number and a greater variety of products capable of satisfying a people relatively simple and unaffected by the demands and expectations of Western consumerism. Internationally it is no longer an isolated country. It maintains diplomatic relations with some seventy-five countries and takes active, if somewhat impotent, part in the activities of the United Nations. Furthermore, since 1977 Albania has succeeded in establishing a new grouping of 'Marxist-Leninist' parties, most of which previously supported China and have now taken the Albanian side in the 'three worlds' theory controversy.[20] This new grouping may prove particularly useful to Albania should it require vocal support as a result of direct Soviet involvement in the Balkans in the post-Tito era. This is a prospect which Albania views with increasing concern.

There is no prospect that China's patronage will be replaced by that of another country. The Socialist Republic of Vietnam is the only country in the socialist group which remains friendly to Albania, but for numerous reasons it is not in a position to help. Also excluded must be any possibility of alliance with non-socialist countries.

'The People's Republic of Albania', declared Foreign Minister Nesti Nase,

> has not traded, and will never trade in principles. The imperialists, the social-imperialists and the other reactionaries are trying in vain to spread diabolical slanders about Albania, they are trying to create the impression that, under pressure of international events, Albania will be compelled either to choose isolation and separation from the world, or abandon the road it has been following until now. We declare openly and in no uncertain terms: Nobody should cherish the illusion that 'Albania is an isolated country', that it 'cannot live without foreign aid', or that it will be compelled to stretch a begging hand to anybody.[21]

THE PARTY OF LABOUR OF ALBANIA

Organisation

The present statute of the Party is that adopted at its First Congress, in 1948.

The Party is based and operates on the principle of democratic centralism.[22] The new constitution of the Republic, promulgated in 1976, recognises the special status of the Party as the 'sole directing political power in State and society'.

The lowest level in the Party's hierarchy is the basic cell, similar in its role and activities to those in the other socialist countries. Three persons or more can form a basic Party cell in a place of work or higher educational establishment. The functions of a cell are: recruitment of new members, supervision and direction of activities in its own area, dissemination and implementation of Party directives, and administration of local Party affairs. The basic cell elects a secretary or, in the case of large membership (over thirty), secretariat; its elected officials are its links with higher Party bodies.

The Party is organised according to the country's territorial subdivisions, i.e. there are village, rural, urban, city and district committees, with central apparatus in Tirana.

The highest organ of the Party, according to the statute, is the Party Congress, which should meet once every four years.[23] Delegates to the Congress are elected by Party conferences at rural, city, regional and district levels. The Congress at its final session elects the central Party Control, the Central Revision Commission and, most importantly, the Central Committee. The Central Committee directs all Party activities between congresses, administers Party funds, represents the Party in its relations with other parties in other countries, but above all it is responsible for the supervision of the lower Party organisations. The Central Committee elected at the Seventh Congress of the PLA, held in Tirana on 1–7 November 1976, consists of seventy-seven full members and thirty-nine candidate members. Among the members of the Central Committee are five married couples, including Enver Hoxha and his wife, Mehmet Shehu and his wife, and Kysni Kapo and his wife.

The Central Committee at its first meeting after the Congress elects the Political Bureau and the Secretariat.

The Secretariat is responsible for the smooth functioning of the Party and the work of the departments of the Central Committee, departments which in their functions closely correspond to those of ministries. The departments play a crucial role in the degree of control and supervision the Party exercises over the non-Party organisations.

The real power lies with the Political Bureau, which is the policy-making body of the Party. The Political Bureau elected at the Seventh Congress consists of twelve full members and five candidate members.

Membership

In 1977 the membership of the PLA was just under 3 per cent of the population. Of the total number of Party functionaries in all establishments, 40 per cent were under the age of 30; 31 per cent belonged to the 31–40 age group; 21 per cent were 41–50; and 8 per cent were over 51 years of age.[24]

Although the membership of the Party has increased over the years (see Table 3.1), the PLA has also undergone several small purges and at least one major purge, during the various stages of the Ideological and Cultural Revolution. During the period 1967–70, 1323 members and 434 candidates were expelled from the Party, while 1047 have been demoted to candidate status.

TABLE 3.1 Membership of the PLA

Year	Membership
1943	700
1948	45,382
1952	44,418
1956	48,644
1961	53,659
1966	66,327
1971	86,985
1977	101,500

Sources: History of the PLA (1971) pp. 327, 369, 411, 474, 572; E. Hoxha, *Report to the 6th Congress of the PLA* (1971) pp. 179–80; E. Hoxha, *Report to the 7th Congress of the PLA* (1977) p. 89.

Composition

Only limited statistical data on the social composition of the PLA is available. Table 3.2 shows that, in accordance with the policy of 'revolutionisation', the percentage of labourers in the Party has increased over the years, while that of white-collar workers has declined. Also since 1967, there has been a deliberate drive to increase the representation of women, who in 1971 constituted 22·05 per cent, in 1972 24 per cent, in 1975 26 per cent, and in 1976 27 per cent of the total membership.

TABLE 3.2 Social composition of the PLA

	Labourers	Collective peasants	White-collar workers
1970	35·2	29·0	35·8
1971	36·4	29·7	33·9
1975	37·7	29·2	33·1
1976	37·5	29·0	33·5

Sources: R. F. Staar, *Yearbook on International Communist Affairs* (1971) p. 3; (1973) p. 3; (1976) p. 1. E. Hoxha, *Report to the 6th Congress*, pp. 180, 182. E. Hoxha, *Report to the 7th Congress*, p. 89.

GOVERNMENT

The Constitution

Since the end of the Second World War Albania has had two constitutions. The first post-war constitution was adopted on 14 March 1946 and was based largely on the Yugoslav Constitution. Although it described Albania as a 'state of workers and labouring peasants' it made no reference to the role played by the Party or any other political organisations. The Constitution was amended on 4 July 1950 and in many respects made closely to resemble the Constitution of the Soviet Union. Further amendments were made in 1955, 1960 and 1963. The new constitution, consisting of 112 articles, that was approved by the People's Assembly on 28 December 1976 differs considerably from the previous one and is unique not only among the socialist countries but also in the world as a whole. Article 1 describes Albania as the Socialist People's Republic (instead of the People's Republic, as hitherto). The PLA is defined as the sole directing political power in state and society and Marxism-Leninism its sole ideology (article 3). Unlike in any other of the socialist countries, the First Secretary of the PLA is also the Commander-in-Chief of the Armed Forces and the Defence Council (article 89). The Constitution prohibits the establishment of foreign bases and the stationing of foreign troops on Albanian soil (article 91) and it explicitly prohibits anyone from signing or accepting the capitulation or occupation of the country (article 90). The document states that private property has been abolished and is forbidden in Albania, and that, when the general interest requires, even personal property may be converted into State property (article 24), which is the highest form of socialist property (article 18). Citizens are not required to pay taxes or levies of any kind (article 31) and the sexes are to enjoy equal rights (article 41).

The Constitution stresses that the State recognises no religion whatever and supports atheist propaganda (article 37). It prohibits the creation of religious, fascist and anti-democratic organisations and propaganda (article 55). Parents are responsible for the upbringing and communist education of their children (article 49), education that combines lessons with productive work and physical and military training (article 32). The document also prohibits 'granting concessions to and the creation of, foreign economic and financial companies and other institutions or ones formed jointly with bourgeois and revisionist capitalist monopolies and states' (article 28). Under the Constitution not only do deputies to the People's Assembly enjoy immunity from prosecution, but, in addition, and without precedent anywhere in the world, members of the local people's councils enjoy immunity within the territorial unit under the council's administration (article 96). Officials in Albania participate directly in production work and are paid salaries in fair ratio with other workers, a provision aimed at 'preventing the creation of a privileged stratum'. The pay ratio is set by law (article 9).

The unusual provisions of this constitution, which make it a unique legal document, are perhaps best explained by the statement that, whereas the old constitution was the constitution of the building of the foundation of socialism, the new document is the constitution of the complete construction of the socialist society.[25]

The People's Assembly

According to the Constitution, power in Albania derives from and belongs to the people. The document establishes the People's Assembly as the legislative branch of the government and refers to it as the highest organ of State power. Members of the Assembly are elected from a single list of Democratic Front candidates, one candidate for each seat, for a term of four years, in a ratio of one member for every 8000 inhabitants (for election results, see Table 3.3). The 250-member Assembly meets twice a year, for sessions lasting four to seven days. Bills become law by simple majority vote in the Assembly, but an amendment to the Constitution requires a two-thirds majority. In practice, all bills and constitutional amendments have until now been approved unanimously.

TABLE 3.3 Albanian election results, 1958–78

Year	Entitled to vote	Positive votes	%	Negative votes
1958	780,061	779,935	99·80	126
1962	889,875	889,868	99·90	7
1966	978,161	978,063	99·99	98
1970	1,097,123	1,097,013	99·99	110
1974	1,248,530	1,248,528	99·99	2
1978	1,436,289	1,436,285	100·00	0

Note: According to the announcement from the Central Electoral Commission during the 12 November 1978 elections, 1,436,288 electors, over 99·99 per cent of the voters, took part in the election. One elector did not cast his vote. 1,436,285 electors voted for the candidates of the Albanian Democratic Front, equal to 100 per cent of all voters. Three ballot papers were found to be void.

Sources: Assembly of Captive European Nations, *Survey of Developments*, v (1958) and xii (1962) New York; BBC, *Summary of World Broadcasts*, 13 July 1966, 22 Sep 1970, 10 Aug 1974 and 15 Nov 1978.

The People's Assembly, under the provisions of the constitution, elects the Presidium, which acts on its behalf between sessions. It is made up of a president, two vice-presidents, a secretary and ten members. The President of the Presidium performs the function of a titular head of State. The Presidium, apart from conducting the affairs of the Assembly between sessions, executes several other functions. It calls the Assembly into session, ratifies international agreements, exercises the right of pardon, issues decrees, receives letters of credence, appoints and recalls diplomatic envoys, and interprets the laws. It also directs and controls the activity of the people's councils.

The Council of Ministers

The People's Assembly, according to the Constitution, also appoints the supreme executive and administrative organ of State, the Council of Ministers. This is usually done on the recommendation of its Chairman after consultations with the Party's Political Bureau. The Council of Ministers is composed of the Chairman, five deputy chairmen, the Secretary-general, fourteen ministers, and the Chairman of the State Planning Commission. As a rule, the members of the Council of Ministers are appointed from among the ranks of the deputies to the

People's Assembly. It is a unit constitutionally responsible for the activities of the ministries, other central organs of State administration and the executive committees of the people's councils. It prepares the national plan and the budget, which have to be approved by the People's Assembly. After approval, which is granted unanimously, the Council is responsible for implementation. It also directs the monetary system, and is responsible for the protection of citizens' rights and the maintenance of public order; the direction and organisation of the armed forces; and, in effect, the administration of the entire economic and cultural life of the nation.

Local government

The constitutional agencies of the central government at village, city, regional and district levels are the people's councils. Elected every three years from a single list of agreed candidates, they are responsible to their constituencies and to the higher organs of State power. Under the provisions of the Constitution, the councils are charged with economic and cultural matters and direct the affairs of the administrative organs under their jurisdictions. The councils meet in session twice yearly and between sessions each council's work is carried on by an executive committee elected from among its membership. The committee supervises and administers the activities of a number of permanent departments, which are responsible not only to the council but also to corresponding sections of the higher levels of the bureaucracy.

Article 95 of the Constitution stipulates that a higher people's council may dissolve a lower-level people's council, appoint the provisional executive committee and decide on the elections for a new council. Similarly, a higher people's council may dismiss the executive committee of a lower council and order new elections. These provisions are based on the principle of democratic centralism, which is common to all Marxist regimes but, is rarely to be found in their Constitutions. (The 1977 Soviet Constitution for the first time defines that the 'Soviet State is organised and functions on the principle of democratic centralism'.)

Party—State relations

Although the Constitution determines the role of the PLA within the political structure of the country, only about 3 per cent of the population are members of the Party. The Party dominates and supervises the direction and activities of the central and local government, not only as of right but also through a comprehensive system of multiple office-holding, with considerable concentration of power among the members of the Political Bureau. Thus, the holders of the most important government posts – the Prime Minister, the deputy prime ministers, and the ministers in charge of such crucial ministries as Defence, the Interior and Finance – are the top Party officials (see Table 3.4).

TABLE 3.4 Government posts held by the members of the PLA Political Bureau, July 1978

Enver Hoxha	First Secretary of the Central Committee
Ramiz Alia	Secretary of the Central Committee
Adil Carcani	First Deputy Prime Minister
Kadri Hazbiu	Minister for Internal Affairs
Hekuran Isai	Secretary of the Central Committee
Hysni Kapo	Secretary of the Central Committee
Spiro Koleka	Deputy Prime Minister, Deputy Chairman of the People's Assembly
Pali Miska	Deputy Prime Minister
Manush Myftiu	Deputy Prime Minister
Mehmet Shehu	Prime Minister, Minister for People's Defence
Haki Toska	Minister of Finance

Multiple office-holding has been standard practice since the foundation of the current Albanian regime. In 1978 seven of the twenty-two members of the Council of Ministers were members or candidate members of the Political Bureau, eleven were members or candidate members of the Central Committee, and the remaining four were regular members of the Party. With every key position occupied by a Political Bureau member, the Party elite maintained direct control over the entire governmental structure, applying the principle that 'the more the revolution advances and deepens, the more the leading role of the Party must be strengthened and perfected in every sphere of life and state and social activity'.[26]

Mass organisations

Cultural, professional and mass organisations in Albania are subordinate to the PLA. Their major functions are to popularise, explain and implement the Party line in their respective areas of concern in such a way as to enable the Party directives to be correctly understood and enacted by all segments of the population, thus ensuring that the Party line prevails in every aspect of the nation's life.

The Democratic Front, founded in 1942 as a successor to the National Liberation Front, is, after the PLA, perhaps the most powerful and important mass organisation in the country. As an umbrella organisation for professional, political and cultural groups, its aim is to give expression to the political views of the entire population and to serve as a mass political educator. The Front, according to its statute, unites the people with the Party in the struggle to build socialism and defend the fatherland. In practice the Democratic Front is a Party instrument expressly designed for the political control of the entire population.

The Union of Albanian Working Youth, founded in 1941, is the PLA's youth branch. Organised in the same way as the Party, the Union has a parallel structure. Its main function is to prepare young people for future Party membership. It is also responsible for the implementation among the country's youth of all Party directives and policies. Its membership consists of school pupils, university students, young workers and peasants, up to the age of eighteen. The Union organises labour brigades to work on construction projects and special assignments: for example, it was given responsibility for closing down all the places of worship in the country after the launching of the Cultural Revolution in 1967.

The United Trades Unions of Albania, founded in 1945, is composed of three general unions: the Trade Union of Workers of Industry and Construction, the Trade Union of Workers of Education and Trade, and the Trade Union of Workers of Agriculture and Procurements. Its main tasks are to carry out the political and ideological education of the workers, to implement Party directives and to increase labour productivity by fulfilling work norms.

The Women's Union of Albania, founded in 1943, controls and supervises the political and social activities of women. It is responsible for their ideological training and for securing equal social and political rights. In a country which has been traditionally dominated by men, the emancipation of women has been one of the major developments. They now share responsibility in the Government at all levels and can enter all the professions and work side by side with men for equal pay.

INTERNAL AFFAIRS

Education

One of the more important problems to be overcome by the new post-war regime was that of reducing the highest percentage of illiteracy in Europe (90 per cent in 1938). By 1963 illiteracy had been eliminated among the population up to the age of forty, and in 1970 universal education with an eighty-year period of study was achieved. In 1957 the first university in the country's history was opened in Tirana. The university has seven faculties, five scientific-research institutes and several annexes in the regions.

In June 1969 the government introduced educational reform aimed at revolutionising schools and higher education and at making 'a decisive contribution to the training and education of the new man with comprehensive Communist traits, loyal to the end to the Party's cause'. The new system, which is similar to that in China, closely links learning with productive work and with physical and military education and gives absolute priority to Marxism-Leninism. The structure of the academic year in all secondary schools is as follows: six and a half months of academic study, two and a half months of productive work, one month of military training and two months of vacation. The degree courses at the institutions of higher education last from three to five years. University students spend seven months of every year at the university, two months in production work, one month in physical culture and military training, and two months on vacation.

Religion

Before the foundation of the People's Republic, the majority of the population, about 70 per cent, belonged to either the Sunni or Benktashi Islamic sects. The Orthodox and Roman Catholic denominations claimed 20 and 10 per cent of the population respectively. Although the 1946 constitution and its amended version of 1950 guaranteed freedom of conscience and religion, measures were taken to limit the activities of the religious denominations. The religious communities had to be recognised by the State, and their statutes and leaders approved by the Council of Ministers. All pastoral letters and messages had to be vetted by a censor before they were made public. In 1951 the regime cancelled its diplomatic relations with the Vatican and, following the pattern established in other socialist countries, organised the Independent Catholic Church of Albania. In 1967, in his speech launching the second stage of the Ideological and Cultural Revolution, Enver Hoxha formulated a new policy towards private and organised religion. He called for intensified struggle against religious beliefs and assigned the anti-religious mission to the youth movement. By the end of May 1967, religious institutions were forced to hand over to the government 2169 mosques, churches and other places of worship, most of which were converted into museums, swimming pools, concert halls or centres of cultural interest. Religious feasts and other customs related to religion were replaced by new festivities and customs socialist in content.[27] No public or private worship is allowed in Albania. Officially the entire population is atheist and the regime has declared Albania the first atheist nation in the world, its only religion 'Albanism'.

Economy

Albania's economic activity is governed by a series of five-year plans prepared by the State Planning Commission under the guidance of the PLA. During the six five-year plans (i, 1951–5; ii, 1956–60; iii, 1961–5; iv, 1966–70; v, 1971–5; vi, 1976–80), the Albanian economy has made substantial progress in all areas, with production in the industrial sector expanding much more rapidly than agriculture.

The progress was mainly owing to large-scale aid, loans and credits – from Yugoslavia during the immediate post-war period, from the Soviet Union and Eastern Europe from 1948 to 1961, and from China from 1961 to 1978.

Albania's industrial sector is based on the exploration of oil, copper, chromium and iron-nickel, the processing industries, hydroelectric power stations and food and textile plants. Since 1961, with China's technical and financial assistance, nitrate-fertiliser and superphosphate plants at Fier and Lac have been added to the country's small industrial base. Only limited attempts have been made to establish other heavy industries, primarily owing to the small market within Albania and the lack of technical expertise. In 1975, in comparison with 1970, industrial production increased by 52 per cent, at an average annual rate of 8·7 per cent.[28]

The country's industry is poorly balanced, not only in a technical sense but also in terms of essential domestic needs and the availability of foreign outlets for its products. Another important problem, which has increasingly attracted the attention of the Albanian leadership, is that of poor workmanship (especially in the manufacture of consumer goods), workers' apathy and alienation.

The total volume of investments envisaged by the 1971–5 plan was not carried out in full and in 1976 the Ministry of Construction was instructed to put an end to 'the irrational dispersal of the principal means of construction, to extension of time limits in building projects, and to exceeding the funds and material provided'. At the Seventh Congress of the PLA, in 1976, Enver Hoxha reported that 'the practice of starting construction work without preliminary studies, specifications and accurate designs, which has frequently been the case, has cost and is still costing the people's economy dearly'.[29]

Albania's agricultural sector was entirely socialised by the end of 1970. There are no private farms in the country and agricultural organisation consists of two types of farms: State farms and collective farms.

State farms were established during the immediate post-war period on land confiscated from large landowners. In 1970 there were thirty-three State farms, with an average size of 3052 hectares. Managers and workers of State farms are salaried government employees.

Collective farms began to be organised through the forcible consolidation of private holdings and against strong peasant resistance in 1946, and was not completed until 1970. Although the land, machinery and livestock of a collective farm is owned collectively by the peasants working on it, the farms are under strong governmental and Party control, through the local organisation of the PLA and the local people's council. A collective farm is nominally governed by its chairman, treasurer and a small group of other officers elected by an annual general meeting. The meeting also establishes work norms for the farm members, its budget, investment policies and production plans. In practice the officers are responsible for the farm's activities to local councils and Party organisations. The collective is assigned and obliged to fulfil centrally determined production tasks. Members of a collective farm receive income on the basis of the quantity and quality of work performed.

In 1973 there were 459 collective farms with an average size of 837 hectares, cultivating 80 per cent of the arable land of Albania. The remaining 20 per cent of the land was cultivated by the State farms.

Members of collective farms and employees of State farms are entitled by law to a private plot for their personal use. The plots vary in sizes depending on the terrain, from 1000 to 1500 square metres per family (about 10,750–16,150 square feet). Each family is also entitled to maintain for its own use a few domestic animals, a cow or a pig and a few sheep or goats.

EXTERNAL AFFAIRS

Between 1961 and 1969, Albania underwent a period of self-imposed diplomatic isolation, participating only in the proceedings of the United Nations and its agencies. Although still formally a member of Comecon, it declined to take part in its activities after October 1961. A founding member of the WTO, since 1961 it has similarly refused to participate in its military exercises and proceedings. On 13 September 1968, the Albanian government officially withdrew from the WTO, in protest at the invasion of Czechoslovakia. Albania views NATO, the WTO, Comecon and the EEC with equal suspicion and contempt, as the basic instruments of the expansionist policy of the two super-powers.

Albania was invited, but refused, to participate in the Conference on Security and Co-operation in Europe in August 1975. As a result, it was the only European country that did not sign the Final Act of the Conference. The Conference was dismissed by Albania as nothing more than a device employed by the two super-powers to legitimise their respective spheres of influence in Europe and ensure their freedom to pursue their 'aggressive imperialistic policies towards China and Albania as well as the peoples of Asia, Africa and Latin America'.

Albanian–Soviet relations have shown no signs of improvement since the split in 1961. The USSR has made several offers to restore normal relations and has offered the Albanians substantial economic aid. This has been refused by the Albanian leadership, who, echoing China, have accused the Soviet Union of being a 'militaristic fascist state' which exploits its allies through such organisations as Comecon and the Warsaw Pact and collaborates with the United States to thwart national liberation movements and popular revolutions throughout the world.

The one area where Albania has predictably shown an interest in better relations has been the Balkans. The resumption, in May 1971, of diplomatic relations with Greece ended the technical state of war that had existed between the two countries since 1940. In July 1977 direct air communication was opened between Tirana and Athens and the trade protocol for 1978 envisages trade worth $28 million between the two countries.[30]

Ties with Romania and Turkey have also been strengthened, and a cultural exchange with the latter was signed in April 1978.

Yugoslav–Albanian relations visibly improved in the aftermath of the Soviet invasion of Czechoslovakia. However, they came to a gradual halt as the Yugoslav–Chinese rapprochement progressed. With China's cancellation of economic aid to Albania and her increasing support for

Yugoslavia's non-alignment, there is little prospect of an improvement of contacts between Tirana and Belgrade. From the Yugoslav point of view, relations with Albania present a special problem because of the large number of Albanians living in Yugoslavia (over 1 million), most of them in the Kosovo area, close to the Yugoslav–Albanian border. The situation of the Albanian minority in Yugoslavia has improved considerably in the last decade, especially since 1970, and today it enjoys genuine equality with the other nationalities in Yugoslavia. However, beneath the surface latent tensions still exist, and these, especially if given encouragement from outside, could erupt.

Overall, however, since 1971 Albania has shown overt concern for the Balkan region. The strengthening of relations between the Balkan states would in Albania's view improve its own security and reduce the prospect of direct Soviet involvement in the region in the future.

BIOGRAPHIES

Enver Hoxha, First Secretary of the Central Committee of the PLA, was born on 16 October 1908 in Gjirokastra to a middle-class Muslim family. He began his revolutionary activities while still at the Lycée Français in Korça, a town which was the strongest revolutionary centre in the country. He finished at the Lycée in 1930 with outstanding results and was awarded a scholarship by the Albanian government to study in France. In 1931 he enrolled at the Faculty of Natural Sciences at Montpellier. His scholarship, however, was suspended in 1934 when the Albanian authorities found that some time earlier he had joined the Communist Party of France. Afterwards, for a period, he worked on the staff of *L'Humanité*, to which he contributed articles denouncing King Zog's regime in Albania. He later became private secretary to the Albanian consul in Brussels and continued his law studies, but never completed them. In 1936 he returned to Albania and became a teacher, first in a high school in Tirana and later in the Lycée Français in Korça. He also joined the trade-union movement of Korça and became a leading member of the communist group there. After the Italian invasion he continued his activities underground, leading the communist group in Tirana. After the unification of the various communist groups into the Albanian Communist Party in 1941, he was elected Secretary of the provisional Central Committee and later, in 1943, its General Secretary. He still holds the equivalent post in the PLA. In 1942 he was elected the leader of the partisan National Liberation Front.

When the regular National Liberation Army was formed, he became its Commander-in-Chief, with the rank of Colonel-general. At the Congress in Përmet in May 1944, he was elected Chairman of the Anti-Fascist National Liberation Council, and in October 1944, at its second conference, he was appointed head of the democratic government of Albania. In this capacity he entered Tirana on 28 November 1944 and outlined the government's domestic and foreign policies. After the war, in addition to the post of Prime Minister (1944–54), he also held the portfolio of Minister of Foreign Affairs (1946–53). Since 1954 he has concentrated on Party work.

In 1945 Enver Hoxha married a partisan girl, Nexhmija Xhangolli, born to a Muslim family in Diber. She has been a member of the Albanian Communist Party since its inception, a member of the Central Committee since 1948 and of the Political Bureau since 1971. Mrs Hoxha has held a number of ministerial and important Party posts and since March 1978 has been Minister for Foreign Trade. The Hoxhas have three children: Ilir (born 1948), Sokol (born 1951) and Pranvera (born 1954).

Mehmet Shehu, Prime Minister and Minister of People's Defence, was born on 10 January 1913 in the village of Corush. He was educated first at the American Technical College in Tirana, which he left in 1932, and later at the military academy in Naples, from which he was excluded after taking part in pro-communist activities. He fought in the Spanish Civil War as a commandant of the fourth battalion of the 'Garibaldi Brigade', and while in Spain he joined the Communist Party. After the collapse of the Civil War, he was interned in France, from 1939 to 1942. During his internment he joined the Italian Communist Party. After his return to Albania in 1942, he became a Member of the Albanian Communist Party and formed a partisan unit in his locality. In August 1943 he became commandant of the First Shock Brigade. He was appointed Chief of the General Staff of the People's Army after the liberation and later attended the Voroshilov Military Academy in the USSR. Following the fall of the Koçi Xoxe group he became Deputy Prime Minister (1948–54) and Minister for Internal Affairs (1948–54). When, in 1954, the office of Prime Minister was separated from that of General Secretary of the Party, Mehmet Shehu became Prime Minister. In 1974 he was appointed Minister of People's Defence. He has been a member of the Political Bureau since 1948.

BASIC FACTS ABOUT ALBANIA

Official name: Socialist People's Republic of Albania (Republika Popullore Socialiste e Shqipërisë).

Area: 28,748 sq. km. (11,101 sq. miles).

Population (1979): 2,594,600.

Population density: 88·6 per sq. km.

Population distribution: 34 per cent urban, 66 per cent rural.

Membership of the PLA (Partia e Punes) (1977 est.): 101,500.

Administrative division: 26 districts.

Ethnic nationalities (1955 census): Albanians, 96·9 per cent; Greeks, 2·5 per cent; Yugoslavs, 0·4 per cent; others, 0·1 per cent.

Populations of major towns (1977): Tiranë (the capital), 192,000; Shkodër, 62,400; Durrës, 60,000; Vlorë, 55,500; Elbasan, 53,300.

National income by sector: industry, 44·2 per cent; agriculture and forestry, 34·6 per cent; construction, 10 per cent; transportation and communications, 3·2 per cent; retail and wholesale trade, 6·8 per cent; others, 1·2 per cent.

Main natural resources: chrome, copper, iron, nickel, coal, oil and timber.

Foreign trade (1964, no figures are available for the total value of trade after that date): exports, £21,401,428 ($59,924,000); imports, £35,045,714 ($98,128,000); total, £56,447,142 ($158,052,000).

Main trading partners: China, Czechoslovakia, Poland, GDR, Romania, Italy.

Rail network: 302 km.

Road network (1977 est.): 4000 km.

Universities: 1, State University of Tirana (16,420 students in 1978).

Foreign relations: diplomatic relations with over 75 countries; 22 diplomatic missions resident in Tirana;, member of the United Nations since 1955.

NOTES

1. *History of the Party of Labour of Albania* (1971) p. 17.
2. N. C. Pano, *The People's Republic of Albania* (1968) pp. 41–2.
3. *History of the PLA*, pp. 122–3.
4. Ibid., p. 156.
5. Ibid., p. 207.
6. Ibid., p. 241.
7. Ibid., p. 264.

8. Ibid., p. 266.
9. Ibid., p. 273.
10. Ibid., pp. 305–19.
11. Ibid., p. 369.
12. *Pravda*, 29 Oct 1961.
13. *History of the PLA*, pp. 496–500.
14. *Hsinhua News Bulletin*, 25 Apr 1961; quoted in Pano, *Albania*, p. 147.
15. J. Prybyla, 'Albania's Economic Vassalage', *Eastern Europe*, xvi, no. 1 (Jan 1967) 9–14. In a note to the Albania Embassy in China, the Chinese Foreign Ministry has claimed that 'the agreements concluded between China and Albania (since 1954) call for an outlay by the Chinese Government of more than 10 billion yuan renminbi', which amounts approximately to £3,076,923,000 or $6,061,538,000 (at July 1978 exchange rate). For the full text of the note, see B. Szajkowski (ed.), *Documents in Communist Affairs – 1979* (1979) pp. 388–393. For authoritative comment see M. Kaser, 'Note on Chinese Aid to Albania', ibid., pp. 424–6.
16. For the Albanian account of the development of the dispute, see 'Letter from the Central Committee of the Albanian Workers' Party and the Council of Ministers of the People's Socialist Republic of Albania to the Central Committee of the Communist Party of China and the State Council of the People's Republic of China', in Szajkowski (ed.), *Documents – 1979*.
17. 'Note of the Ministry of Foreign Affairs of the People's Republic of China to the Embassy of the People's Socialist Republic of Albania', ibid. (note 15).
18. The first overt sign of the dispute was the publication by the official organ of the PLA Central Committee, *Zëri i Populit* (The Voice of the People), on 7 July 1977, of the article 'The Theory and Practice of the Revolution'. China replied on 1 November 1977 with the publication in the CPC Central Committee newspaper, *People's Daily*, of a 35,000 word editorial entitled 'Chairman Mao's Theory of the Differentiation of the Three Worlds is a Major Contribution to Marxism-Leninism'. For texts of both, see B. Szajkowski (ed.), *Documents in Communist Affairs – 1977* (1978).
19. E. Hoxha, *Report Submitted to the 7th Congress of the PLA* (1977) p. 72.
20. The new grouping includes the Marxist-Leninist parties of Brazil, New Zealand, West Germany, Italy, Spain, Portugal, Greece, France, Switzerland and Benin.
21. Speech to the Thirty-second Session of the United Nations General Assembly, Albanian Telegraphic Agency, 7 Oct 1977.
22. The principles of democratic centralism can be summarised as follows:

    (1) election of all leading party bodies, from the lowest to the highest;
    (2) periodical reports of party bodies to their party organisations and to higher bodies;
    (3) strict party discipline and subordination of the minority to the majority;
    (4) the decisions of higher bodies are obligatory for lower bodies.

23. Two congresses met after periods of more than four years. Six years lapsed between the Third (1955) and Fourth (1961) Congresses (1961) and again six years between the Sixth (1971) and Seventh (1976) Congresses.
24. Hoxha, *Report to the 7th Congress*, p. 95.
25. Ibid., p. 12

26. Ibid., p. 23
27. *History of the PLA*, p. 625.
28. Hoxha, *Report to the 7th Congress*, p. 80
29. Ibid., p. 57
30. BBC, *Summary of World Broadcasts*, 4 Apr 1978.

BIBLIOGRAPHY

Albania: Geographical, Historical and Economic Data (Tirana: Naim Frashëri Publishing House, 1964).
Amery, J., *Sons of the Eagle: A Study in Guerrilla War* (London: Macmillan, 1968).
The Facts About Soviet—Albanian Relations (Tirana: Naim Frashëri Publishing House, 1964).
Frasheri, K., *The History of Albania: A Brief Survey* (Tirana: Naim Frashëri Publishing House, 1964).
Griffith, W. E., *Albania and the Sino-Soviet Rift* (Cambridge, Mass.: Massachusetts Institute of Technology Press, 1963).
Hamm, H., *Albania – China's Beachhead in Europe* (London: Weidenfeld and Nicolson, 1963).
History of the Party of Labour of Albania (Tirana: Naim Frashëri Publishing House, 1971).
Hoxha, E., *Our Policy is An Open Policy, the Policy of Proletarian Principles* (Tirana: 8 Nëntori Publishing House, 1978).
——, *Report Submitted to the 6th Congress of the Party of Labour of Albania* (Tirana: Naim Frashëri Publishing House, 1971).
——, *Report Submitted to the 7th Congress of the Party of Labour of Albania* (Tirana: 8 Nëntori Publishing House, 1977).
Marmullaku, R., *Albania and the Albanians* (London: C. Hurst and Co., 1975).
Pano, N. C., *The People's Republic of Albania* (Baltimore: Johns Hopkins Press, 1968).
Prybyla, J., 'Albania's Economic Vassalage', *East Europe*, XVI, no. 1 (1967) 9–14.
Skendi, S. (ed.), *Albania* (New York: Praeger, 1958).
——, *The Albanian National Awakening, 1878–1912* (Princeton, N.J.: Princeton University Press, 1967).
——, *The Political Evolution of Albania, 1912–1944* (New York: Mid-European Studies Center, Mar 1954).
Staar, R. F. (ed.), *Yearbook on International Communist Affairs* (Stanford, Calif.: Hoover Institution Press) (annual).
Szajkowski, B. (ed.), *Documents in Communist Affairs – 1977*; *Documents in Communist Affairs – 1979* (annual: 1977–9, Cardiff: University College Cardiff Press; 1980– , London: Macmillan)
Tang, P. S. H., *The Twenty-Second Congress of the Communist Party of the Soviet Union and Moscow—Tirana—Peking Relations* (Washington, D.C.: Research Institute on the Sino-Soviet Bloc, 1962).
Twenty Years of Socialism in Albania (Tirana: Naim Frashëri Publishing House, 1964).

4 People's Republic of Angola

MICHAEL WOLFERS

Angola is one of the largest and potentially one of the wealthiest countries in Africa, but its people came to independence after suffering from Portugal one of the longest and most debilitating of all forms of European colonialism. Geographically Angola serves as a transit route for mineral exports from, to the east, landlocked Zambia, and, to the north, Zaire, which has very limited access to the Atlantic through a shipping channel within Angolan territorial waters. Angola had its first Portuguese colonial settlement in 1575 (independence came 400 years later), but for centuries was mainly of interest to Portugal as a source of slaves, or as a dumping ground for exiled criminals.[1] Portugal conducted military campaigns at the end of the nineteenth century and in the early decades of the twentieth century to establish effective occupation, developed a railway system serving coastal ports and began a largely unsuccessful programme of free white rural settlement.[2] Diamond extraction, initiated in 1913, became of commercial importance after 1920, and petroleum extraction, beginning at low level in 1956, had by 1973 overtaken coffee as the main source of foreign revenue. A post-Second World War boom in the coffee grown with forced labour on plantations and a subsidised settlement policy encouraged Portuguese immigration in the last twenty-five years of colonialism, but the majority of these new immigrants – for the most part, illiterate Portuguese peasants – remained in the towns in competition and conflict with African workers and left Angola during the pre-independence unrest of 1974 and 1975. Nationalist and anti-Portuguese risings in 1961, in Luanda in February and in the coffee plantations of the north in March, brought military reinforcement by Portugal and some belated development as new roads were built for military purposes, education services were expanded and labour

Angola: provincial boundaries

conditions eased, but without dampening the demand for full independence. In the 1960s Portugal relaxed a policy of protecting Portugal's domestic industries and allowed the modest growth of manufacturing and processing industry in Angola.

Angola has a narrow, dry coastal lowland extending along the Atlantic seaboard, followed by a sub-plateau strip and a large central plateau (*planalto*), which is the most densely populated area, to the north of which lies rain forest and tropical savannah, where many of Angola's twentieth-century coffee plantations were established, and to the south of which lies arid and desert land used traditionally for cattle herding and later for commercial ranching. The continental shelf provides rich fishing grounds.

Angola has about one hundred ethnic groups, with the majority of the population coming within nine ethno-linguistic groups.[3] Of the total population in 1960 of 4,830,449, it was estimated that 500,000 were Bakongo (speaking Kikongo), 1,200,000 were Mbundu (speaking Kimbundu) and 1,700,000 were Ovimbundu (speaking Umbundu). These linguistic differences have become less important with labour mobility and the growing use of Portuguese as a vehicular language through education. In the towns many young people do not speak a traditional African language.

THE BIRTH OF MODERN NATIONALISM 1953–60

The rise of modern Angolan nationalism has usually been seen as the creation of the cultural movement of the 1940s, which was certainly an important factor, but nationalism was not the creation solely of intellectuals, some of whom spent crucial years outside Angola, in Portugal or other countries.[4] It has been correctly ascribed to *assimilados*, the official designation until 1961 of Africans who fulfilled legal and social requirements to become registered as Portuguese citizens (not to be confused with *mestiços* – the term still used to describe persons of mixed white and African ancestry). But even *assimilados* could be in very modest circumstances in colonial society, and an important current in the birth of Angolan nationalism came from workers on the fringe of Luandan society. Even for the *assimilado* intellectuals, what distinguished them and made them effective future leaders was the degree to which they rejected Portuguese attempts to absorb them socially and chose instead to identify with their African backgrounds. With the increase after the Second World War of

Portuguese immigration, competition with Africans for low-skill and unskilled jobs developed in the towns. In this context, sports and recreational associations played a significant part in mobilising African efforts towards change.[5] About 1953, the Party for the United Struggle of the Africans of Angola was founded secretly with a nationalist programme, and in 1956 the MPLA (the Movimento Popular de Libertação de Angola – Popular Movement for the Liberation of Angola) was founded as an umbrella for anti-colonial and anti-imperialist forces.[6]

Among those who played important parts in the preparation for this step were Agostinho Neto, then imprisoned in Portugal, and Amílcar Cabral, founder of the liberation movement for Guinea-Bissau and Cape Verde, who was then working in Angola. But the MPLA's initial meetings took place clandestinely in a small house in Luanda and were co-ordinated by Ilídio Tomé Alves Machado, a postal clerk, who was the MPLA's first President. Machado was arrested in 1959 by the PIDE (the International Police for the Defence of the State), the political police of the time, tried in 1960 for alleged subversion and imprisoned at Tarrafal on Santiago island in Cape Verde. The MPLA's manifesto,[7] drawn up secretly and dated 10 December 1956, was a long and sophisticated defence of African rights and denunciation of Portuguese colonialism, which would not fall without 'a revolutionary struggle'. The first part of the manifesto stressed that no African could remain indifferent to the struggle in the colonies against the world imperialist front. The struggle would achieve victory through a single front of all anti-imperialist forces in Angola, through a broad 'Movimento Popular de Libertação de Angola', but would not mean the affiliation of all Angolan patriots to a single organisation or association: 'The movement will be the sum of activities of thousands and thousands of organisations (of three, more than three, dozens or hundreds of members in each) which will be created throughout Angola.'

Development through cells and front organisations was possible until the PIDE began to seek out the MPLA leadership, some of whom escaped into exile. The wave of arrests in 1959 included dozens of Africans and *mestiços*, and a handful of progressive Europeans who then or later were active in the MPLA. The prisoners included clerks, students and nurses, and the arrests led to the 'trial of fifty' in 1960 and imposition of long prison sentences. Agostinho Neto, who had qualified as a doctor in 1958 and returned from Portugal to Angola in December 1959, opened a medical practice in Luanda, which also served as a cover for his underground leadership of the MPLA. He was arrested in his consulting room on 8 June 1960 (a protest from villagers in his home area was savagely repressed by the Portuguese authorities, with much loss of life among the villagers). Neto was held in Luanda, then in Lisbon and then in Cape Verde, where he spent much of 1961.

ARMED STRUGGLE, 1961–74

In December 1960 in a sequence of trials against some of the PIDE prisoners, a military court sentenced one group of twenty who were accused of activities against the external security of the State. This group included eight male nurses – among them António Pedro Benje, Agostinho Mendes de Carvalho and Manuel Bernardo de Sousa – and the accused were condemned to long prison sentences and loss of political rights for fifteen years. In January, 1960, Mendes de Carvalho's younger brother José (Zeca), then a schoolboy, and three friends left Luanda to cross the northern frontier. Zeca Mendes was in search of military training; he reached Morocco (one of the first African countries to aid the MPLA militarily), was in the first MPLA contingent to be trained and later became one of the MPLA's leading military commanders. He eventually died on 14 April 1968 in an attack he led on a Portuguese military post at Karipande on the Eastern Front of Angola. He is best known under his *nom de guerre* of Hoji Ya Henda.

Meanwhile, in Luanda, from about August 1960, groups of older African workers were preparing an insurrection under the leadership of men such as Neves Adão Bendinha (who worked for a building company), Paiva Domingos da Silva and Francisco Santana, who were drilling virtually unarmed squads in the Luanda townships. Under the impression that the political prisoners of the December trial, still imprisoned in Luanda, were about to be transferred to Cape Verde, three groups of these inadequately armed militants attacked at dawn on 4 February 1961 the colonial prisons, a PIDE post and the official radio station. One group was largely destroyed in the Portuguese counter-attack, but others were able to escape into hiding and then to the bush north of Luanda and maintain armed struggle. A separate insurrection with civilian targets, including whites and *mestiços*, was launched on 15 March 1961 in the northern coffee plantations by a predominantly Bakongo movement which was later to become the FNLA (the National Front for the Liberation of Angola) and to oppose the MPLA's efforts at national liberation. In view of the intense secrecy with which it was sought to prepare all political and military operations, it is scarcely surprising that events of this period are still occasionally obscure and that allegiances were not clarified until some time later.

The PIDE repression forced the MPLA's political leadership into exile first in Conakry, under the shelter of the Republic of Guinea, and then in Kinshasa, Zaire, which was more accessible to Angolan refugees who had poured out of their own country to escape massive repression and slaughter by Portuguese troops brought into Angola. In 1962 the MPLA began its transformation from an umbrella organisation into a formal political movement, and to train men for the EPLA (People's Army for the Liberation of Angola). A crucial event was Agostinho Neto's release from prison in March 1962 in Portugal, where he was put under restricted residence. The MPLA, with the help of some progressive Portuguese, contrived Neto's escape with his family to Casablanca, from where he moved to Kinshasa. At this time there occurred the defection from the MPLA of a faction led by Viriato da Cruz (one of the pioneers of modern Angolan poetry), who was formally expelled in July 1963. Meanwhile the MPLA's first national conference was held in Kinshasa in December 1962 and it elected a ten-member executive, under Neto's presidency, including Lúcio Lara and Iko Carreira who were to remain key leadership figures during the long years of guerrilla warfare waged by thousands of Angolans, most of whom were of peasant origin.

In July 1963, unfavourable conditions in Kinshasa led the MPLA Steering Committee to transfer to Brazzaville, from where it co-ordinated military operations in its First Region, in northern Angola, and in its Second Region, in the enclave Cabinda province. In 1966 the Third Region, in eastern Angola, was established, with offices in Zambia and Tanzania to arrange supplies. At various times in the course of the guerrilla struggle the MPLA offered to ally with other opponents of Portuguese rule – on the basis of a national effort and particularly to gain access to Angola across the Zaire border – but the FNLA and a southern breakaway, UNITA (the National Union for the Total Independence of Angola), formed in March 1966, were unable to overcome their tribalist bias. The MPLA had diplomatic contacts with several socialist and friendly countries who gave material support. Among these were the People's Republic of China and the Soviet Union, but the latter was a more consistent backer, particularly after 1964. In January 1968, Neto announced at a press conference in Brazzaville that the Movement had begun to transfer its headquarters to one of the regions it controlled inside Angola. The MPLA was still developing its political line, and in February 1968 a regional assembly was held for the

First Region (covering Luanda, Cuanza Norte, Uíge and Zaire provinces) and the Second Region (covering the Cabinda province), and in August a regional assembly was held in the Third Region (Moxico and Cuando-Cubango provinces). The struggle then advanced in 1968 into a Fourth Region (Lunda and Malange provinces) and by May 1969 into a Fifth Region (central provinces). In February 1972 a Sixth Region (Moçâmedes and Huíla provinces) was established.

From 1972 to 1974 the Movement underwent an internal crisis, reminiscent of the crisis of ten years earlier, although some aspects were positive. One result of the 1968 regional assemblies was the demand that a full congress of the MPLA be held. A plenary assembly of the Steering Committee, held from 27 September to 3 October 1971, appointed a commission to prepare for a congress, but this coincided with increased military action by the Portuguese and some military reverses for the MPLA – to the point where the organised structure of military command had almost broken down. In August 1972 a 'readjustment movement' was initiated on the Eastern Front, as a searching examination of the political, military and organisational levels of the MPLA, and resulted in the creation of a regional military staff and more effective discussion between the political leadership and the mass of MPLA supporters. The 'readjustment movement' was aimed at the adoption of a theory of revolution and a political principle incorporated into the MPLA's basic documents was: 'The masses are the point of departure and arrival of all the actions and structure of the organisation.' A similar process took place on the Northern Front at the end of 1973.

The criticism and self-criticism that took place at this period was regarded by the MPLA as constructive, but the political leadership faced in late 1972 and early 1973 a destructive take-over attempt by Daniel Julio Chipenda. Chipenda, a member of the Movement's executive and of Umbundu origin, was reported by the MPLA to have plotted with some members, including guerrilla fighters, in an attempt to use tribalism to destroy MPLA unity and to oust the main leadership. By June 1973 Chipenda had been suspended and some of his associates had been detained by the MPLA, but Chipenda had external, non-Angolan support, and by August 1973 he had formalised his opposition in what was called the 'Eastern Revolt'. When, on 25 April 1974, the fascist regime in Portugal fell – with the Armed Forces Movement removing Marcello Caetano's administration – the MPLA was still seeking to resolve its internal problems.

The situation was further complicated when on 11 May 1974 a group of MPLA personalities meeting in Brazzaville issued a statement – with nineteen signatories – criticising what it alleged were undemocratic methods of leadership, and suggesting that a congress would aim to 'restore the political principles of MPLA, eliminate presidentialism within the organisation to the benefit of a collegial leadership as a fundamental condition for our politico-military action', and would also allow the proclamation of 'a broad united front for national independence, integrating all the parties and organisations that really exist in the country, and all personalities and individuals sincerely animated by the desire to bring about complete independence'.[8] It is perhaps not surprising that this statement was an echo of the 1956 manifesto, as if nothing had been learned during the intervening years. The Brazzaville group were mostly intellectuals, some of whom had for one reason or another withdrawn from or been out of touch with the armed struggle. This Brazzaville group, who became known as the 'Active Revolt', included several individuals who had taken part in the first MPLA national conference, in 1962. It included such early nationalists as the Revd Domingos da Silva, Mário de Andrade, Eduardo dos Santos, Hugo Menezes, Gentil Viana, the military commander Floribert Monimambu, and later Joaquim Pinto de Andrade. (Many of the signatories to the 'Active Revolt' statements were afterwards to undertake self-criticism and to be reintegrated into the MPLA or to take up jobs in independent Angola.)

The MPLA's political leadership was enormously encouraged by an initiative taken by the key military commanders from the Eastern and Northern Fronts – especially the former – in proclaiming on 1 August 1974 the FAPLA (People's Armed Forces for the Liberation of Angola), which linked all military and people's defence forces in an autonomous institution subordinated to the political direction of the MPLA, meaning Neto and his colleagues; the names of eighty-three commanders appeared on the proclamation, which signified the isolation of Chipenda from the MPLA's military forces.

Under pressure from African heads of State, the MPLA tactically agreed to take part in a conference in Lusaka in August with the two factions, but withdrew from the conference saying that FNLA members had been included in the Chipenda delegation and that a congress should be held in Angola rather than Zambia. (Chipenda was officially expelled from the MPLA in December 1974, and by February 1975, with some troops that followed him, he joined the FNLA, although within that grouping also he remained a factionalist, organising his troops on the basis of personal loyalty to him and not to the FNLA northern leadership.)

Considerable clarification was achieved by an inter-regional conference of MPLA militants, held in Moxico in Angola from 12 to 20 September 1974. The conference was an attempt to fuse what might loosely be regarded as internal MPLA (activists who had been operating clandestinely in the cities or had been released from prison at the end of April and beginning of May 1974, and guerrilla fighters from the First Region – relatively isolated from the leadership, because access across the Zaire–Angola border was denied) and external MPLA (activists in the liberated areas who had escaped Portuguese administrative control, and guerrilla fighters on the Eastern Front or from the Lusaka and Dar es Salaam delegations). Some of the Eastern and Northern Front commanders had met for the first time in August, in the context of the abortive Lusaka 'Congress', and the former political prisoners in the Portuguese gaols were to some extent an unknown quantity, as were young delegates from Luanda. The main aim of the inter-regional conference was to devise an MPLA strategy that would avoid the risk that the gains of the national liberation struggle would be lost at the last moment in neocolonial solutions for Angola; furthermore, the MPLA strongly insisted that Cabinda was an integral part of Angola, and asserted that it would be included in the MPLA's defence of Angola's territorial integrity.

Another question discussed was the MPLA's racial policy. A small group, including Nito Alves, a guerrilla from the First Region, argued that Angola after independence should deny full citizenship rights to whites and even *mestiços*, but this view was rejected in favour of the MPLA's traditional non-racism (in August 1968, for example, the inter-regional assembly had decided that white Angolans could be 'sympathiser' members of the MPLA). The 1974 conference adopted revised statutes and rules of discipline[9] – on classic democratic centralist principles – and elected a Central Committee of thirty-five, headed by Agostinho Neto. The Central Committee elected a ten-member Political Bureau, made up of Agostinho Neto, President; Lopo do Nascimento, Secretary; Lúcio Lara (Tchíweka); Carlos Rocha (Dilolwa); José Eduardo; Joaquim Kapango; Rodrigues João Lopes (Ludy); Pedro Maria Tonha (Pedalé); Jacob Caetano João (Monstro Imortal); and Henrique Teles Carreira (Iko).

INDEPENDENCE AND THE FORMATION OF THE PARTY 1975–7

In October 1974, after the principle of Angolan independence had been recognised by Portugal, the MPLA agreed to a cease-fire in the liberation war. On 8 November 1974 the MPLA's first official delegation arrived in Luanda. In January 1975 agreement was reached at Alvor in Portugal that independence would be proclaimed in Angola on 11 November 1975, and that an administration by a Portuguese High Commissioner and transitional government of FNLA, MPLA and UNITA would take office on 31 January, with the task of organising general elections within nine months. Neto returned to Luanda on 4 February 1975, to a massive popular welcome. By July the transitional government had broken down, and Zaire and South Africa began active intervention to support FNLA and UNITA respectively. On the night of 10–11 November 1975, Agostinho Neto proclaimed the independence of the People's Republic of Angola and a constitution and on the following day he was invested as President by Lúcio Lara, speaking on behalf of the Central Committee of the MPLA.[10] Military intervention by Zairean and South African regular troops continued, and the Communist Party of Cuba, meeting on 5 November 1975, decided to send combat troops to aid the MPLA (these were in addition to a contingent of specialist instructors who had been sent in response to a request made by the MPLA in mid 1975). By February 1976 the Zairean troops and FNLA forces, with British and American mercenaries, had been routed, and the South African troops had begun a strategic withdrawal towards the southern border of Angola; by 27 March 1976 they had been driven out of Angola entirely. Although Lúcio Lara in May 1975 led an MPLA delegation to China, which had received MPLA delegations in earlier years and had provided military training for some MPLA guerrillas, China, within the framework of the broader Sino-Soviet dispute, gave priority to the MPLA's opponents.

Independence and the establishment of peace provided the conditions under which, for the first time, the MPLA could begin to create party structures. During the guerrilla war the political leadership had deliberately avoided any attempt to form a cadre party, because it wished to maintain, albeit within the framework of socialist objectives, the broad anti-colonialist and anti-imperialist front with which it had begun in 1956. The Central Committee elected in September 1974 had last met in plenary session in February 1975 (meetings were required by statute to be held every six months) and that meeting dealt with

immediate questions of defence and organisation. The MPLA's independence constitution[11] had opened by setting out the basic principle of
'building a prosperous and democratic country entirely free from any
form of exploitation of man by man, thereby fulfilling the aspirations of
the masses', and had stressed the primacy of the MPLA, but it had not
institutionalised Marxism-Leninism. In October 1976 the MPLA
Central Committee held its third plenary session, to delineate Angola's
course towards scientific socialism. At one stage before the meeting it
had looked as if the MPLA might announce a decision to form a party
from the Movement, but it was felt in the Political Bureau that that
would be premature. The pressing need to establish State administration, against a background of warfare in the first months of
independence and a near collapse of the economic and commercial
structure of the country, had left the MPLA badly understaffed with
cadres. Much of the burden of political mobilisation had been left with
Lúcio Lara and his staff, while his other politically experienced
colleagues had to shoulder the additional burden of government duties.
The formula announced by the Central Committee after its third plenary
session was that in the third quarter of 1977, at the latest, the First
Congress of the MPLA should be held, to 'study and decide upon the
creation of a Party guided by Marxism-Leninism, the ideology of the
proletariat'.[12]

The third plenary session also drew attention to internal problems
that had arisen in the MPLA, and urged militants to combat divisive-
ness, sectarianism and opportunism. The resolution did not publicly
blame Nito Alves on this score, but it was noticeable that an attempt was
made to control his behaviour by abolishing his Ministry of Internal
Administration (to which he had been appointed in November 1975).
Alves, who had been co-opted to the Political Bureau during the second
national liberation war, had abused his position both as a minister and
as a member of the Political Bureau, and, unannounced, an inquiry was
instituted. Pending its findings he remained in the Central Committee,
where he had a small number of supporters. Alves, albeit with more
sophisticated arguments and techniques, played a role not unlike
Chipenda's, but in reverse. Whereas Chipenda had tried to enlist
personal support in the southern part of the Eastern Front against the
North, Alves sought to advance himself (through his connections in the
Northern Front and with some elements among the former political
prisoners and Luanda clandestine networks) against the main body of
the MPLA political leadership and the former guerrilla fighters from the
Eastern Front. The inquiry report was presented to a Central

Committee meeting held on 20 and 21 May 1977, when Nito Alves and another member of the Committee, José Van Dunem, a former political prisoner, were expelled. The Alves group then attempted a *coup d'état*, which had been in preparation for some eight months and was launched on the morning of 27 May 1977.[13] The coup was foiled the same day by loyalist action, but among the victims of the Alves group were Saydi Mingas, a member of the Central Committee and Minister of Finance, and four senior military commanders, two of whom were also members of the Central Committee. In the ensuing investigations, Jacob Caetano João (Monstro Imortal) in the Political Bureau and Eduardo Ernesto Gomes da Silva (Bakaloff) in the Central Committee were found to have been implicated in the Alves conspiracy. At the Central Committee's sixth plenary meeting, held in August, two other members were suspended after they admitted concealing foreknowledge of the intentions of the Alves group.

The MPLA proceeded to a reassignment of posts in the civil administration and within political structures to eradicate the *Nitista* (from *Nito* Alves) tendency, then resumed nationwide preparation for the delayed First Congress. A series of preparatory meetings was held in the provinces; Congress documents and theses[14] on the main sectors of national life were prepared, and key issues were discussed in seminars and assemblies of workers, soldiers and MPLA militants. The MPLA's political leadership was concerned whether the level of political experience was such as to justify the early formation of a vanguard party and whether the change to a cadre party might in fact demobilise Angolans who had grown up in the broader MPLA front. The Central Committee third plenary meeting, in October 1976, had decided on the creation of a party school, with the purpose of training militants in Marxist-Leninist theory. Some progress had been made, with schools in several provinces, courses for political activists and workers generally – and even a special pilot course held for the most senior political, military and civil leaders. Congress documents recognised that 'The thousands of members of MPLA have not had an equal opportunity of contact with historical materialism and dialectical materialism. Their adherence to scientific socialism is empirical and relies much on the trust they place in MPLA and in the guidance of Comrade President Agostinho Neto.' The formula proposed to Congress was a cadre party with membership categories able to absorb most activists in the MPLA, and the retention of mass organisations – for women and trade unionists, for example – which were outside the formal party and membership of which did not raise the question of Marxist-Leninist ideology. Entry conditions to the party allowed for a shorter probationary period for those of working-class origin than for those of other class backgrounds. Congress met in Luanda from 4 to 10 December 1977, with delegates from the leadership, from all provinces, from FAPLA and from the mass organisations, in accordance with MPLA statutes. The Mandates Committee reported that 41 per cent of delegates had taken part in the first national liberation war, 20 per cent had been in the clandestine internal struggle and 30 per cent had been political prisoners of the colonialists.

On 10 December 1977, the twenty-first anniversary of the MPLA's foundation, the First Congress closed with the foundation of the MPLA Partido do Trabalho (MPLA Workers' Party) and a programme drawn up 'with a basis in a Marxist-Leninist interpretation of the fundamental tasks for which the Party must struggle'. Congress resolutions established that the Party must be 'guided by the scientific ideology of the proletariat, Marxism-Leninism'.[15] During several hours of the night of 9–10 December, delegates elected the Party's first Central Committee, consisting of forty-five full members and ten alternate members (of twenty-two MPLA Central Committee members attending Congress as delegates, twenty-one were elected as full members of the Party Central Committee and one as an alternate member) and Agostinho Neto was elected unopposed as President of the Party.

At a mass rally in Luanda on the afternoon of 10 December, Neto announced that the next ordinary congress was scheduled for 1985, with an extraordinary congress in 1980 to analyse progress to date, particularly on the economic plan for 1977–80 discussed at the First Congress, and possibly to enlarge the Central Committee to seventy-five members. On 14 and 15 December 1977 the Party Central Committee met and elected the Political Bureau, substantially the same as the MPLA Political Bureau elected in September 1974 (see end of previous section and Table 4.2), and formed a Central Committee Secretariat (see Table 4.1).

THE MPLA WORKERS' PARTY

Organisation

The statutes of the Party are those adopted at the MPLA Congress in December 1977, but much of the organisational detail and internal structure was being clarified during 1978. In all fields of activity the Party defines the political line to follow and bases its action on Leninist

TABLE 4.1 Secretariat of the Central Committee of the MPLA Workers' Party, December 1977

Afonso Van Dunem (Mbinda)	Department of Revolutionary Orientation
Ambrósio Lukoki	Department of Education, Culture and Sport
Ilídio Machado	Department of Administration and Finance
José Eduardo dos Santos	Department of National Reconstruction
Lopo do Nascimento	Department of Political and Ideological Education
Lúcio Lara	Department of Organisation
Pascoal Luvualu	Department of External Relations

methods of Party functioning, with democratic centralism. Membership is open to Angolan citizens above the age of eighteen who do not exploit the labour of others, and who know and accept the programme and statutes, give material support through payment of subscriptions, study and apply the principles of Marxism-Leninism, and possess irreproachable political and moral revolutionary qualities. Membership is in two categories, of militant and aspirant (probationary), and sympathisers in the mass organisations may give voluntary contributions and put forward their names for membership.

The Party is structured according to criteria of territory and production; institutions at the base are formed in factories and enterprises, schools, agricultural co-operatives, villages, military units, residences, and so on. The basic institution is the cell, formed in all work and living places where there are more than three militants or aspirants, and a cell may have up to thirty members. Where there is more than one cell, a Party committee is formed to direct and co-ordinate the cells. The institutions at the base are grouped according to the territorial principle, in sectors, neighbourhoods, municipalities, communes and provinces, in accordance with the administrative division of the People's Republic of Angola.

The senior leadership bodies of the Party are:

(1) the Assembly of Militants, at the base;
(2) the Conference, for institutions from commune to provincial level;
(3) the Congress, at national level.

Congress is the supreme body and ordinarily meets every five years. Conferences are called once every two years and assemblies once each year. The youth organisation is linked to the Party under an autonomous statute and its local bodies are guided by the corresponding Party echelon.

Delegates to Congress are elected by Assemblies of Militants and by conferences. Congress includes full and alternate members of the Central Committee in enjoyment of their rights, and the Central Committee has the right to call other elements or bodies to the Congress. Congress has power to elect the full and alternate members of the Central Committee, the President of the Party and members of the Central Control Commission. The Central Committee ensures the general guidance of the Party, within the framework of Congress decisions, between congresses; elects the eleven full and three alternate members to the Political Bureau, of which the Party President must be a member; and meets in ordinary session every six months (the statutes provide for seventy-five full members and twenty-five alternates, but in 1977 forty-five and ten, respectively, were elected). The Central Committee chooses its Secretariat, which is answerable to the Political Bureau and dependent on Political Bureau orientation.

Composition

During 1978, composition of the Party was being determined through a system of administrative vetting of members of the Movement before the Party was formed and through consultation with work colleagues of candidates. By decision of the First Congress of the MPLA, the Central Committee in 1978 launched a 'rectification movement' with the aim of refining the Party, strengthening ideological cohesion and improving working methods. In 1978, while the campaign was proceeding the Party leaders explained that it was aimed at combating petty-bourgeois ideology, its vices and manifestation.

Mass organisations

Mass organisations are effectively directed by the Party through Party members within those mass organisations. The Party youth body guides and controls the Organisation of the Angolan Pioneer, an institutionalising of a children's grouping formed in 1963. The mass organisation for women, the Organisation of the Angolan Woman, was founded in Kinshasa in March 1962 by MPLA women militants. The National Union of Angolan Workers was formed in the 1950s independently of the MPLA, but by the early 1960s it had become closely linked to the MPLA and became increasingly an MPLA organ, headed by a member of the political leadership, although the distinction on paper is retained in the Party programme.

GOVERNMENT

Constitution

The independence constitution[16] of November 1975 has been amended in points of detail, notably by the third and sixth plenaries of the MPLA Central Committee, in October 1976 and August 1977, respectively. The changes adjust the balance of power between the President, MPLA and the Council of the Revolution, the highest legislative body pending the election of a People's Assembly. In the original constitution the Prime Minister presided over the Council of Ministers, but in the 1976 amendment[17] this responsibility was transferred to the President, who was also given power to appoint Provincial Commissioners, whereas previously appointment was by the Council of the Revolution on the recommendation of the MPLA. In the same amendments the power of the Council of the Revolution to appoint a provisional President of the Republic in the case of death, resignation or permanent incapacity was transferred to the Central Committee, which would designate a provisional President from among its members. The composition of the Council of the Revolution was also amended to give the Central Committee greater representation and influence.

In the 1977 constitutional amendments the President of the Republic was further given power to appoint members of the government, whereas previously the power had constitutionally lain with the Council of the Revolution acting on the recommendation of the MPLA.

The People's Assembly

The independence constitution stated that an elected People's Assembly should be the supreme State body, but that pending its creation the Council of the Revolution, representing political, military and civil leadership, should act as the supreme organ of State power. Legislation passed in February 1976 initiated the first stage of the electoral process, which began with elections for people's neighbourhood committees in the Luanda commune on 27 June 1976. These elections were in part unsuccessful (through manipulation by the Nito Alves group[18]) and in October 1976 the Central Committee postponed the subsequent stages until more effective preparation had been made for valid elections.

The Council of Ministers

Under the revised constitution the President of the Republic appoints the Council of Ministers (the Political Bureau decides which Ministers form part of the Council of the Revolution to the maximum of three non-members of the Central Committee). The government until December 1978 comprised a Prime Minister, three deputy prime ministers, ministers, deputy ministers and secretaries of state. After an extraordinary meeting of the Central Committee in December 1978 the posts of Prime Minister and deputy prime minister were abolished. In July 1979 the central government was remodelled to allow a maximum of eighteen ministries and five secretariats of state; a Ministry of the Interior was created to replace the former Directorate of Information and Security of Angola (DISA). The Governor of the National Bank of Angola is not in the government structure but is regarded as part of the governmental team.

Local government

The People's Republic of Angola is administratively divided into *provincias* (provinces), *concelhos* (Councils), *comunas* (communes), *bairros* (neighbourhoods) and *povoações* (villages), and at the various levels there are commissioners and commissions. Under the People's Power Law 1/76 of 5 February 1976,[19] the commissions are to be elected and commissioners, excepting provincial commissioners (see above, under 'Constitution'), are to be appointed on the proposal of the corresponding MPLA committee, but the electoral process has been delayed (see above, under 'The People's Assembly').

Party–state relations

The Constitution vests sovereignty in the Angolan people and in-stitutionalises the MPLA as their legitimate representative. The third and sixth plenaries of the MPLA Central Committee confirmed the primacy of the Central Committee and Political Bureau over govern-ment departments (a position which was reinforced in the Party programme and by the Party Central Committee at its second session held in July 1978). The right of the Party to supervise government is further manifested in a system of multiple office-holding (see Table 4.2).

TABLE 4.2 Government posts held by members of the Angolan Political Bureau, January 1978

António Agostinho Neto	President of the Republic
Ambrósio Lukoki	Minister of Education
Carlos Rocha (Dilolwa)	Second Deputy Prime Minister
Henrique Teles Carreira (Iko)	Minister of Defence
João Luís Neto (Xietu)	Deputy Minister of Defence
José Eduardo dos Santos	First Deputy Prime Minister
Lopo do Nascimento	Prime Minister
Pedro Maria Tonha (Pedalé)	Provincial Commissioner for Huambo Province
Rodrigues João Lopes (Ludy)	Director of Information and Security of Angola

Note: of the two other members, António dos Santos França (Ndalu) held a senior appointment in the armed forces, and Lúcio Lara (Tchiweka) was responsible for party organisation.[20]

INTERNAL AFFAIRS

Education

The country inherited from colonialism a narrow urban-based educational system, which strongly favoured the Portuguese settlers and left the Angolan population with an overall illiteracy rate of 85 per cent (considerably higher for those over the age of fifteen) despite an expansion in primary education after 1961. In December 1975 education was made entirely free by law. A nationwide literacy campaign was launched in January 1976, drawing on experience of MPLA campaigns in the liberated areas during the anti-colonial war. In April 1976 experimental educational reform was begun, with the change from a school year beginning in September to a school year with three terms – from 15 April to 30 June, 15 July to 30 September, and 1 October to 31 December – and with part of the vacation period, principally the month of January, devoted to agricultural or industrial production. A provisional unified structure provided for three educational cycles of two years each, with a division for an additional two years of vocational studies as a preparation for further study or employment. The tertiary sector was to give priority to the training of agricultural and technical cadres.

A more elaborate educational scheme was adopted by the First Congress of the MPLA in December 1977, with four classes at first level, two classes at second level and two classes at third level, providing eight classes to be extended later to a ten-class basic education. A related system of adult education was proposed to operate until illiteracy had been eradicated. Middle education on an approximately four-year basis would be through technical institutes and training schools and higher education on a four- or five-year basis through an enlargement of the existing university structure. Education would be profoundly tied to political training and would at all levels aim at providing technical–professional qualifications.[21]

Religion

In the late colonial period, census returns showed under half the population as Christian (with Catholics outnumbering Protestants by more than three to one) and more than half following traditional African beliefs. Constitutionally the People's Republic of Angola is a secular state with complete separation of the State and religious institutions, but all religions are respected and the State provides protection for churches and places and objects of worship so long as the adherents comply with State laws. In January 1978, on the principle that the information services must be national, the government closed down in Luanda a Church broadcasting station that had originally been established under a concordat between Portugal and the Catholic Church. No effort has been made to discourage or prevent worship, but education is 'scientific and materialist', and the third plenary session of the MPLA Central Committee recommended legislation to prevent any attempt to set faith or religious belief against the revolutionary transformation of society, the education of new generations or the carrying out of citizens' duties.

Economy

Angola's economy is guided according to a provisional plan for 1978–80 adopted at the First Congress of the MPLA in December 1977.[22] During the national reconstruction phase, the target is to restore the production levels of 1973 – particularly in the agricultural sector, as 85 per cent of the population live in the countryside – and 1978 was designated as Agriculture Year. The main sources of foreign revenue are petroleum exports, principally by the United States Gulf Oil Corporation under royalty agreements; diamonds, mined by an operating company in which, since August 1977, the Angolan government has a 60·85 per cent controlling interest; and coffee, which is effectively a State monopoly. The government strongly encourages production and consumption co-operatives for farming and for retail trade in basic foodstuffs, although there is a supporting system of State shops to ease current shortages and distribution problems (1976–8) and a system of national controlled prices for basic items.

EXTERNAL AFFAIRS

Angola achieved independence under the MPLA and had immediate support from socialist countries (with the exception of China) and from progressive African states. The invasion by South African troops in support of the MPLA's opponents had the effect of increasing independent African sympathy with the MPLA, and Angola was admitted to the Organisation of African Unity (OAU), with the requisite approval of a simple majority of the membership, in February 1976. Angola was particularly concerned about its immediate neighbours (apart from the People's Republic of the Congo, which had supported the MPLA for more than a decade), and in April 1976 Zambia recognised the People's Republic of Angola, after withdrawing support for UNITA. Relations between Angola and Zaire remained more difficult, as each country accused the other of supporting opponents of its neighbour's government, but, after a series of bilateral meetings at head of State, ministerial and official level, agreement was reached in principle in July 1978 for diplomatic relations. Since independence Angola has provided material and diplomatic aid to liberation movements, notably the South West Africa People's Organisation, in Namibia; the Patriotic Front, in Zimbabwe (Rhodesia); and the African National Congress, in South Africa. Angola's request for admission to the United Nations was initially vetoed by the United States, but later this opposition was withdrawn and after formal approval in the General Assembly Angola took its UN seat in December 1976.

António Agostinho Neto, President of the MPLA Workers' Party and the Republic, and Commander-in-Chief of the FAPLA, was born at Cachicane village in the Icolo e Bengo region near Luanda in 1922. He attended secondary school in Luanda and then worked in the colonial health services. He left Angola in 1947 to study medicine in Portugal. He was arrested for political activities in 1951 and 1952 and again in 1955, after which he remained imprisoned until June 1957. He qualified as a doctor in October 1958, married Maria Eugénia da Silva and returned to Luanda in December 1959 and opened a medical practice, which served as a cover for his clandestine leadership of the MPLA. He also established an international reputation for his poems (several of which were written in prison and smuggled out by Maria Eugénia, when she was his fiancée). He was again arrested in June 1960 and held in various prisons before being sent to Cape Verde, where he worked as a doctor under police surveillance. He was re-arrested in Cape Verde in 1961 and transferred to prison in Portugal. After an international campaign on his behalf, he was released in March 1962 and put under restricted residence. He escaped from Portugal with his family and went to Casablanca and shortly afterwards to Kinshasa, where in December 1962 he was elected President of the MPLA at its first national conference – he had earlier been 'honorary president'. He was the political leader of the MPLA's armed struggle for national liberation and became President of the People's Republic of Angola at independence on 11 November 1975. In December 1977, at the First Congress of the MPLA, he was elected President of the MPLA Workers' Party. Dr Neto died of cancer on 11 September 1979 while on a visit to the USSR.

Lopo Fortunato Ferreira do Nascimento, Prime Minister until December 1978, was born in Luanda in 1940 and attended commercial schools. He was arrested by the colonial political police in 1959 and again in 1963 and was released in 1968. He was a trade unionist and organised brewery workers while working clandestinely in MPLA action groups. In 1974 he was incorporated into the MPLA leadership and went to the Northern Front, where he was attached to the MPLA's Department of Information and Propaganda. He took part in the inter-regional conference of militants held in eastern Angola in September 1974 and was elected to the Central Committee, and in turn to the Political Bureau, as Secretary. He was the MPLA's nominee as Prime Minister in the presidential council of the Angolan transitional government that held office from the end of January 1975 until shortly before independence. In November 1975 he was appointed Prime Minister in the first government of the People's Republic of Angola. In December 1977 he was elected to the Central Committee of the MPLA Workers' party, and in turn to the Political Bureau and as a member of the Secretariat of the Central Committee.

Colonel Iko Carreira (Henrique Alberto Teles Carreira), Minister of Defence, was born in Luanda in 1934. He attended secondary school in Luanda and went to study law in Portugal, where he worked clandestinely in MPLA cells. In 1961 he fled from Portugal to join the armed struggle for national liberation. In December 1962 he was elected to the MPLA executive at the Movement's first national conference. He served first on the Cabinda Front and then from 1968 on the Eastern Front, where he operated in the areas of Luso, Lumege and Munhango. At the inter-regional conference of militants in September 1974 he was elected to the Central Committee, and in turn to the Political Bureau; he was Defence Council Co-ordinator. In November 1975 he was appointed Minister of Defence. On 1 August 1974 he headed the list of guerrilla fighters who signed the proclamation of the FAPLA, and on 1 August 1976 he was given the rank of Column Commander in the first formal commissionings in the armed forces. In December 1977 he was elected to the Central Committee of the MPLA Workers' Party, and in turn to the Political Bureau. In March 1979 he was made Colonel.

BASIC FACTS ABOUT ANGOLA

Official name: People's Republic of Angola (República Popular de Angola)

Area: 1,246,700 sq. km. (481,350 sq. miles).

Population: 5,673,046 (1970 census), 6,353,000 (mid 1975 UN est.).

Population density: 5·1 per sq. km. (on 1975 est.)

Population distribution (1970): 14·9 per cent urban, 85·1 per cent rural.

Party of government: MPLA Workers' Party (MPLA Partido do Trabalho), founded 10 December 1977. Membership unknown.

Administrative division (1978): 17 provinces.

Population of major towns (1960): Luanda (the capital), 224,540 (1970 provisional census, 475,328); Lobito, 50,164; Huambo (formerly Nova Lisboa), 38,745; Benguela, 23,256.

Main natural resources: crude oil, diamonds, iron and timber.

Main cash crops: coffee, sugar, cotton and tobacco.

Foreign trade (1976): exports, 34,869 million escudos ($1057 million); imports, 22,009 million escudos ($659 million); total, 56,878 million escudos ($1716 million).

Main trading partners (1974–5): Portugal, USA, FRG.

Rail network (1972): 3049 km.

Road network (1972): main 25,093 km.; secondary 28,718 km.

Universities: 1, University of Angola (Luanda and Lubango) (1109 students in 1977).

Foreign relations: more than 30 diplomatic missions resident in Luanda; member of OAU, Non-Aligned Movement and UN since 1976.

NOTES

1. For background on the colonial period, see D. M. Abshire and M. A. Samuels (eds), *Portuguese Africa – A Handbook* (New York: Praeger; London: Pall Mall, 1969), and D. L. Wheeler and R. Pélissier, *Angola* (New York: Praeger; London: Pall Mall, 1971).

2. For detailed investigation of race relations and white settlement, see G. J. Bender, *Angola under the Portuguese – The Myth and the Reality* (Berkeley, Calif.: University of California Press; London: Heinemann, 1978).

3. For ethnic and cultural analysis and description, see J. Redinha, *Etnias e Culturas de Angola* (Luanda: Instituto de Investigação Científica de Angola, 1975).

4. For a sympathetic account of the MPLA, see B. Davidson, *In the Eye of the Storm – Angola's People* (London: Longman, 1972; Harmondsworth: Penguin, 1975). For painstaking background on modern nationalism, including the FNLA and UNITA, see J. A. Marcum, *The Angolan Revolution*, vol. I: *The Anatomy of an Explosion, 1950–1962* (Cambridge, Mass., and London: MIT Press, 1969), and vol. II: *Exile Politics and Guerrilla Warfare, 1962–1976* (Cambridge, Mass., and London: MIT Press, 1978). Interesting sidelights are given in M. de Souza Clington, *Angola Libre?* (Paris: Gallimard, 1975) and R. Davezies, *Les Angolais* (Paris: Éditions de Minuit, 1965).

5. Angolan literature provides a social context for 1960, in, for example, J. L. Vieira, *A Vida Verdadeira de Domingos Xavier* (Lisbon: Edições 70, 1974), or English translation by M. Wolfers, *The Real Life·of Domingos Xavier* (London: Heinemann, 1978).

6. Sequence and dating for the clandestine and guerrilla period differ on points of detail in the secondary sources, but see MPLA, *História de Angola* (Algiers: Centro de Estudos Angolanos, 1965). As far as possible I have followed the best available evidence, usually MPLA documents, including statements from participants made after the fall of colonialism, when the need for secrecy lessened.

7. A recent republication of the original text is 'Documentação: Manifesto do

MPLA', *Novembro – A Revista Angolana*, I, no. 3 (1977) 1–5.
8. See P. Petrucci, 'Angola: Appel pour un Congrés du MPLA', *Afrique–Asie*, no. 58 (1974). For comment on this crisis, see B. Davidson, 'The Politics of Armed Struggle: National Liberation in the African Colonies of Portugal', in B. Davidson, J. Slovo and A. R. Wilkinson, *Southern Africa: The New Politics of Revolution* (Harmondsworth: Penguin, 1976) pp. 83–4.
9. MPLA, *Estatutos, Lei de Disciplina, Membros do Comité Central e do Bureau Político* (Luanda: Departamento de Informação e Propaganda, 1975).
10. Speeches and texts in *Documentos da Independência* (Luanda: Ministério da Informação, 1976) in Portuguese, French and English.
11. Ibid.
12. MPLA, *Documentos – 3.ª Reunião Plenária do Comité Central do MPLA* (Luanda: Secretariado do Bureau Político do MPLA, 1976), or unofficial English translation of main speeches and resolutions, *Documents MPLA Central Committee Plenary 23–29 October 1976* (London: Mozambique, Angola and Guiné Information Centre, 1977).
13. See MPLA, *Informação do Bureau Político sobre a Tentativa de Golpe de Estado de 27 de Maio* (Luanda: Departamento de Orientação Revolucionária, 1977), or English translation in MPLA, *Information Bulletin*, I, no. 4 (July 1977), or extract in unofficial translation 'How the Angola Coup was Crushed', *African Communist*, no. 71 (1977) 35–51.
14. MPLA, *Documentos e Teses ao I Congresso* (Luanda: Jornal de Angola, 1977), or, for summary and extract in unofficial English translation, 'MPLA: The Story of the First Congress', *People's Power*, no. 11 (1978) 33–49 (London: Mozambique, Angola and Guiné Information Centre).
15. Principal Congress speeches and resolutions are published as 'Documentação', *Novembro – A Revista Angolana*, I, no. 7 (1977) 1–44.
16. *Documentos da Independência*.
17. See sources in note 12 above.
18. See sources in note 13 above.
19. *Lei do Poder Popular, Lei No. 1/76* (Luanda: Conselho da Revolução, 1976).
20. In December 1978 Lopo do Nascimento was dismissed as Prime Minister and Carlos Rocha resigned as Second Deputy Prime Minister. Their places in the Political Bureau were taken by Evaristo Kimba, Provincial Commissioner for Cabinda Province, and Pascoal Luvualu, member of the Secretariat of the Central Committee.
21. See sources in notes 14 and 15 above.
22. MPLA, *Orientações Fundamentais para o Desenvolvimento Económico-social da República Popular de Angola no Período de 1978/1980* (Luanda: Imprensa Nacional de Angola, 1977).

BIBLIOGRAPHY

In addition to secondary sources listed in the notes, much published work on Mozambique, Guinea-Bissau and Cape Verde is of relevance to Angola, and the Portuguese colonial background is relevant to all four countries. A useful bibliographical sketch up to 1975 is G. J. Bender and A. F. Isaacman, 'The

Changing Historiography of Angola and Mozambique', in C. Fyfe (ed.), *African Studies since 1945 – A Tribute to Basil Davidson* (London: Longman, 1976).

A critical view of United States intervention in the pre-independence and immediate post-independence period is J. Stockwell, *In Search of Enemies – A CIA Story* (New York: W. W. Norton, 1978). Accounts of European mercenary involvement in the war against Angola in 1975 and 1976 are given in R. Valdes Vivo, *Angola: Fin del Mito de los Mercenarios* (Havana: Empresa de Medios de Propaganda, 1976), and W. Burchett and D. Roebuck, *The Whores of War – Mercenaries Today* (London: Penguin, 1977). A Soviet journalist's view of the independence period, with some historical background, is Oleg Ignatyev, *Secret Weapon in Africa* (Moscow: Progress Publishers, 1977). A sympathetic view of Cuba's involvement in support of Angola in 1975 and 1976 is the Colombian writer G. García Márquez's 'Operación Carlota', widely published in Spanish and French, and translated into English by P. Camiller as 'Operation Carlota', *New Left Review*, no. 101–2 (1977) 123–37. A contemporary class analysis from an MPLA viewpoint is J. Slovo's three-part interview with Lúcio Lara, 'Angola: Colonialismo e Libertaçào', *Tempo*, no. 400 (1978) 41–8; no. 401 (1978) 39–46; and no. 402 (1978) 45–52; or the two-part English translation 'How the Angolan Revolution was Built', *The African Communist*, no. 74 (1978) 18–36, 'The Angolan Revolution Main Phases in the Development of the MPLA', *The African Communist*, no. 75 (1978) 53–73. The present author is writing a political study of the first years of independence.

5 People's Republic of Benin

SAMUEL DECALO

Benin – until 1975 known as Dahomey – is one of Africa's smaller states and by far the continent's most unstable polity. During its eighteen years of independence from French colonial rule, the country has experienced six coups and numerous other military upheavals; ten civilian or military presidents have risen to power and six different constitutions have been promulgated. What distinguishes the current regime – which rose to power by military coup in 1972 – is both its declaration of a Marxist–Leninist state and its continuance in office despite several attempts to dislodge it.

The country stretches from a 125-km. palm-fringed littoral to the Niger River, some 675 km. inland. Much of the original rain-forest has been cleared, and, apart from the quartzite north-western Atakora range (highest altitude 655 metres), the topography presents no serious barriers to the development of internal communications. A paved coastal road connects Benin with both Nigeria and Togo (and on to Ghana), while a paved road and a railway link the coastal areas with Parakou in the interior. The latter centre is also an important transshipment juncture for freight to and from landlocked Niger, further north.

The population is a mosaic of over sixty different ethnic groups at differing stages of development.[1] A sharp dual cleavage has existed from pre-colonial days, dividing the more populous and advanced coastal groups (the Fon, Yoruba, Adja and so on) from the interior elements, with whom contact had been minimal; and the aggressive and expanding Fon (centered around Abomey and their former powerful Danhomé kingdom)[2] from the Yoruba and allied groups in Porto Novo and the coast. Ethnic animosities between the two dominant southern populations still exist, a legacy of over a century of constant warfare and

87

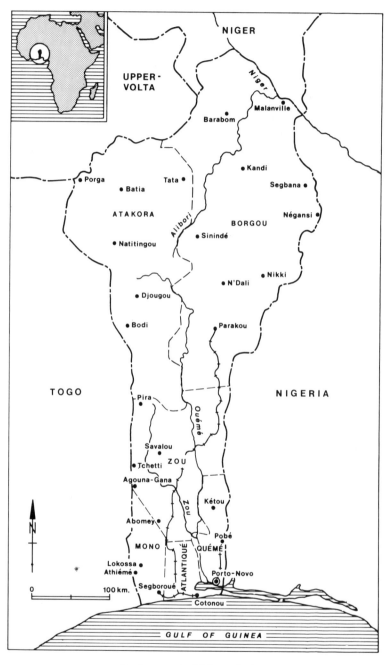

Benin: provincial boundaries

mutual competition. Strong resentments have built up in the less advanced and never-unified north[3] against the south as a whole, aggravated by the haughty and domineering attitudes of southern administrators recruited into the colonial civil service. Both shortly before independence and during a particularly harsh political crisis in 1970, the cry was raised in Parakou, capital of the north, for (unrealistically) secession from Dahomey.

The perpetuation of these historic animosities and the entrenchment of existing socio-economic disparities between the country's various populations have spawned deep feelings of regionalism and intense political allegiances to ethnic–regional leaders.[4] This has meant that at all times, under civilian or military rule, political leadership has been assessed by the bulk of the population in the countryside more in terms of its ethnic composition and credentials than in terms of its political content or programme.[5] In like manner, urban elements have usually placed ethnic considerations above class interests, while modern structures, such as the unions and armed forces, have been violently polarised along ethnic–personalist lines, adding to the tumult of Beninois politics.

Exacerbating Benin's internal divisions is the country's abject economic non-viability and continuing dependence on France. Though various mineral deposits are known to exist, they are mostly unexploitable, owing to their distance from the coast or poor ore content. Agriculture has for long been stagnant and hefty negative trade balances have piled up annually. Budget-balancing subsidies from France and some foreign public aid from other Western countries (and since 1972 from the East and from OPEC) have not sufficed to soothe a deep economic malaise affecting all strata of society or to make a serious impact on the economy. The high upward mobility of the coastal populations and their thirst for educational facilities, social services and public employment have placed severe strains on all governments to date. The fact that up to 80 per cent of the national budget must be set aside for the payroll of a grossly bloated civil service, and that only a trickle of private or public capital reaches the country sharply delimits the range of economic options available to any regime in power, including the current one.

BACKGROUND TO THE 1972 REVOLUTION

Much of the political history of Benin between 1945, when politics was legalised in the French colonial empire, and the 1972 revolution, is the story of a three-cornered tug-of-war for political supremacy, between the country's three ethnic–regional leaders.[6] And, as each of these political giants tried in turn, while in office, to demote, purge or exile his rivals, the political scene came to be punctuated by unionist–student riots, upheavals and military interventions. Though a plethora of other political aspirants presented their credentials to the electorate, none made the slightest dent on the stranglehold of the triumvirate over their respective ethnic fiefdoms. In the last electoral contest (1970) the veteran and respected politician and ex-President Dr Émile-Derlin Zinsou (elevated to power by the armed forces and then deposed) competed against the triumvirate as a 'non-regional' national candidate and humiliatingly garnered only 3 per cent of the vote cast.[7] The permanence of ethnic allegiances, despite governmental immobility, corruption and mismanagement while in office, is attested to by the fact that each regional leader obtained exactly the same percentage of the vote in 1970 as in the 1960 elections.

As the struggle for power spawned seemingly insoluble constitutional crises and administrative chaos, the military forces were inexorably drawn into the political vortex to preside over extra-constitutional successions (as in 1963 and 1965). From the outset politicised and polarised into factions supporting each of the three political camps,[8] by 1967 the armed forces had rapidly lost whatever semblance of corporate unity they had formerly possessed. Drawn into the very centre of the political arena by the 1965 assumption of power by Chief of Staff General Soglo (in the aftermath of a paralysing constitutional stalemate), the officer corps disintegrated into a series of competitive personalist cliques, one of which seized power in 1967.[9] A brief experiment to impose on the country a non-regional President (Zinsou) collapsed in 1969 under a new personalist coup.

With the officer corps in a hopeless state of disarray and divided internally into mutually hostile factions, the old triumvirate was recalled back from exile in France. In May 1970 – after an election that confirmed that regionalism was still the dominant force in Benin – a unique constitutional arrangement was finally hammered out. Under it each of the three leaders was to hold executive power for a period of two years in rotation, while participating in a collegiate Presidential Council. Despite its potential for friction, the formula achieved a major advance when in May 1972 the country's first-ever peaceful political succession took place. Barely five months later, however, the armed forces – for long regarding themselves not merely as arbiters, but as the fount, of political power[10] – again intervened in the political scene, placing the triumvirate under house arrest, where they still remain. In their place Lt Col. Kerekou set up an increasingly radicalised military regime that wrenched the hitherto ideology-free Benin onto a socialist course.

The causes of the 1972 *coup détat* were varied and convoluted.[11] The motivations of the clique that mounted it were not solely, or even primarily, ideological, as was *ex post facto* rationalised. Certainly a more militant mood had been sweeping the armed forces and urban masses, exacerbated by the conservative policies of the Presidential Council. Nationalistic frustrations played a major part as well: frustration at the fact that Benin – once regarded as the intellectual pacesetter and Latin Quarter of French Africa – had been unable to produce alternative leadership hierarchies to those at the helm of the nation for over two generations; and frustration at Benin's perennial economic quasi-pauper status and acute dependence upon French largesse. Finally, purely internal military factors, interfactional competitions, jealousies and personal animosities, were an important ingredient, as in all previous military upheavals. The divergent multiple motives behind the coup go a long way in explaining the reason why the 'revolutionary' phase of Kerekou's regime (since 1974) was so delayed; they also form a background for the understanding of the continuing strains and internal upheavals within the officer corps once the socialist option was embarked upon. Despite the revolution, Benin's armed forces remain divided on a multiplicity of planes, much as in pre-revolutionary days, preserving the country's unenviable reputation for instability and political tumult.

The radical option in pre-revolutionary Benin

Given Benin's pre-1972 pattern of ethnic–regional political allegiances, ideological parties of whatever hue tended to be stillborn. Though urban elements – especially organised labour, students and the intelligentsia – were slowly to become susceptible to class appeals, at election time they deviated but little from the ethnic voting pattern of their rural brethren. Thus, though Justin Ahomadegbé – the perennial leader of Benin's Fon – was widely regarded as ideologically militant (at least, as compared with the other two leaders in the triumvirate) this did not win him measurable support from the Yoruba and Adja populations of southern Benin. Likewise, Hubert Maga, the supreme *status quo* politician of the northern populations, consistently counted in his entourage several radical northern youth leaders – some of whom had held office in militant student associations in France.[12] Attempts to create nuclei of non-ethnic socialist parties invariably failed to attract popular interest. In one early attempt (in 1959) a Parti de la Revolution Socialiste du Benin collapsed when it could not gather more than fifty members.

The radical option began to be more forcefully expressed in the late 1960s via the increasingly unruly student organisations and the trade unions. Thoroughly politicised and under the sway of militant leaders, teachers and political aspirants locked out of positions of authority by Benin's power hierarchy, their periodic confrontations with the government acquired a distinctly Marxist rhetoric. Their main targets were French expatriate capital and entrepreneurs, invariably viewed as crassly exploitative. Aware of the power of labour and youth to mount acutely destabilising strikes, all regimes in Cotonou attempted to keep a tight reign over these constituencies (or to appease them), but by the time the Presidential Council came to power the situation was volatile and intolerable. The schools (both primary and secondary) had become hotbeds of radical demonstrations and open calls for revolutionary change and violence. During 1971 and 1972 the Council was forced to crack down strongly on the overt challenges to its authority but was unable truly to soothe the unrest in the educational establishment. Following the rise to power of Kerekou, youth and (to a lesser extent) labour were at the forefront of the societal groups that welcomed the coup, though the slow radicalisation of the new regime was to lead a resurgence in student–government confrontations.

THE PEOPLE'S REPUBLIC

The ambigous motivations behind the 1972 *coup d'état* precluded the radicalisation of the new regime until 1974. Beninois socialism was at its inception merely a series of *ad hoc* nationalistic decrees only later anchored to the legitimacy of a more comprehensive doctrine, Marxism–Leninism. Indeed, hardly any observer was able to predict that the military upheaval was different from all previous ones, or that it would lead to any lasting systemic change. None of the key leaders of the coup were known Marxists, though most were to grasp at Marxism and elevate it to official State ideology.

Benin socialism was therefore at inception nothing more than a general socially acceptable catch-all phrase expressing pent-up nationalistic frustrations. It obtained form, substance, direction and theory under the multiple pressures of radical elements in the educational establishment (who had imbibed Marxism while students in France), from several extremely militant self-exiled ideologues (including several protégés of Guinea's Sekou Touré), who flocked home after the 'revolution' (and returned to Guinea disenchanted with the insincerity of the regime), and in response to the urgent pragmatic need to adopt the radical garb of the urban masses – ultimately the sole clientele of the new regime.

In part reflecting the officer corps's pent-up but rudderless grievances at the *ancien régime* and in part a very opportunistic adoption of an ideology that could not but evoke support in the urban areas, the doctrine's chequered history, half-hearted application and major internal inconsistencies reflect its multifaceted origins. Stripped of jargon, the core of Beninois socialism revolves around a number of tenets enunciated by Kerekou in 1974. These include (1) economic independence via the nationalisation of most means of production in the hands of the State; (2) transformation of society – via various structures and reforms – into a model socialist alliance of farmers and workers; (3) a realignment of Beninois foreign policy towards the progressive bloc; and (4) democratic centralism under the leadership of Kerekou. These tenets are also *mutatis mutandis* an integral part of Benin's 1977 Fundamental Law.

The 'revolutionary' phase of Kerekou's rule did not commence until the second anniversary of the 1972 revolution. During 1974–6, a series of nationalisation measures brought under State control large segments of the national economy. The banking sector, oil-distribution network, educational establishment, road haulage, insurance, tourist facilities and selected commercial and industrial enterprises were in quick succession absorbed into the public sector of the economy. Yet the nationalisation left untouched several large French firms, which still dominate aspects of Beninois commercial life. Moreover, extending State control to its utmost practical limits involved the expropriation of assets valued at a mere 2000 million CFA (Commonauté Financière Africaine) francs, or $8 million, reflecting the smallness of the Benin modern sector and, especially, the weakness of its industrial segment. By comparison, French public assistance to Benin in 1974 – temporarily frozen pending assurances of compensation – exceeded this sum; indeed, French aid in the years 1970–4 (fully 40 per cent of all public funds coming into the country) amounted to 10,200 million CFA francs.[13]

Hand in hand with the nationalisations in the modern sector came an administrative reorganisation of local government; edicts setting up revolutionary structures at all levels of society, to motivate, educate and mobilise the peasantry and workers; a series of social laws (regulating dress, bar-hours, the proper way of addressing 'revolutionary' letters, and so on); and, in November 1975, the change in the country's name and flag. With the growth of opposition to Kerekou's rule (in his roles of military officer, northerner and leader of the Marxist option), legitimation was sought through the creation of the People's Revolutionary Party of Benin in May 1976 and the promulgation of a new Fundamental Law in August 1977.

Notwithstanding the above radical changes in the image of Benin, the transformation is still superficial and skin-deep. The regime has given much more attention – at least until recently – to the trivial, tangential and structural aspects of a Marxist-Leninist state.[14] The detailed outward trappings of the new order contrast sharply with the relatively lifeless structures, largely apathetic and uninvolved peasantry, the non-socialist comportment of leaders of the revolution, opportunistic utilisation of radical rhetoric by cadres and the continued dependence on France and the West in general. The economy has reacted sluggishly to the directives of the new leadership, and a combination of drought in the north and flooding in the south has further complicated efforts to bring about greater development and self-reliance. Opposition from both within the country (the officer corps, civil service, unionists), and from emigré groups in Europe and West Africa, has resulted in the continuation of tumult and unrest in Beninois post-revolutionary life, with the January 1977 airborne assault on Cotonou[15] underscoring the very real threat to the revolution from abroad.

THE PARTI DE LA RÉVOLUTION POPULAIRE DU BENIN

The PRPB, or People's Revolutionary Party of Benin, was created on 30 November 1975 and its first extraordinary congress was held in Cotonou on 15–17 May 1976. The Congress ratified the Party's constitution and internal organisation, and elected its executive officers. The constitution specifies that the dominant forces in the Party are, and will continue to be, the working class, the poor and middle peasants and artisans.

The Congress, whose membership was chosen in a more or less *ad hoc* manner, established a twenty-seven man Central Committee (with a majority of civilian members) entrusted with Party affairs in between congresses. The executive organ of the Central Committee is a six-man Political Bureau headed by Kerekou. Its most powerful figures (apart from Kerekou) are Major Michel Alladayé and Lieutenant Martin Azonhiho, both members of the military government.

There are no reliable figures about the current membership of the PRPB, which is still very weak at the grass-roots level. Estimates are of the order of 6000, but this figure, if accurate, is likely to include a sizable inactive contingent not necessarily militant.

According to Benin's 1977 Fundamental Law (article 52), the Central Committee of the PRPB selects and submits its choice for the Presidency of the Republic (and for other executive offices) to the National Revolutionary Assembly of Benin for confirmation.

GOVERNMENT

The constitution

On 23 May 1977 the draft Fundamental Law of Benin was published by the PRPB Central Committee, minutely defining the organisation of the State and paving the road for the 'people's democratic revolution' – the second of three evolutionary stages in terms of official doctrine. The first stage – the 'revolutionary movement of national liberation' – was deemed to have been attained by the very nature of the 1972 coup, while the subsequent stage was defined as that of the socialist revolution.

The Fundamental Law is a lengthy document containing eleven chapters and 160 articles.[16] It affirms the 'people's revolutionary dictatorship' but specifically (article 24) protects the private property of expatriates and foreigners (if their activities are beneficial to the national economy). It specifies the creation of a National Revolutionary Assembly of directly elected people's commissioners, which formally elects the head of State (on the advice of the PRPB Central Committee), who in turn selects a governing National Executive Committee in accordance with specific guidelines; the constitution also provides a very detailed structural and functional outline of a pyramid of local government from the provincial to the village level. The Law 'rigorously' prohibits 'all acts of regionalism' (article 3), reiterates the Republic's philosophical foundation in Marxism-Leninism applied in a 'creative' manner in accord with Benin's realities (article 4) and enjoins labour (1) to study Marxism-Leninism, (2) to practice democratic centralism, and (3) to undertake criticism and self-criticism (article 7). It prohibits 'preaching against the Benin revolution under the pretext of defence of one's religion and its particularistic and egotistical interests' (article 12) and spells out the rights and duties of citizens.

The Fundamental Law was tendered as a proposal to the National Revolutionary Council for approval after 'broad democratic consultations'. These were eventually deemed to have been carried out, and the promulgation of the constitution on 26 August 1977 effectively made it the law of the land. Until the erection of the structures specified in the constitution, existing organs were to remain in force; several of the latter, however, merely changed name, transforming themselves into the structures specified by the constitution.

The executive

The President of the Republic, as defined by the Fundamental Law, is elected by the National Revolutionary Assembly at the proposal of the Central Committee of the PRPB. He is elected for a renewable term of three years, and holds executive powers. The President of the Republic nominates his National Executive Council (cabinet) on the advice of both the PRPB Central Committee and the National Revolutionary Assembly. The Executive Council must include in its membership the president of the executive organs of the provincial administrations and certain other specified officials.

With the promulgation of the Fundamental Law on 26 August 1977, the existing Revolutionary Military Government became *de facto* the National Executive Council (usually referred to as the government or the Cabinet). Table 5.1 lists its members.

There have been several shuffles and purges within the military government since the 1972 *coup d'état*, reflecting residual factional tensions in the officer corps. Particularly noteworthy was the liquidation of the popular and powerful Major Michel Aikpé (at the time Minister of the Interior) in June 1975, and the purge, a few months earlier, of Capt. Janvier Assogba (Minister of Civil Service), who mounted an attempted putsch.

Within the current government, neither Lt Col. Ohouens nor Lt Col. Rodriguez, despite their high rank, are part of the inner circle of power, which includes Lt Col. Kerekou, Major Alladayé and Lt Azonhiho. The last, once a very close associate of Kerekou, has in the past two years been shunted aside in favour of Alladayé.

The legislature and elections

There have been no elections in Benin since 1970, nor has there been a

TABLE 5.1 Membership of the Beninois National Executive Council

Lt Col. Mathieu Kerekou*	President of the Republic
Lt Col. Barthelemy Ohouens	Minister of Industry and Handicraft
Lt Col. Richard Rodriguez	Minister of Equipment
Major Michel Alladayé*	Minister of Foreign Affairs and Co-operation
Isidore Amoussou	Minister of Finance
Major François Dossou*	Minister-delegate to the Presidency: Planning, Statistics and Foreign Aid
Capt. Djibril Moriba	Minister of Justice, Legislation and Social Affairs
Capt. Augustin Honvoh	Minister of Technical and Higher Education
Capt. Vincent Guezodje	Minister of Primary Education
Capt. André Atchadé*	Minister of Trade and Tourism
Capt. Issifou Bouraima	Minister of Health
Capt. Leopold Ahovéya	Minister of Transport
Capt. Adolphe Biaou*	Minister of Civil Service and Labour
Capt. François Kouyami	Minister of Youth, People's Culture and Sport
Capt. Martin Azonhiho*	Minister-delegate to the Presidency: Interior and National Orientation
Lt Philippe Akpo	Minister of Rural Development and Co-operatives

*Denotes member of the PRPB Political Bureau.

legislative organ since the 1972 *coup d'état*. The Fundamental Law of 26 August 1977 provides for a National Revolutionary Assembly composed of 'people's commissioners' elected for three-year terms. Their number and manner of election is subject to future legislation. Until the election of the new Assembly, the existing National Revolutionary Council serves as Benin's deliberative body.

The National Revolutionary Council (Conseil National de la Révolution)

The Council was formally created on 1 September 1973 and installed in office on 19 October 1973. It is headed by President Kerekou and has sixty-nine members, of whom thirty-three are military personnel of all ranks (including the military members of the Government); six are prefects of Benin's provinces, twelve are other members of the provincial revolutionary councils, and seventeen are representatives of the civil service, the police and paramilitary organs. The Council has had a checkered history since its creation, and its membership has been shuffled and purged a number of times.

Local government

With its consolidation in power, the Kerekou regime declared that one
of its prime objectives was to achieve an administrative decision-making
decentralisation in the countryside to meet the expressed needs of
farmers, the bulk of the population. Several *ad hoc* decisions were taken
and in February 1974 came the administrative reorganisation of local
government. Most of these changes and several subsequent ones were in
due course entrenched in the country's Fundamental Law.

In the administrative reforms the number, names and boundaries of
the former prefectures and sousprefectures were left intact, though the
prefectures were retermed provinces (still under prefects) and the
sousprefectures districts (under district chiefs). The country thus remains
divided into forty districts, grouped into six provinces. The latter, with
their administrative headquarters, are as follows:

Province	*Headquarters*
Ouémé	Porto-Novo
Atlantique	Cotonou
Mono	Lokossa
Zou	Abomey
Borgou	Parakou
Atakora	Natitingou

At each level (down to that of the village or town quarters that are the
basic units) revolutionary councils were established, each with executive
organs, charged with various administrative functions. These duties, the
composition of the executive organs and the relations between the
various levels of local government are laid out in great detail in thirty-
five or so articles of the Fundamental Law.[17]

The Fundamental Law provides for the creation at every level of
government (provincial, district, urban commune, village or urban
quarter) of revolutionary councils. These councils are the Conseils
Provinciaux de la Révolution (CPR), the Conseils Révolutionnaires de
District (CRD), the Conseils Communaux de la Révolution (CCR) and
the Conseils Révolutionnaires Locaux pour les Villages et Quartiers de
Ville (CRL). Each council is headed by an executive organ, called,
respectively, a Comité d'État d'Administration de la Province (CEAP),
a Comité Révolutionnaire d'Administration du District (CRAD), a
Secrétariat Exécutif du Conseil Communal de la Révolution (SECCR),
or a Secretariat Exécutif du Conseil Révolutionnaire Local. All

members of these organs are elected for a period of two years, and each organ is under the supervisory control of the one above it (see Figure 5.1).

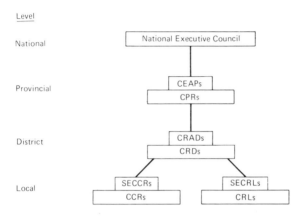

FIGURE 5.1 Administrative organisation of Benin

Each of the executive organs is in turn controlled by a Permanent Committee. In the case of the CEAPs, the Committee is composed of a president (the prefect of the province), elected by the National Assembly on the recommendation of the Party Central Committee and a *de facto* member of the Conseil Exécutif National; two vice-presidents, elected from the larger provincial organ at the recommendation of the Party Central Committee; and any other members deemed necessary. The CEAP itself also includes a secretary-general, representatives of the 'diverse branches of activities and services' in the province, two members of the armed forces, and five other members, elected from the CPR. With minor variations this is also the composition of the district, *commune* and local organs. According to eye-witnesses, much of the structural reorganisation of Benin is not yet complete, and the organs (especially at the grass-roots level) are listless and moribund. Popular participation is minimal, elections largely a *pro forma* ratification of Party choices, and local participation in decision-making, planning and development negated by constant interference from higher organs and/or unwillingness of the local bodies to take any concrete initiatives.[18]

OPPOSITION GROUPS

Opposition to the Kerekou regime abounds in Benin and stems from several sources. First, the officer corps itself is sharply divided on a variety of planes, including the ideological, ethnic and regional. As noted previously, personal ambitions, competitions and corporate jealousies have always been an integral part of Benin military life. Even the core issue of whether the armed forces should continue to play a dominant political role polarises the corps into opposing camps. Secondly, resistance to the new regime exists among disaffected supporters, notables, chiefs and political lieutenants of the country's ethnic leaders, who were totally ousted from positions of influence after the 1972 coup. They have usually, in light of the general radical-isation of public opinion in the urban areas, been very cautious in their attempt to canvass support for a return to the former *status quo*. Thirdly, a significant section of the largely southern bureaucracy (many of its members supporters of Ahomadegbé) have been disaffected both by the militancy of socialist Benin and by attempts to pack the civil service with northerners who may be expected to support Kerekou. It was these southerners who took to the streets when the popular southern Major Michel Aikpé was murdered, in June 1975, and it is also from this stratum that most defections from the regime have occurred, swelling the Beninois émigré communities in neighbouring Togo and in France. So serious, and embarrassing, has been the outflow from Benin of skilled personnel that in 1975 the regime imposed stiff exit requirements at the country's borders and confiscated the property of those who refused to heed an amnesty. Finally, an anti-Kerekou Front for the Liberation and Rehabilitation of Dahomey, structurally the only organised opposition, has been established in Paris and Brussels, with underground cells in Porto Novo and Cotonou. It is led by ex-President Zinsou and is also active in Senegal, Ivory Coast, Gabon and Togo. Zinsou's supporters include émigrés in Europe and West Africa, and disaffected elements in Benin. The organisation has been accused of sponsoring several plots against Kerekou, including the still mystery-shrouded airborne attack on Cotonou airport on 16 January 1977.

MASS ORGANISATIONS

Youth

Benin's student and youth associations have traditionally been either linked to the regional political machine of the country's ethnic leaders or, especially in the coastal cities and prestigious lycées, highly politicised. This process of politicisation (of both primary and secondary schools), aided by the destabilising role youth played during the coup of 1963, greatly escalated in the late 1960s and early 1970s. Frequent student–government confrontations, over both academic and political issues, brought about the closure of Benin's educational establishments on several occasions during 1969–72, and the selective ban of student associations. In November 1971, for example, the Union Général des Étudiants et Élèves was banned (and schools closed) after the latter issued a call for a massive strike and social upheaval, demanding that workers, soldiers and policemen 'transform Dahomey into a battlefield'.[19]

The unruly student associations dissolved by the previous Presidential Council government were reinstated shortly after the 1972 *coup d'état*. Continued friction and demonstrations against the Kerekou regime (over its laxity in bringing radical change) brought about their later dissolution and efforts to impose greater control over youth in general.

In January 1978 the **PRPB** announced plans to create a four-tier youth organisation encompassing all (not just students) between the ages of four and forty. The avowed purpose of this reorganisation was to 'safeguard the unity of the people'. The plan envisaged an organ for children between the ages of six and fifteen; one for pupils between the ages of thirteen and twenty; one for students aged eighteen to thirty; and a national structure for young workers, farmers, intellectuals and soldiers between the ages of fifteen and forty. These structures are not yet operative.

Trade unions

There are ten central confederations of labour, with a total of 167 unions. These are all grouped into the Comité de l'Unité Syndicale

(Labour Unity Committee). All factories and intermediate-size enterprises and the various branches of the civil service have local Committees for the Defence of Revolution set up to 'detect and expose all acts of sabotage against the Revolution and all threats to the Revolutionaries'.[20] Attempts have been made to appease unionists by giving them a greater role in management, better working hours (an uninterrupted 7 a.m.–2 p.m. day) and by unfreezing wages, which had been outstripped by inflationary pressures. Nevertheless, organised labour has been a constant source of worry to the regime, as to all governments before it. For, though labour has become radicalised and many support the United Front and the Dahomey (later Benin) League, both Marxist pressure groups, the allegiance of the unionists to the new regime is hardly assured. Thus, after the June 1975 liquidation of Major Michel Aikpé, massive labour walkouts and demonstrations drove the military regime into a virtual state of seige. Moreover, the underground Front for the Liberation and Rehabilitation of Dahomey is active among Benin's labour and has been able to disseminate tracts calling for the overthrow of Kerekou.

THE ECONOMY

Benin possesses one of the weakest economies in francophone Africa. Only a few mineral ores are known to exist (chrome and gold near Natitingou, iron in the Atakora mountains and near Kandi, marble at Dadjo, and so on) but most is inexploitable. About 87 per cent of the population live solely off agriculture, which is largely stagnant.[21] Only a minor manufacturing sector exists, including a palm-oil industry, cotton gins, two shrimp-processing plants and a recently constructed cement factory. Importing increasingly large quantities of processed goods and machinery (see Table 5.2) and exporting mostly primary products (see Table 5.3), Benin's balance of trade has been in deficit since 1927. Indeed, since independence the median coverage of imports by exports has been 41·3 per cent, with the ratio as low as 16·1 per cent in 1975 (see Table 5.4).

The negative balance of payments has been covered largely by direct capital transfusions from the French Treasury, which has likewise assisted Benin with its chronic budgetary deficits. Financial constraints, and the fact that Benin's bloated civil service consumes up to 80 per cent of the national budget, have imposed severe limitations upon economic planning, while Benin's few resources and political instability have attracted little risk capital.[22]

TABLE 5.2 Benin: principal commodities imported, 1971–5

Commodity	Quantity (tons)					Value (CFA francs million)				
	1971	1972	1973	1974	1975	1971	1972	1973	1974	1975
Tobacco	3,065	3,043	2,301	2,833	2,901	927·9	1,265·6	1,568·2	2,415·9	3,337·1
Cement	49,301	51,550	59,631	82,729	45,307	356·2	373·3	420·1	1,176·8	582·0
Petroleum products	63,478	82,722	67,158	66,262	86,200	767·5	1,010·3	1,416·2	2,250·2	2,579·2
Pharmaceuticals	594	721	704	1,756	648	705·6	690·3	926·6	1,898·9	1,083·2
Cotton cloth	5,450	5,126	4,555	3,302	4,842	3,971·8	3,338·2	3,424·0	3,310·6	4,533·2
Clothing	985	830	910	1,460	1,305	1,404·6	862·3	1,387·2	3,149·9	2,877·2
Iron, steel	11,189	19,397	12,542	17,411	12,870	1,037·4	1,643·8	1,480·4	2,645·6	2,070·5
Mechanical machinery	1,604	2,159	3,098	7,383	2,737	1,280·7	1,655·0	1,690·6	4,526·5	2,989·5
Electrical machinery	1,406	2,361	2,419	3,945	5,238	759·6	1,330·2	1,060·8	2,141·3	2,425·2
Road haulage	4,569	3,733	3,868	4,116	6,090	1,935·0	1,972·2	1,970·1	2,362·9	3,851·7
Total	250,563	297,804	272,322	285,326	272,656	21,201·8	23,509·7	24,859·2	35,529·9	42,080·2

TABLE 5.3 Benin: principal commodities exported, 1971–5

Product	Quantity (tons)					Value (CFA francs million)				
	1971	1972	1973	1974	1975	1971	1972	1973	1974	1975
Peanuts	3,658	3,704	3,311	4,605	1,779	241·5	187·2	820·6	489·0	256·6
Cotton	32,951	38,653	33,191	46,037	11,724	2,607·8	2,971·3	3,187·0	5,204·0	1,541·9
Karite	9,179	11,758	3,158	13,161	500	275·1	182·3	101·4	458·5	29·5
Cacao	19,259	12,320	15,291	3,694	1,610	2,806·8	1,780·5	2,443·0	1,205·0	642·0
Cement	3,001	—	1,685	37,841	45,645	238·0	—	19·4	469·3	555·5
Total	160,409	142,422	112,589	146,574	118,705	11,648·1	9,189·2	9,794·3	10,240·3	6,790·5

TABLE 5.4 Benin: imports/exports, 1960–75 (CFA francs million)

Year	Imports	Exports	Balance	Exports as percentage of imports
1960	7,643	4,513	− 3,130	59·0
1961	6,275	3,579	− 2,696	57·0
1962	6,627	2,699	− 3,928	40·6
1963	8,249	3,155	− 5,094	38·3
1964	7,762	3,254	− 4,508	42·0
1965	8,491	3,367	− 5,124	39·8
1966	8,270	2,585	− 5,685	31·2
1967	11,983	3,750	− 8,233	31·2
1968	12,211	5,505	− 6,706	45·0
1969	14,129	6,693	− 7,436	47·3
1970	17,660	9,062	− 8,598	51·3
1971	21,202	11,648	− 9,554	54·9
1972	23,510	9,189	− 14,321	39·0
1973	24,859	9,794	− 15,065	39·4
1974	35,174	10,240	− 24,934	29·1
1975	42,080	6,791	− 35,289	16·1

Benin's revolutionary regime has sought to reorganise the country's economy and uplift its productivity by a series of nationalisations in 1974–6 and by efforts to revive the stagnant agriculture sector – the mainstay of the economy. The nationalisations (with compensation) promptly dried up sources of foreign investment, caused unrest among the local expatriate community (though many stayed on as State employees), and brought about a decline in productivity and, inevitably, greater opportunities for corruption.[23] On the other hand, several of the larger French firms, vital for Benin's commercial links with the outside world, were largely untouched.

Concomitant with the centralisation of the productive sector in State hands, the regime has mounted campaigns to mobilise the population behind drives for greater productivity. Despite a great deal of patriotic fanfare, revolutionary slogans and sporadic organisational effort in the countryside, the farmers do not appear yet to have become mobilised or socio-politically conscious and not much change is visible in the countryside. In part this is a function of the intense preoccupation of the revolutionary regime with mere structural change and rhetoric, though certainly adverse climactic conditions (severe drought in the north, flooding in the south, and the like) have also acted to limit the potential of the countryside to uplift itself economically.[24] Meanwhile the cost of living has doubled (between 1969 and 1976), unemployment in the coastal cities remains high, the rural–urban exodus continues unabated, and real per capita income has been *declining* since 1971 at the rate of 2–3 per cent per year. So long as France is willing to pick up the tab, as she has for so long in the past, the regime in Cotonou is to some extent insulated from the immediate negative implications of Benin's chronically ill economy; yet it is this very dependence upon France that revolutionary Cotonou is so anxious to end.

RELIGION AND EDUCATION

Religion

The most reliable figures on religion in Benin are contained in the 1961 census. According to this, 65 per cent of the population held a variety of animist beliefs, 13 per cent were Moslem and 15 per cent professed Christianity (12 per cent were Catholic and 3 per cent Protestant). The Moslem areas are concentrated in the vicinity of Porto Novo (among segments of the Yoruba, as well as the small Hausa community) and in the north, in the Bariba and Dendi areas. Their numbers are small, since northern Benin was largely bypassed by the Fulani invasions of the nineteenth century, which so affected neighbouring northern Nigeria. Christianity is mostly the religion of the educated coastal populations and was spread through missionary schools. The most well known of the various animist cults in Benin is Voudou (from which the Haitian offspring stems); and the historic slave port of Ouidah is the centre of the python cult, which has its temple facing the local cathedral.

Catholic missionary activity commenced practically as soon as regular European contact with Benin began, the first systematic evangelical effort being launched in 1634 in Ouidah. Despite this the missionary effort did not reach the north of the country until 1939, when a mission was set up in Kandi. The Protestant effort in Benin commenced only in the middle of the nineteenth century, seeping into the country from neighbouring British colonies. In 1942 proselytising moved to the north, with the establishment of a mission in Djougou. In 1974 the Catholic archdiocese of Cotonou (encompassing all Benin and Niger) had 450 schools and 2500 staff. In the same year there were 257 Protestant missions in the country, with 1200 staff.

The Catholic missions and schools played a dominant role during the colonial era in educating Benin's future political elite, and at least one leader – Sorou Migan Apithy – rose to prominence with active and powerful Church support. Owing to budgetary constraints and other factors – both during the colonial era and after independence – fully half of the country's schoolchildren attended Catholic (i.e. private) schools. With the rise to power of the Kerekou military regime, the situation was judged intolerable, and by means of several decrees (1974–6) all private (Catholic, Protestant, Moslem) educational establishments were nationalised. Since the government had neither the staff nor the resources to replace the expatriate personnel, the latter were asked to stay in their posts as employees of the State educational system, financed by French funds.

The Kerekou regime has acted in other ways to reduce the power of the Church in Benin; this power is viewed both as an undesirable foreign cultural influence and as a tool of French neo-colonialism, not to speak of its negative role in Marxist doctrine, which Kerekou accepts. In mid 1976 religious holidays (such as Christmas, Easter, Pentecost and the Moslem Tabaski) lost their status as legal holidays and were replaced by civil days of commemoration (Armed Forces day, the Feast of Productivity, and so forth). A month later Kerekou publicly admonished the Archbishop of Cotonou for interfering in Benin's political life by denying that sorcerers were responsible (as Kerekou had claimed) for the drought in northern Benin and other national calamities.[25] A number of minor religious sects (such as Jehovah's Witnesses) have been banned from Benin. The Fundamental Law specifically rejects religious grounds for opposition to any State edict or action, and Kerekou has clearly indicated that organised religion is barely tolerable in the People's Republic.

Education

The natural interest of the coastal populations (Fon, Yoruba) in education, and the long history of missionary educational activities in Benin have given the country one of Africa's more advanced educational systems. It has also produced a large number of Beninois intellectuals, professionals and other skilled personnel, many of whom reside abroad.

Benin's current education rate stands at around 33 per cent. The spread of education (and educational facilities) is, however, extremely uneven. In 1969 over 90 per cent of Cotonou's school-age children attended primary schools, but the relevant percentage for Tanguiéta in the far north-west was 17 per cent. This gross imbalance has improved somewhat with the rise to power of the northern-oriented regime of Kerekou, but is still sharp. Table 5.5 reproduces some educational statistics for the period 1971−6. Fully 40 per cent of the national budget has been devoted by the government to direct and indirect expenditures on education.

TABLE 5.5 Benin: selected educational statistics, 1971−6

	1971−2	1973−4	1976
Primary education	186,000	244,000	332,000
Secondary education	27,000	32,500	54,000
Technical education	2,000	2,600	2,900
Teacher training	2,553	2,900	3,100
Higher education (local)	600	1,180	1,800

As we have already seen, a large number of the country's schools were, until 1976, private missionary establishments. When these were nationalised, the school year was revised, to run from mid February to December (to suit the countryside's need for labour during the new vacations) and simple khaki uniforms became obligatory for all primary-school pupils.[26] Since, in Kerekou's view, 'revolutionary schooling is one of the absolute priorities of any revolutionary state',[27] the content of education has also been somewhat modified and an effort is made to redirect higher education (producing surplus intellectuals) into agricultural and industrial fields of study.

FOREIGN AFFAIRS

For a small, impoverished country with few global interests, Benin has always had a highly individualistic foreign policy and relatively extensive diplomatic service. Over the years there have been sharp vacillations in Benin's relations with her immediate neighbours, the Organisation of African Unity (OAU), the Organisation Commune Africaine et Malgache (OCAM), and the Council of the Entente. However, the core of Benin's foreign policy until the 1972 coup had been the maintenance of the warmest possible relations with France and the EEC – sources of the bulk of private and public capital coming into the country – and the avoidance of anything but minimal contacts with the East. Benin's dependence on France and her concomitant conservative domestic and foreign policies had in turn generated little interest in her in the East.

The 1972 *coup d'état* and, especially, the declaration for Marxism-Leninism dramatically transformed Benin's foreign policy and diplomatic relations, opening the country to a host of influences from which it had hitherto been remarkably insulated. The reorientation to the East brought into Cotonou a wide array of new embassies, missions, loans and technical assistance, from countries as disparate as Libya, Kuwait, Saudi Arabia, Guinea, the People's Republic of the Congo, China, Cuba, Romania and North Korea. Though quantitatively the new foreign aid reaching Benin since 1972 is quite modest, qualitatively it has radically transformed the image of Benin. And the new rhetoric emanating from Cotonou, along with the country's voting record at the UN, has placed Benin squarely with the other socialist countries of Africa.[28]

On the other hand, relations with France and Western Europe continue to be assiduously cultivated and continuous domestic diatribes against neocolonialism (which never mention France by name) have not been matched by meaningful attempts at disengagement from the former mother country. Indeed, in a 1976 agreement Benin even continued military co-operation with France.

The natural strains of such a dual posture, coupled with the establishment of anti-Kerekou émigré communities in Europe and West Africa eventually took their toll. Franco-Benin relations plummeted to a nadir in 1977, when Benin accused the French Ambassador – as well as the governments of Gabon, Senegal, Ivory Coast and Morocco – of active complicity in airborne assault on Cotonou airport in January.[29] Although relations were eventually patched up, for pragmatic reasons, they are no longer at the same level of symbiotic amity as prior to the 1977 assault.

The growth of anti-Kerekou opposition abroad has also greatly strained relations with Togo, normally extremely amicable, which was accused of aiding and abetting subversive elements. On the other hand, relations, and economic co-operation, with neighbouring Nigeria have expanded.

BIOGRAPHIES

Lt Col. Mathieu Kerekou, President of the Republic, Chief of Staff of the Armed Forces, Chairman of the PRPB and its Political Bureau, was born on 2 September 1933 near Natitingou in north-west Benin. Kerekou is a member of the Somba, a minor ethnic group in the region. He was educated in Kati (Mali) and Saint-Louis (Senegal) following which he received military training at Frejus and at the École Militaire de Saint-Raphaël. Transferred to the budding Dahomean Army in August 1961 (from the French colonial forces) with the rank of Second Lieutenant, Kerekou served until 1963 as President Hubert Maga's aide-de-camp. He received his first operational command in March 1963. A prominent member of a clique of northern junior officers revolving around the (also Somba) mercurial Major Maurice Kouandété, Kerekou was promoted Captain in 1965. Vice-president and then President of the Comité Militaire Révolutionnaire, following Kouandété's 1967 *coup d'état*, Kerekou then attended senior staff officers courses in France and was not involved in Kouandété's 1969 *coup d'état*. Upon his return he was promoted Major and commander of the elite Ouidah-based paracommando force, and in July 1970 became Deputy Chief of Staff under Colonel Paule Émile de Souza.

Kerekou played a moderating role during the February 1972 military upheaval, but eventually moved against the civilian Presidential Council in the coup of 26 October 1972. In 1974, after a period of growing radicalisation, he proclaimed Benin a People's Republic. Essentially moderate and pragmatic in orientation, Kerekou has been hard-pressed to keep in line the various factions within the armed forces. He has survived several attempted coups from within the army, intense foreign and domestic opposition to his socialist policies, and a foreign-initiated airborne invasion of Cotonou in January 1977.

Major Michel Alladayé, Minister of Foreign Affairs (1972–) and of Co-operation (1976–), and a member of the PRPB Political Bureau, was born in 1940 in the Fon centre of Abomey. He commenced his military career after attending Cotonou's Lycée Victor Ballot. He attended courses at France's École Militaire de Saint Cyr and the École Supérieur Technique du Génie, Versailles, and in 1963 returned home to take command, as Lieutenant, of the First Engineer Corps, based in Kandi. Promoted to Captain in 1967, he was transferred to the Engineer Unit, Army General Staff Command, later becoming Commander and Director of Military Engineers of the Benin armed forces. A powerful figure in the clique that formed behind Major Mathieu Kerekou when the latter mounted his 1972 *coup d'état*, Alladayé was appointed Foreign Minister after the takeover and in 1976 also assumed the International Co-operation portfolio. Architect and chief spokesman of Benin's new radical foreign policy, Alladayé has by his allegiance to President Kerekou survived the various purges of the officer corps, though he is on bad terms with the President's former close confidant Lt Martin Dohou Azonhihou, Commander of the Gendarmerie.

BASIC FACTS ABOUT BENIN

Official name: People's Republic of Benin (Republique Populaire du Benin).

Area: 112,622 sq. km. (47,144 sq. miles).

Population (1976 est.): 3,228,000, increasing at the rate of 2·8 per cent per year.

Population density: 28·6 per sq. km.

Population age distribution: under 15, 46·7 per cent; 15–29, 22·6 per cent; 30–44, 16·1 per cent; 45–59, 9·1 per cent; 60 and over, 5·5 per cent.

Official language: French.

Membership of the PBRB: 6000 (1977 est.).

Population distribution: 13 per cent urban, 87 per cent rural.

Administrative division: 6 provinces, divided into 40 rural and urban districts.

Ethnic nationalities: 60 ethnic groups, traditionally falling into 12 larger cultural families, of which the largest (1976 est.) are the Fon (960,000), Adja (250,000), Bariba (200,000), Yoruba (185,000), Aizo (105,000), Somba (100,000) and Fulani (75,000).

Population of major towns (1976 est.): Cotonou (modern commercial centre of Benin) 175,000; Porto-Novo (the capital) 97,000; Natitingou, 49,000; Abomey, 38,000; Ouidah, 26,000; Parakou, 21,000.

Main natural resources: cotton, cacao, karite, cement, palm oil.

Foreign Trade (1975) in millions of CFA francs: imports, 39,956 ($182·9 million); exports, 6354 ($29·0 million; balance of trade, −33,602 ($153·8 million). Average imports/exports 15·9 per cent.

Currency: the CFA franc (pegged at 0·02 French franc).

Main trading partners: France, FRG, United Kingdom, USA, Netherlands.

State budget (1977): 18,710 million CFA francs ($74 million).

Per capita income (1970, latest official figures): $67 per annum.

Per capita GNP (1974 World Bank est.): $120.

Gross domestic product (1976): primary sector (agriculture, fisheries, forestry) 29 per cent; secondary sector (industry) 14 per cent; tertiary sector (services, trade, transport) 57 per cent.

Rail network: 3 lines, totalling 579 km.

Road network: 6550 km. (roads and tracks), of which 700 km. are paved.

Cotonou Airport traffic (1976): 2090 commercial flights; passengers arriving and departing 49,149; freight traffic 3413 tons; mail traffic 226 tons.

Education (1976): education level 33 per cent, with 332,000 children at primary schools, 5400 in secondary schools, and 3400 students in universities at home and abroad.

Universities: 1, National University of Benin, at Abomey-Calavi (9 km. northwest of Cotonou), with 1800 students in 1976.

Foreign relations: diplomatic relations with over 46 countries; 6 diplomatic missions residing in Cotonou; member of the UN, OAU and OCAM.

NOTES

1. See R. Cornevin, *Histoire du Dahomey* (1962).
2. W. J. Argyle, *The Fon of Dahomey* (1966); I. A. Akinjogbin, *Dahomey and its Neighbours* (1967); M. J. Herskovits, *Dahomey* (1938).
3. J. Lombard, *Structures du Type 'Feodal' en Afrique Noire* (1965).
4. See D. Ronen, 'Preliminary Notes on the Concept of Regionalism in Dahomey', *Études Dahoméennes*, no. 2 (1967), and *Dahomey between Tradition and Modernity* (1975).
5. S. Decalo, 'The Politics of Instability in Dahomey', *Geneva—Africa*, VII, no. 2 (1968).
6. Justin Ahomadegbé, of royal Danhomé descent, leader of the Fon; Sorou-Migan Apithy, leader of the Yoruba and Adja; Hubert Maga, leader of the northern populations and especially the Bariba. For biographies of them, as well as those of other leaders of Benin, see S. Decalo, *Historical Dictionary of Dahomey* (1976). See also M. Staniland, 'The Three-Party System in Dahomey', *Journal of African History*, XIV, nos 2—3 (1973).
7. S. Decalo, 'Full Circle in Dahomey', *African Studies Review*, XIII, no. 3 (Dec 1970).
8. S. Decalo, 'Regionalism, Politics and the Military in Dahomey', *Journal of Developing Areas*, VII, no. 3 (Apr 1973).
9. R. Lemarchand, 'Dahomey: Coup within a Coup', *Africa Report*, June 1968.
10. 'Dahomey: Kerekou's Coup', *West Africa*, 6 Nov 1972. *West Africa*, 20 Nov 1972, cites Kerekou as stating, 'The ousted civilian leadership held its power from the Army. The Army has taken back what it gave.'
11. S. Decalo, 'The Army in a Praetorian State: Dahomey', in his *Coups and Army Rule in Africa* (1976).

12. M. Glélé, *Naissance d'un État Noir* (1969).
13. 'Benin', in *Africa Contemporary Record, 1974–5*.
14. See S. Decalo, 'Ideological Rhetoric and Scientific Socialism in Two Peoples' Republics: Benin and Congo/B', in C. Rosberg and T. Callaghy (eds), *African Socialism in Subsaharan Africa* (Berkeley, Calif.: Institute of International Studies, 1979); G. Malirot, 'Le Dahomey Sortira-t-il un Jour du Marasme Actuel?', *Eurafrica*, July–Aug 1975.
15. See *West Africa*, 24 and 31 Jan 1977.
16. For the full text, see 'Benin: La Loi Fondamentale', *Afrique Contemporaine*, no. 93 (Sep–Oct 1977).
17. Articles '76–102, ibid., pp. 29–32.
18. M. Wolfers, 'Letter from Cotonou', *West Africa*, 16 Dec 1974; S. Morgan, 'Will Kerekou Return to the Barracks?', *Africa*, no. 73 (Sep 1977).
19. *Africa Research Bulletin*, Political Series, Dec 1971.
20. *New York Times*, 23 Nov 1975.
21. See S. Amin, *L'Afrique de l'Ouest Bloquée* (1970).
22. See 'Dahomey', in International Monetary Fund, *Surveys of African Economics*, vol. III (1970).
23. For one example, see *Le Monde*, 1 Dec 1976.
24. 'Breaking out of the Gloom', *Africa*, no. 75 (Nov 1977); 'Benin', in *Africa Contemporary Record*, 1976–7. See also 'La Revolution Beninoise en 1977', special issue of *Europe-Outremer*, Mar 1977.
25. *Jeune Afrique*, 10 Sep 1976.
26. 'Benin', in *African Contemporary Record*, 1976–7.
27. P. Leymarie, 'Benin, An 2', *Afrique–Asie*, 29 Nov 1976.
28. Thus, for example, Benin sided with Libya in the latter's 1977 desert skirmish with Egypt, took a strong position on the 1975 anti-Zionism resolution, led off the African rejection of Patrick Daniel Moynihan's anti-Amin comments, and recognised the Algiers-based Sahara Democratic Republic.
29. *West Africa*, 16 and 23 Jan 1978. Benin also boycotted the 1977 OAU meeting, because it was being held in Libreville, Gabon.

BIBLIOGRAPHY

Akinjogbin, A., *Dahomey and Its Neighbours* (Cambridge: Cambridge University Press, 1967).
Amin, Samir, *L'Afrique de l'Ouest Bloquée: L'Économie Politique de la Colonisation* (Paris: Éditions de Miniut, 1970).
Argyle, W. J., *The Fon of Dahomey: A History and Ethnography of the Old Kingdom* (Oxford: Clarendon Press, 1966).
Banque Centrale des États de l'Afrique de l'Ouest, *Indicateurs Économiques Dahoméens*, quarterly.
'Bénin', in *Africa Contemporary Record* (London: Rex Collings, annual).
'Bénin: La Loi Fondamentale', *Afrique Contemporaine*, no. 93 (Sep–Oct 1973) 23–35.
'Bénin, Le Dossier de l'Agression Mercenaire', supplement to *Afrique – Asie*, no. 37 (1977) 31–82.
'Benin's Way Ahead', *West Africa*, 1 May 1978, pp. 845–6.

Bentsi-Enchill, Nii K., 'Remember Benin', *West Africa*, 16 Jan 1978, pp. 92–3.
'Breaking out of the Gloom', *Africa*, no. 75 (Nov 1977).
Beynel, J., 'L'Organisation Judiciare au Dahomey', *Penant*, no. 740 (Apr–June 1973).
Cornevin, R., 'Coups d'État en Chaine au Dahomey', *Revue Française d'Etudes Politiques Africaines*, no. 99 (Mar 1974) 52–65.
——, *Histoire du Dahomey* (Paris: Berger-Levrault, 1962).
'Dahomey', in International Monetary Fund, *Surveys of African Economies*, vol. III (Washington, DC, 1970) pp. 143–219.
'Dahomey: l'Armée au Pouvoir', special issue of *Europe–France Outremer*, December 1972.
'Dahomey Diary', *West Africa*, 30 Dec 1967, p. 1664, 6 Jan 1968, pp. 15–16.
'Dahomey: Kerekou's Coup', *West Africa*, 6 Nov 1972, pp. 1479–81.
Decalo, S., 'The Army in a Praetorian State: Dahomey', in his *Coups and Army Rule in Africa: Studies in Military Style* (New Haven, Conn.: Yale University Press, 1976).
——, 'Dahomey 1968–1971: Return to Origins', *Geneva–Africa*, X, no. 1 (1971) 76–91.
——, Full Circle in Dahomey', *African Studies Review*, XIII, no. 3 (Dec 1970) 445–58.
——, *Historical Dictionary of Dahomey* (Metuchen, N.J.: Scarecrow Press, 1976).
——, 'The Politics of Instability in Dahomey', *Geneva–Africa*, VII, no. 2 (1978) 5–32.
——, 'Regionalism, Politics and the Military in Dahomey', *Journal of Developing Areas*, VII, no. 3 (Apr 1973) 449–78.
——, 'Ideological Rhetoric and Scientific Socialism in Two Peoples' Republics: Benin and Congo/B', in C. Rosberg and T. Callaghy (eds), *African Socialism in Subsaharan Africa* (Berkeley, Calif.: Institute of International Studies, 1979).
Dictionnaire Bio-bibliographique du Dahomey, vol. I (Porto-Novo: Institut de Recherches Appliquées du Dahomey, 1969).
Glélé, M. A., *Naissance d'un État Noir: L'Evolution Politique et Constitutionelle du Dahomey, de la Colonisation à Nos Jours* (Paris: Pichon et Durand-Auzias, 1969).
——, *La République du Dahomey* (Paris: Berger-Levrault, 1969).
Herskovits, M. J., *Dahomey: An Ancient West African Kingdom* (Evanston, Ill.: Northwestern University Press, 1967), 2 vols. (Repr. of 1938 ed.)
'Kerekou's Dahomey', *West Africa*, 12 Feb 1973, p. 195; and 19 Feb 1973, pp. 240–1.
Lagarde, ., 'Benin's Push for Prosperity', *West Africa*, 15 May 1978, pp. 421–2.
Lemarchand, R., 'Dahomey: Coup within a Coup', *Africa Report*, June 1968, pp. 46–54.
Leymarie, P., 'Benin, An 2', *Afrique–Asie*, 29 Nov 1976.
Lombard, J., *Structures de Type 'Feodal' en Afrique Noire: Études des Dynamismes Internes et des Relations Sociales Chez les Bariba du Dahomey* (Paris: Mouton, 1965).
Malirot, G., 'Le Dahomey Sortira-t-il un Jour du Marasme Actuel?', *Eurafrica*, July–Aug 1975.

Morgan, S., 'Will Kerekou Return to the Barracks?', *Africa*, no. 73 (Sep 1977).
Oké, F. M., 'Des Comités Électoraux aux Parties Politiques Dahoméens', *Revue Française d'Études Politiques Africaines*, no. 45 (Sep 1969) 45–57.
Olodo, J. K., 'Les Institutions de la République Populaire du Benin', *Revue Juridique*, XXXII, no. 2 (Apr–June 1978) 759–92.
'La Révolution Beninoise en 1977', special issue of *Europe-Outremer*, Mar 1977.
Ronen, D., 'Preliminary Notes on the Concept of Regionalism in Dahomey', *Études Dahoméennes*, no. 2 (1967).
——, 'The Colonial Elite in Dahomey', *African Studies Review*, XVII, no. 1 (Apr 1974) 55–76.
——, *Dahomey between Tradition and Modernity* (Ithaca, NY: Cornell University Press, 1975).
Staniland, M., 'The Three-Party System in Dahomey', *Journal of African History*, XIV, nos 2–3 (1973) 291–312, 491–504.
Terray, E., 'Les Révolutions Congolaise et Dahoméenne de 1963: Essai d'Interprétation', *Revue Française de Science Politique*, XIV, no. 5 (Oct 1964) 917–42.
Thompson, V., 'Dahomey', in G. M. Carter (ed.), *Five African States. Responses to Diversity* (Ithaca, NY: Cornell University Press, 1963) pp. 161–262.
Wolfers, M., 'Letter from Cotonou', *West Africa*, 16 Dec 1974.

6 People's Republic of Bulgaria

LESLIE HOLMES

Bulgaria is a relatively small and ethnically homogeneous state, bounded by Romania, Yugoslavia, Greece and Turkey. It is the only one of the four communist Balkan states to have remained consistently loyal to Moscow – a fact explained partly by the traditional amicability between the two countries, partly by the leader's (Zhivkov's) lack of interest in asserting his country's autonomy, and partially by the fact that Bulgaria has usually felt a need for a powerful supporter in territorial claims against her neighbours. Thus, a common ideology in the Balkan communist states has not overcome traditional territorial and nationalistic rivalries.

By any criteria, the economic achievements of the Bulgarians under communist rule have been very impressive, so that the country has by now a relatively well developed industrial base. On the other hand, there has been far less liberalisation and democratisation of the political system than in many other communist states.

BULGARIA PRIOR TO SEPTEMBER 1944

The most important date in the history of modern Bulgaria is 9 September 1944, when a *coup d'état* overthrew the government and established a new political order in which the communists were gradually to assume dominance. In this section we consider the build-up to this event.

In the 1870s, what is now Bulgaria had been part of the Turkish (Ottoman) Empire for almost five centuries. As a result of the Russo-Turkish War and the ensuing Treaty of San Stefano (1878), however, a large, autonomous Bulgaria should have come into existence. But before

116

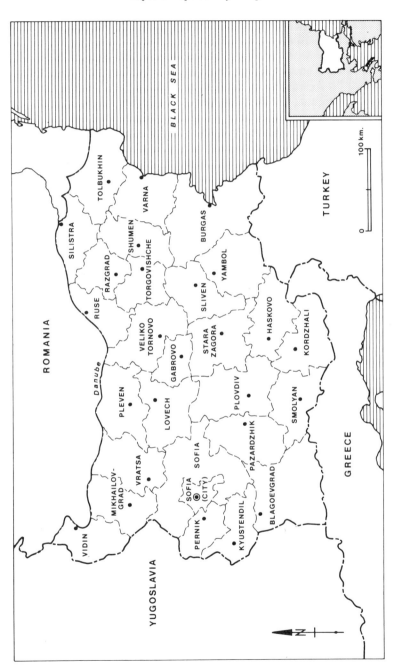

Bulgaria: provincial boundaries

this could come about, Britain and Austria insisted on a new treaty; the resulting Treaty of Berlin (also 1878) essentially divided the Bulgaria of the earlier document into three parts. The northern part became an autonomous principality of Bulgaria, the south-eastern part (eastern Rumelia) was to be administered by a Christian prince responsible to the Turkish Sultan, whilst the southern part, including Macedonia, was returned to Turkish rule. The Treaty of San Stefano had raised nationalist hopes for a unified, autonomous Bulgaria and this came nearer to realisation when in 1885 a popular uprising in eastern Rumelia led to the inclusion of the province in the Bulgarian principality; the Macedonian issue remained unresolved and still is today.

With support from the powerful Austro-Hungarian Empire, in 1908 the principality of Bulgaria declared itself totally independent of Turkey; Bulgaria was now a monarchy under Tsar Ferdinand. It sided with the Germans and Austrians during the First World War – as so often in history, because of Balkan rivalries. Following the defeat and collapse of the Austro-Hungarian Empire, Bulgaria lost some of its territory to the new state of Yugoslavia and to Greece and Romania.

In the period between the two world wars, Bulgaria remained a monarchy (under Tsar Boris), and witnessed various violent changes of government. In 1923, the peasant-oriented Agrarian government under Stamboliisky was overthrown and replaced by a rightist coalition. After a period of turmoil, something like a constitutional democracy emerged by the early 1930s. This development was very short-lived, however, and a military coup overthrew the existing arrangement in May 1934. Although the military were able to upset the political system, they were incapable of exercising power themselves. Instead, power accumulated in the hands of Tsar Boris, whilst the role of the constitutional representative bodies declined drastically.

Bulgaria's position in the Second World War was an odd one. The Bulgarian government's perceptions of the country's interests in the Balkans led it to side with the Germans in 1939. When the Germans invaded the USSR in 1941, the Bulgarians preferred not to take sides or become involved in the conflict; consequently, they declared war on Britain and the USA but not on the Soviet Union. But this position did not protect Bulgaria from Soviet invasion once the fortunes of Germany and the USSR were reversed. In August 1944, the Red Army entered Romania, and at the beginning of September declared war on Bulgaria. By this time, Bulgaria was being governed by a three-man Regency Council, since Tsar Boris had died in 1943 and his successor (Simeon II) was a minor. Initially very anti-Soviet, the position of this council changed considerably when Muraviev replaced Filov as its head at the beginning of September 1944; Bulgaria now denounced the Germans and attempted to negotiate an armistice with the Western Allies. But this did not placate the Soviets, who entered Bulgaria on 8 September; in such a situation, there was little point in the Muraviev government attempting to resist the Soviet-backed Fatherland Front when it made a bid for power on 9 September, and the coup succeeded with a minimum of fuss.

The Fatherland Front was a coalition of various anti-fascist parties, though dominated by the communists and the left wing of the Agrarians. It had been proposed by veteran communist Georgi Dimitrov in 1941 (he was at that time in Moscow), and took shape in the late summer of 1943 when a National Committee was created.

Before moving on to the first days of the new regime, something needs to be said about the development of the communist movement. Interest in Marxism developed in Bulgaria in the late nineteenth century, and a quasi-Marxist party – the Bulgarian Social Democratic Party – was founded in 1891. Within a year this had split into two parties, which merged again in 1894 to form the Bulgarian Workers' Social Democratic Party. However, the tensions between the orthodox Marxists, led by Blagoev, and the less radical wing (under Sakuzov) continued, and in 1903 the Party split into a 'broad' and a 'narrow' faction. The latter was headed by Blagoev, and eventually, in 1919, became the Bulgarian Communist Party; it played an important role in the newly created Communist International. The Party suffered badly after the 1923 coup, and particularly after an attempt by some of its members to assassinate the Tsar in 1925; as some of the older members (for instance, Dimitrov) pointed out to their younger, terrorism-oriented comrades, the failure of such tactics usually plays into the hands of the State coercive forces. In 1927, the BCP split into an illegal Communist Party and a legal Workers' Party. This division lasted until the end of the 1930s, when the BCP merged with the by-then underground Workers' Party. The Party took an anti-German stance in 1941, but its effectiveness was not helped by the fact that many of its leaders (including Dimitrov and Chervenkov) were abroad – mainly in the USSR. Moreover, many Bulgarians were satisfied with their government's policy at this stage, since it meant minimal involvement in the war and was conducive to Bulgarian territorial claims; only later, when the Soviets were approaching, did popular perception of and attitudes towards the communists change.[1]

In terms of membership, the communists were second only to the

Agrarians. But this is not to say that there was a large movement; even if we combine the membership of both the Communist Party and the Workers' Party, membership in the period up to September 1944 never exceeded its 1932–3 peak of just over 30,000[2].

SEPTEMBER 1944 TO DECEMBER 1948 – THE CONSOLIDATION OF COMMUNIST POWER

For two years after the overthrow of the Muraviev government, Bulgaria formally remained a monarchy. Following a referendum in September 1946, however, the National Assembly proclaimed Bulgaria a republic. This transition from monarchy to republic was achieved with far less bitterness and bloodshed than the transition to *de facto* communist rule. In analysing this process, the reader should bear in mind that, although there was an Allied Control Commission in Bulgaria from 1944 until 1947 – with British, American and Soviet representatives – it was headed by a Soviet. Indeed, Churchill had revealed in his famous 'percentage' agreement with Stalin in 1944 that he was not particularly interested in this ex-Axis power, and neither Britain nor the USA seriously objected when the Soviet Army occupied Bulgaria from 1944 to 1947. This Soviet presence was of considerable psychological – as well as more tangible – value to the Bulgarian communists.

After 9 September 1944, the new three-man Regency Council included only one communist (Pavlov), and only two of the sixteen members of the Council of Ministers were communists. However, as in other East European states, the communists were astute in their choice of governmental portfolios, taking over ministries through which opposition could be suppressed with the authority and power of the State (i.e. the Ministries of the Interior and Justice). Very soon, opposition elements were being imprisoned or even executed.[3] At the same time, the communists began to exert pressure on their coalition partners in the Fatherland Front government – particularly the powerful and popular Agrarians. In January 1945, under pressure from both domestic and Soviet communists, the Agrarians were forced to expel their leader from the party; this act was symbolically highly significant, since it revealed that the communists were intent on ensuring that their coalition was only with people of very similar outlook to their own. The new Agrarian leader was the man who had headed it during the war, N. Petkov. But Petkov soon proved to be as hostile to the communists as his predecessor had been. In August 1945 he requested the British and American missions to Bulgaria to secure a postponement of the imminent elections, believing that these would be manipulated by the communists unless supervised by the Allies. This postponement was obtained, at which point Petkov and many other Agrarians left the coalition and formed an opposition Agrarian Party; this division of the party into participatory and oppositional wings was emulated by the smaller Social Democratic Party. When the elections were held a few months later they were boycotted by this opposition – who also rejected the proposal of both the Americans and the Soviets to participate in the Fatherland Front government.

Another election was held in October 1946, and this time the opposition parties participated. They obtained almost 30 per cent of the vote, and for a few months acted as a real opposition force within the National Assembly. But as the influence of the Western allies in Bulgaria declined – notably after the Paris Peace Treaty (February 1947) – so the communist suppression of opposition increased. On the day after the US Senate had ratified the Peace Treaty (June 1947), Petkov was arrested. He was subsequently tried and executed; his death symbolised the end of tolerated opposition in Bulgaria.[4] In organisational terms, the ending of opposition and the consolidation of communist power culminated in 1948. In February, the Second Congress of the Fatherland Front unanimously adopted a programme for the building of a socialist Bulgaria. Within a few months, all the oppositional political parties had been disbanded, the loyalist wing of the Social Democrats had been merged with the Communist Party, whilst the loyalist Agrarians (under Obbov, then Traikov) declared themselves representatives only of the poor and middle (as opposed to all) peasants, and committed to socialism.

One question that naturally arises is why the communists felt it necessary to dispose of all opposition forces. Although writers such as Brown and Oren have emphasised the amount of support enjoyed by Petkov and other opposition leaders, the fact remains that the overwhelming majority of Bulgarians supported the Fatherland Front.[5] Moreover, many Bulgarians were very sympathetic towards the USSR – especially given Western support for Greece, which had various territorial disagreements with Bulgaria.[6] Whilst a definitive answer cannot be given to this question, we can refer to three factors which must have played an important role in the decision effectively to eradicate opposition. First, the communists had suffered often brutal suppression at the hands of various inter-war Bulgarian governments, and it is not inconceivable that they had some fear of what could happen again in the future.[7] Secondly, there was no real tradition of parliamentary democracy in Bulgaria, so that the communists did not feel any cultural pressure to make concessions to liberal-democratic ideology for self-legitimation. Finally, there was no need to tolerate an opposition; once the Western allies had essentially written off Bulgaria as part of the Soviet bloc, the indigenous communists could set about implementing the radical change in society to which they were committed; given that the majority of the electorate appeared to be in favour of this, there was little reason to take heed of minority views.

What changes were set in motion in these early days? The most important policies were those relating to the economy. By 1946, the government was already working on a two-year plan for economic development, and this was approved in April 1947. There was further nationalisation of industry – a process which had started in the nineteenth century – and this was accelerated considerably in December 1947; by 1948, 90 per cent of industrial output was from State or co-operatively owned enterprises.[8] Banking, too, came into full State ownership. In agriculture, the pre-1944 developments in co-operative farming were encouraged, although at this stage the emphasis was more on reforming land ownership. Thus, a law of March 1946 limited the amount of land that any one family could own, and this resulted in the confiscation of vast areas belonging to the Church and wealthier peasants.

DECEMBER 1948 TO JUNE 1958 – THE TRANSITION TO SOCIALISM

The Fifth Congress of the BCP (December 1948) resolved that Bulgaria was now to embark upon the full-scale construction of socialism. The term socialism in this context largely referred to the production relations in society, so that our analysis should begin with a consideration of the economic changes over the next decade.

The commitment to a planned development of the economy was put on a firmer basis with the adoption of the first five-year plan. This was to have covered the years 1949–53, but in the event was fulfilled – in industry at least – a year early. The plan provided for a major re-orientation within industry, away from the dominant light sector and towards heavy branches. Thus, although it was accepted that light industry would account for more output even by the end of the first five-year period, this lead was to be markedly reduced by pouring the lion's share of investment into the heavy sector.

Following Stalin's death in 1953, however, a reform process known as the New Course was instituted in Bulgaria. One major component of this was an acknowledgement that there had been too much emphasis on heavy industry, which was having a detrimental effect on the material incentives required to spur people on towards socialism. Although this did not in practice lead to significant change in the relative apportionments of investment funds within industry, heavy industry did lose out somewhat to other sectors – notably housing construction and agriculture.

As in other states which have tried to industrialise rapidly on the basis of 'primitive socialist accumulation', it was the agrarian community which had suffered most in the early days of modernisation. It had been decided at the Fifth Congress that the poor and middle peasants should be drawn into collective farms. In principle, this was to have been done on a voluntary basis, encouraging peasants to join collectives both by showing them the advantageousness of such an arrangement and by the use of material incentives. In practice, many were coerced into joining – whilst wealthier peasants were branded 'kulaks' and imprisoned. On various occasions, the BCP Central Committee acknowledged that errors were being committed in the collectivisation drive – yet did little to improve matters.[9] The drive was very effective in one sense, since the amount of arable land in collectives increased tenfold (from about 6 to 60 per cent of the total) in the period 1948–52.[10] But, from another viewpoint, collectivisation was much less satisfactory. Many peasants resented the coercion and considered the branding of some of their colleagues as kulaks inappropriate in a country where there had been a high degree of peasant equality prior to September 1944.[11] Their negative attitudes were reflected in the fact that agricultural production fell far below official targets. The situation changed under the New Course. The position of those already in collectives improved, with a reduction in the quotas of production to be supplied to the State and an increase in living standards. The lot of the private peasants worsened in one way – their compulsory delivery quotas were increased – but the pressure on them to join collectives was slackened in the mid-1950s.

By 1958, the situation had changed yet again in the countryside. From 1956, collectivisation was once more strongly encouraged, so that by the time of the Seventh Congress (June 1958), over 90 per cent of arable land was collectively farmed. However, the lot of the peasantry had also noticeably improved by this time, in terms both of living standards and of security.[12]

With such a high level of collective ownership in agriculture and full nationalisation in industry since 1952, the BCP announced at its Seventh Congress that socialism had been achieved, and that Bulgaria was now on the path to advanced socialism.

What had been happening within the BCP during this period? Whereas in the consolidation period the communists had concentrated on eradicating opposition elements beyond their own ranks, attention was now focused on the Party itself. A major purge was implemented in 1949, which resulted in the execution of some communists and the imprisonment or demotion of others. The most notable victim was Traicho Kostov, who was accused of being disloyal and a Titoist, and was subsequently executed; many less well known communists were accused of similar crimes. Some pattern is discernible in this purge; broadly speaking, the so-called 'Muscovite' communists (i.e. those who had trained and lived in the USSR) were disposing of the home-bred members of the Party. Even Anton Yugov suffered at this stage, losing some of his more important posts.

At the same time, 'natural' causes too were changing the face of the Party leadership. In July 1949, the BCP's leader, Georgi Dimitrov, died in Moscow.[13] His presidency of the Council of Ministers was taken over by Vassil Kolarov – who himself died in January 1950 and was succeeded by the Stalinist Vulko Chervenkov; Chervenkov also became Secretary-general of the BCP in 1950.

Chervenkov was the dominant figure in Bulgarian politics from 1950 to 1956, although his position was marginally weakened from 1954 when the first-secretaryship of the Party was transferred to Todor Zhivkov and a gradual release from prison of so-called Kostovites was begun. But opposition to the wilful style of Chervenkov had been building up within the BCP over the years, and other leaders used Khrushchev's attack on Stalinist methods, at the CPSU's Twentieth Congress, as a pretext for removing the leader. At the April 1956 plenum of the Central Committee, Zhivkov criticised the personality cult that had developed around Chervenkov, and later in the month the National Assembly accepted Chervenkov's 'resignation' from the premiership. His successor was Anton Yugov, whose fortunes had changed considerably since their 1949 nadir. Simultaneously, Zhivkov's authority was increased when the Central Committee named him head of the Political Bureau at the April plenum.[14]

For a few months after April the Party experienced a democratisation, with criticism and self-criticism being widely encouraged and practised. But the conservatives within the BCP were unenthusiastic about such developments, and, when liberalisation in Poland and Hungary culminated in uprisings, their calls for a tightening of discipline had to be acted upon. By the end of 1956, most aspects of the Bulgarian 'thaw' were gone, and by February 1957 Chervenkov was again becoming very important in Bulgarian politics (he was appointed Minister of Education and Culture). Later in the year, there was another purge of the BCP's senior ranks; two members of the Central Committee lost their membership – largely, it appears, because they had wanted a continuation of the liberalisation that had followed the April plenum.[15]

In sum, by the time Bulgaria was proclaimed a socialist state, her industry was fully nationalised, agriculture almost wholly collectivised – and there had been major factional struggles within the BCP. The population had not always accepted the transformation gracefully – there were strikes and a riot by tobacco workers in Plovdiv in May 1953, for instance – but neither was there evidence of the extreme alienation that became so visible in Poland and Hungary in the autumn of 1956. Generally, Bulgarian socialism appeared to be working.

JUNE 1958 TO THE PRESENT – ON TO ADVANCED AND DEVELOPED SOCIALISM

According to the official ideology, Bulgaria was transformed into an advanced socialist state by 1971, since when she has been progressing towards developed or mature socialism; it was announced in 1976 that his stage would be reached by 1990, when the full-scale construction of communism would be embarked upon. What actual changes in Bulgaria have been associated with such claims?

At the end of the 1950s, Bulgaria experienced a period of intense activity known as the Great Leap Forward; although the leaders subsequently denied any Chinese influence in their decision to mount the campaign, some had clearly been impressed by Maoist development policies. The main aims of the campaign were to fulfil the plan two years early (i.e. accelerate development); to improve agriculture, largely through the merging of the collectives into a thousand very large units; to improve territorial administration in order both to harmonise with this merging and to decentralise industrial decision-making; and to create jobs for the many unemployed. By the time the Great Leap was terminated (December 1960), very big improvements had indeed been made in the economy (though the original targets for production were not reached) and certain problems, such as unemployment, had been solved. But the policy had also led to much hostility, both within the Party, and amongst sections of the general public; the leadership responded by setting very modest targets in the 1961 plan. This relaxation was short-lived, however, and in 1962 the new twenty-year plan adopted envisaged substantial growth in both industry and agriculture; whilst such growth was not at the level of the Great Leap, the rates were nevertheless formidable.[16] Simultaneously, there were signs – notably the 1962 price rises – that the economy was in difficulties. The population could not be expected to make great efforts and be thus rewarded, so the leadership now began looking for new ways to improve the economy. Over the next three years – and in line with developments in the USSR and other East European states – the Party encouraged a debate on and experimentation in ways to improve management and planning. This resulted in the issuance by the Political Bureau, in December 1965, of a set of theses, which were approved by the Central Committee in the following April; Bulgaria had introduced her own version of economic reform. Briefly, the reform involved the use of more material incentives, and the raising of efficiency through giving more responsibility to the production unit for its own fate.[17] However, it was clear by late 1967 that implementation was proceeding less successfully than had been intended – partly because of opposition to the policy from various quarters – and by the end of the decade the economy had been largely recentralised again.

The 1970s have witnessed further changes in the organisation of the economy, the most important of which have been the concentration of industrial management from the individual enterprise to larger associations, and the creation of about 160 agro-industrial complexes since 1970; the latter are meant to eradicate the traditional differences between the towns and the countryside. At the same time, there has again been a call for paying more attention to the consumer – both in terms of the amount of production (a major concern of the 1971–5 plan) and in terms of the quality of the goods (stressed in the 1976–80 plan). Despite all these developments, the BCP still shows signs· of serious concern about the state of the economy in a developed socialist society, as witnessed in the revival of Party conferences in the 1970s for discussing particular aspects of economic policy.

The Party itself has not remained unaffected by the changes in policy. In the early 1960s, Zhivkov finally disposed of two of his most serious rivals – on one level because of their attitudes towards official policies.

Thus, Chervenkov opposed Zhivkov's intensified de-Stalinisation policy following Khrushchev's further denunciations of the former Soviet leader in 1961, and was soon afterwards deprived of his most important posts on the grounds of encouraging a personality cult, committing errors and using vicious methods. Then, at the Eighth Congress (November 1962), Zhivkov charged Yugov – along with several other leading figures in Bulgarian politics – with having opposed the Great Leap Forward, as well as having abused socialist legality and committed various other crimes. He was therefore deprived of the premiership. At the same time, the security forces were downgraded.

Of course, such events were not merely the result of differences over policies – they also testified to power struggles within the leadership. Since then, Zhivkov's position has been relatively secure, and it was strengthened when he took over the presidency of the Council of State in 1971. However, there have been at least one definite and two probable threats to the senior leader's position since 1962. The definite case was in 1965, when a group of ten men – all with close Party and/or military connections – were discovered to be conspiring against the government. Although charged with being Maoists, the conspirators' motivations are not entirely clear; what does seem certain is that they were all committed to socialism, but that they wanted a Bulgaria more independent of Moscow. Over the next three years, there were various signs that these sentiments were not confined to the ten, and various purges in the Party and another restructuring of the internal security organs were carried out; it seems likely that, apart from internal moves to combat them, such aspirations no longer seemed tenable anyway after the invasion of Czechoslovakia in August 1968. At all events, by the end of that year, Bulgarian party politics again seemed quiet; and at the Tenth Congress (1971), no changes at all were made in the Political Bureau. The two cases of possible opposition both involve men who were, at the time of their removal, considered to be second only to Zhivkov. Thus, at the Ninth Congress (1966), Mitko Grigorov lost his position on the Political Bureau, but without any reason being given; one can only surmise that he was either unpopular and/or considered over-ambitious by Zhivkov. The second case emerged in May 1977, when Boris Velchev lost his Central Committee secretaryship. This time a reason was given – there had been shortcomings in the work of Velchev's department (Party affairs). Whilst this was undoubtedly part of the reason for Velchev's fall, it seems likely that his desires for a more autonomous Bulgaria, and his own ambitiousness, also contributed.[18]

In this period, then, the government used both moral and material incentives to make Bulgaria an industrial state, a task in which it enjoyed some success. But these policies, as well as international developments, did create tensions; these were manifested more within the Party than in the general public.

THE BULGARIAN COMMUNIST PARTY

Structure and functions

The present structure of the BCP is laid down in the fourth statute, first adopted in 1962 and marginally modified since then.[19] Like all communist parties, the BCP operates according to the principle of democratic centralism. For example, there is no direct horizontal linkage between peer groups, all communication formally being via a superior organ.[20]

At the lowest level of the Party is the primary Party organisation. This is usually organised in a place of work, although it may also be based on a small territorial unit such as a hamlet. In line with the Leninist idea that one needs at least two people to form a party cell but at least one more to ensure a majority decision, the minimum number of members of a primary Party organisation is three. This lowest level of the Party has to meet at least once a month, and performs many mobilisation and socialisation functions. It also plays a vital role in recruiting new members. One function in which the role of various primary Party organisations differs is that of control. In the way communists use this word, control means 'checking on' or supervision rather than direction, and the many primary Party organisations (particularly in production units) have a duty to ensure that the administrative and management organs are performing their tasks in accordance with central Party and State directives, to the benefit of society and to the best of their ability. However, the primary organisations in central State bodies (for instance, ministries) do not have the right of control over these organisations, so that it would be wrong to assume that at any given level the Party is higher than the equivalent State body.[21]

Before leaving the primary level, mention should be made of the Party 'groups'. These may be formed in any subdivision of the mass organisations and elected State bodies where there are at least three communists, and their function is to raise the influence of the BCP in these bodies.

Although most of the organisations comprising the first level of the

Party are based on the workplace, the levels above are based on geographical–administrative divisions; hence the Party is structured on a territorial–production principle. The next tier up is the municipal level; then comes the city or regional level; the district level; and finally the central organs of the Party. The highest organ of the municipal, city, regional and district organisations is, in formal terms, the conference; for the central level it is the Congress. However, it is obvious that in practice a body which is to meet every five years (the Congress) or even twice every five years (the district conference) is not going to play a significant part in the decision-making and other roles of the Party, so that one must look to the various smaller elected bodies to see where the real work of the BCP above the primary level takes place. For the work of the Party between conferences and congresses, a committee is elected. But even the committees' role is limited because of their relatively infrequent convocations, so that often the most powerful Party bodies are those made up of the small core of full-time, professional Party workers that staff the bureaux and secretariats of the Party at various levels; these people constitute the Party apparatus. The most important of these at the central level are the Central Committee Secretariat and the Political Bureau. The Secretariat supervises the work of the Central Committee 'departments', to some extent the work of the State bodies approximately equivalent to these departments (for example, ministries), provides information to the Political Bureau, and ensures that lower Party bodies are filled with the most appropriate cadres. The Political Bureau is in practice the top policy-making body in Bulgaria. The secretariats and bureaux at lower levels perform similar tasks on a smaller scale. Thus, they check on the work of subordinate Party organisations and of peer-ranked State bodies; ensure that higher Party and State decisions are implemented; see that important posts in Bulgarian society are occupied by suitable cadres; and participate in local decision-making.

A potential source of confusion is the fact that at the central level there is in addition to the Congress the possibility of a central Party conference. Whereas the Congress is a regularly convened gathering[22] of the faithful, held to receive Party endorsement of the past, present and future policies of the smaller bodies, such as the Political Bureau, a conference can be held at any time to discuss a particular problem or set of problems. Many communist states still provide for the convening of conferences, but several have in practice ceased to implement this form of party democracy. Bulgaria, however, is an exception to this tendency. Although it looked as if she were following the Soviet example when no conference was held for over twenty years after that of 1950, the BCP has held two in the 1970s – the most recent being that on economic questions held in April 1978.[23]

Indeed, it would be fair to say that various changes in the Party rules and practice over the past twenty years or so have revealed at least as many moves towards the more democratic elements of democratic centralism as towards the centralist elements. Thus, whilst there have been indications of growing centralism – the lengthening of the period between the convening of both congress and central committee meetings, for example – symbolically important moves to raise the accountability of the smaller Party organs to the larger membership were made in 1962 and 1971. This said, it would be wrong to infer that these steps were of more than marginal significance in terms of democratising the Party, so that on balance the BCP is still, typically, a predominantly centralised organisation.[24]

Finally, its position in society has undergone theoretical changes since the 1940s. From 1945 to 1954, the BCP was seen as the vanguard of the working people. From 1954 to 1962, the Party broadened the base of its support, playing a leading role in the alliance between workers, peasants and the intelligentsia. In 1962, the BCP became the leader of the whole poeple. But in recent years there has again been a stress on the proletariat, although the concept of leader of the people has not been dropped. Thus, the position of the Party is not unambiguous at a theoretical level, in that it represents simultaneously all sections of society and one section in particular. The theoretical problem is further aggravated by the continued toleration of the other party in Bulgaria, the Bulgarian Agrarian Union. This party is important primarily for the integrative role it plays (i.e. it helps to gain support for the regime from non-communist peasants). Since it accepts the leading role of the BCP, however, and has played no serious opposition role since the 1940s, its importance should not be exaggerated. Despite this, its very existence means that the BCP cannot claim directly to represent the whole population.

Membership

In the liberal democracies, access to the membership of most political parties is relatively open; in the BCP, as in other communist parties, membership is more exclusive. The minimum age of entry is eighteen years, but only persons who have been in the youth organisation may join at that age. The applicant has to be proposed by at least three Party members with a minimum of three years' service to the BCP each, and at least one year's acquaintance with the candidate. If the primary party organisation accepts the proposers' recommendation, the applicant is admitted to the Party, subject to ratification by a superior Party organ.[25]

Even after a person has become a full member of the BCP, his position is not entirely secure. From time to time there is a revision of Party membership in the form of an exchange of Party cards – only satisfactory members have their cards renewed.[26] In addition, there have been more violent and disorderly purges; in 1957, for example, many communists lost their membership and were sent to prison camps, accused of being sympathetic to the ideas behind the 1956 Hungarian uprising.

Despite such events, Table 6.1 reveals that membership of the BCP continues to grow, and that it is, in comparative terms, a 'mass' party.

TABLE 6.1 Membership of the BCP[27]

Year	Membership
1922	38,036
1944	25,000
1945	254,000
1948	495,658
1954	455,251
1958	484,255
1962	528,674
1966	611,179
1971	699,476
1976	788,211
1978	817,000

Note: The above figures are from different months in the respective years; a more consistent mode of presentation is not possible with existing data.

Composition

A glance at Table 6.2 shows that the relative proportions of peasants and industrial workers in the Party have changed dramatically since the early 1950s, so that the group that was once the largest is now the smallest, and vice versa. Another point is that, despite an official policy of increasing the proletarian element in the Party in the 1970s, there is very little sign of this actually occurring. It is interesting to note, however,

TABLE 6.2 Social composition of the BCP[28]

	Industrial workers	Peasants	White-collar workers	Others
1948	26·5	44·7	16·3	12·5
1954	34·1	39·8	17·9	8·2
1958	36·1	34·2	21·7	8·0
1962	37·2	32·1	23·6	7·2
1966	38·4	29·2	?	?
1971	40·2	26·1	28·2	5·6
1976	41·1	23·1	35·6	–
1978	41·8	22·4	30·3	5·5

Note: Only years for which data is available are included; in some cases the figures in the 'others' category have been calculated by the author on the basis of the other data given.

that in an apparent endeavour to play down the number of white-collar/intelligentsia members, the merging of white-collar workers with 'others' that occurred in the presentation of composition data at the Eleventh Congress in 1976 was not repeated in the figures issued in April 1978.

Another policy pursued particularly in the 1970s has been to increase the number of relatively young people in the Party; in January 1978, approximately 40 per cent of Party members were less than forty years of age. Finally, less than 30 per cent of members are female, though over 50 per cent of the total population are.

THE STATE

In most communist states, the Party and State are often not clearly separated – at least, in terms of personnel. Nevertheless, there is a State structure quite distinct from that of the Party and we now consider this and other aspects of the State.

The Constitution

The People's Republic of Bulgaria has had two constitutions – although the first twice underwent significant modifications.[29] This first, commonly known as the Dimitrov Constitution, was formally adopted in December 1947 and bore marked resemblances to the Soviet

Constitution of 1936. Interestingly, it did not refer to the Communist Party – and, indeed, emphasised the nationalist dimensions of the September 1944 uprising.

The second, present constitution was adopted in May 1971, following a nationwide discussion of a draft version which had appeared in March of that year and a national referendum. The commission that produced the draft was headed by Todor Zhivkov; few changes were made to the original version. One important development was the upgrading of the BCP, which was defined as 'the leading force in society and the State'. However, in practical terms the most important innovation in the 1971 constitution was the establishment of a State Council (see below).

The National Assembly

In constitutional terms, the National Assembly is the supreme representative organ of State. This unicameral body comprises 400 deputies, of whom 272 are members of the BCP, 100 are members of the Agrarian Union, and 28 are not party-affiliated; elections to the assembly are to be held quinquennially. The electoral procedure is similar to that in certain other communist states having more than one party. A list of candidates is drawn up by the Fatherland Front, and includes representatives from the two parties and from the mass organisations. Voters either accept or reject the official list. As can be seen from Table 6.3, the overwhelming

TABLE 6.3 Bulgarian election results, 1945–76[30]

	Entitled to vote	Votes cast	Votes for Fatherland Front candidates	%[a]	Negative and invalid votes
1945	4,504,735	4,265,599[b]	3,869,462	90·71[b]	396,137
1946	4,558,322	4,216,000	2,984,000	70·78	1,232,000
1949	4,751,849	4,698,979	4,588,966	97·66	109,983
1953	4,987,587			99·8	
1957	5,218,602	5,206,428	5,204,027	99·95	2,401
1962	5,482,607	5,466,517	5,461,224	99·90	5,294
1966	5,774,251	5,752,817	5,744,072	99·85	8,745
1971	6,168,931	6,159,942	6,154,082	99·90	5,860
1976	6,378,348	6,375,092	6,369,762	99·92	5,330[b]

a This figure is the percentage of support amongst those voting.
b Calculated from the data available.

majority of the electorate both cast their votes and endorse the official list.

The National Assembly is the sole legislative body in Bulgaria, and assumes 'supreme leadership' in both domestic and foreign policy; it also elects the members of the other top State bodies – the State Council, the Council of Ministers and the Supreme Court – and appoints the head of the armed forces.[31]

This said, it should be pointed out that the Assembly now has no presidium (in contrast, for example, to the USSR and Albania); since sessions of the full body take place only about three times annually, one has to look to more regularly functioning bodies to see where the real decision-making power within the State machinery lies.

The State Council

The State Council is a relatively new body, dating from 1971 (although calls for it date back at least to 1968).[32] Previously, the State structure had been virtually a mirror-image of the Soviet State (though lacking a federal infrastructure), with a presidium of the National Assembly similar to the Presidium of the Supreme Soviet. Now, however, this presidium was replaced by the more powerful State Council.[33] It includes representatives from both parties and the mass organisations, and has been headed since its creation by Todor Zhivkov.

The State Council is formally defined as a supreme permanent organ of State power which unites the taking of decisions with their realisation. Hence, it fulfils executive and legislative functions when the National Assembly is not in session, although legislation does require ratification by the Assembly. However, one symbol of the greater power of the Council in comparison with its predecessor is that it can pass decrees and resolutions entirely in its own right (i.e. without needing Assembly endorsement). It also has the right to initiate legislation, and to represent Bulgaria in international affairs. One other important function of the State Council is to supervise the work of the Council of Ministers.

It is indicative of a feeling that power in Bulgaria was becoming too centralised that many of the suggestions made during the discussion of the 1971 draft constitution were for a reduction in the proposed rights of the new body; some of these proposals were incorporated in the final version.[34]

The Council of Ministers

The Council of Ministers – or government – is the principal executive and administrative organ of the State. As such, it is responsible for ensuring that the decisions of its superiors – the National Assembly and the State Council – are implemented, which means that it plays an important supervisory role over ministries and the local State organs. It also has the right to initiate legislation and to pass decrees and resolutions.

The Council of Ministers comprises all the ministers and ministerially ranked officials, not all of whom are members of the BCP. The Council has some twenty-five to thirty members, which is evidently considered by some leaders as too many for effective decision-making, since an inner core of about ten people, the Bureau, was re-established in July 1971. The decisions of this Bureau have the same force as those of the larger Council. Both the Council and its Bureau are currently headed by Stanko Todorov.

Local government

The local agencies of State power and 'people's self-government' are the 'people's councils', which are organised at municipal, area and district level. Deputies to these are elected every two and a half years. The tasks of the councils include the implementation of national policies at local level and making decisions for the locality which are not covered by and not in conflict with central edicts. Their powers have increased since 1971, especially in the area of the local economy. In order to ensure some accountability, the councils are now required to report on their activities to their constituents at least once a year.

Party–state relations

As in all other communist states, there is considerable interpenetration of Party and State in Bulgaria. Whilst we still await a full analysis of this at the local level, Table 6·4 reveals the extent of such overlap at the topmost tier.

Despite the obvious close connections, it should be recalled that not all ministers are members of the BCP. Those who are not are, however, members of the Agrarian Union, whose subservient position to the BCP has already been noted.

TABLE 6.4 Posts held by the members of the Political Bureau of the BCP, July 1978

Full members	
Ognyan Doinov	(Secretary of the Central Committee)
Tsola Dragoicheva	Member of the State Council
Dobri Dzhurov	Minister of National Defence
Grisha Filipov	Member of the State Council; (Secretary of the Central Committee)
Pencho Kubadinski	Member of the State Council; Chairman of the Fatherland Front
Aleksandr Lilov	Member of the State Council; (Secretary of the Central Committee)
Ivan Mihailov	Member of the State Council
Petar Mladenov	Minister of Foreign Affairs
Stanko Todorov	Chairman of the Council of Ministers
Tano Tsolov	First Deputy Chairman of the Council of Ministers
Todor Zhivkov	President of the State Council; (First Secretary of the Central Committee)
Candidate members	
Todor Stoichev	Member of the State Council
Peko Takov	Vice-President of the State Council
Krustyu Trichkov	Deputy Chairman of the Council of Ministers; Chairman of the Committee for State and People's Control
Drazha Vulcheva	Member of the State Council; Minister of Public Education

Note: In addition, all of the above are members of the National Assembly and the Fatherland Front. Purely Party posts are given in parentheses.

Mass organisations

The largest organisation in Bulgaria is the Fatherland Front, which now has over 4 million members. Its purpose is to involve more than just BCP members in political activity; an important task in this connection is the supervision of elections – including the compilation of the list of candidates, and ensuring that people do cast their votes. Other mass organisations include the trade unions (2·5 million members), the Youth League and the Movement of Bulgarian Women – all of which perform functions similar to those of their counterparts in other communist states.

DOMESTIC POLICIES

Education and culture

Bulgaria already had a relatively high literacy rate (about 75 per cent) by 1944, and there had been compulsory education for all since the nineteenth century.[35] Nevertheless, the communists have improved the level of education of the population, especially big strides being made at the tertiary level, in adult education, and in the establishment of kindergartens. Schooling is free, and compulsory for all children between the ages of seven and sixteen; it is intended to provide some form of higher (tertiary level) education for all by 1980. One indication of the growing integration of Bulgaria with the USSR was the ruling in 1975 that all children would have to begin studying the Russian language in their third year of school; previously such courses had begun in the fifth year.

Bulgarian cultural policy has frequently emulated Soviet. Thus, there were mild thaws in the mid 1950s and in the early 1960s. However, there was also a relaxation in the mid 1960s, when liberalisation emerged in many aspects of Bulgarian life. But, since the late 1960s, censorship has again become more rigid, and cultural activity has come under more centralised control (symbolised by the establishment of the Congress of Bulgarian Culture in 1967). Some indication of the involvement of the senior leadership in cultural life is seen in the fact that the Committee on Arts and Culture is headed by Zhivkov's daughter, whilst his son-in-law is in charge of radio and television broadcasting.

Religion

Constitutionally, citizens have the right to religious beliefs as long as there is no political basis to any religious organisation they join. In practice, the State discourages the study and practice of religion (for example, it is forbidden to give religious instruction in the schools), and in 1974 the Central Committee called for an intensification of 'the struggle against religious prejudices and anachronisms'.[36]

Economic policy

Since this aspect of Bulgaria has already been dealt with in the historical section, all that needs to be added here is that Bulgaria has been one of the strongest advocates of a high level of integration within Comecon, and has in the 1970s been concentrating on the production of certain items as part of the international socialist division of labour.[37]

FOREIGN POLICY

There are only two clear cases of Bulgarian foreign policy conflicting with Soviet; in both, the digression was temporary and short-lived. Thus, at the end of the 1950s, Bulgaria was initially very enthusiastic about the Chinese 'Great Leap Forward', whilst in the mid 1960s she appeared to favour an improvement of relations with West Germany when Moscow was reacting coldly to Erhard's proposals for improved relations with Eastern Europe. But, although Bulgarian foreign policy has nearly always mirrored Soviet, the importance attached by the two states to particular parts of the world varies; for Bulgaria, the most important foreign relationships (apart from that with Moscow) are with her Balkan neighbours.

At present, these relations are as good as they have ever been; but the situation is in flux, and some issues have consistently worked against really warm relationships. The most intractable one is the Macedonian question, which has perpetually troubled Sofia's relations with Belgrade. The dispute is basically over whether the inhabitants of Macedonia (a Yugoslav republic) have their own nationality – which the Yugoslavs maintain, and which the Bulgarians accepted with reservations until 1956 – or whether they are ethnically predominantly Bulgarians merely inhabiting a geographical area known as Macedonia (which has been the Bulgarian contention since 1956).[38] Whilst there have been rapprochements between the Yugoslavs and the Bulgarians, this problem has always been in the background; moreover, the recent Chinese visit to Yugoslavia has not helped the situation. Relations with Romania have been relatively good in the 1970s, and there are no significant territorial or ethnic disputes; here too, however, the recent warm welcome given by Ceausescu to the Chinese could augur a souring of relations between Bucharest and Sofia. In contrast, relations with Albania have slightly improved in the 1970s, and the estrangement between Tirana and Peking could help to make Bulgaro–Albanian relations even better. As for relations with her non-communist neighbours, Bulgaria has a better relationship with Greece than with Turkey (for instance, supporting the Greek position on the Cyprus question). However, the USSR's recent overtures towards the new government in

Ankara could well lead to a marked improvement of relations between Bulgaria and Turkey before long.

Space precludes a more detailed analysis of Bulgarian foreign policy. But the general guide to such policy until now has been to consider Soviet attitudes; it remains to be seen whether this will continue to be an accurate indicator.

BIOGRAPHIES

Todor Zhivkov, First Secretary of the BCP and President of the State Council, was born in a village north of Sofia in September 1911. His family were of poor peasant stock and Eastern Orthodox faith. After an elementary education in the village school, he studied graphics. He became a printer, and in 1930 joined the communist youth movement. Zhivkov joined the Party itself in 1932, and in the early 1930s was a Party representative at the State Printing Office. He also, until the late 1930s, rose rapidly in the Party organisation in Sofia, but thereafter, for a period, his biography is obscured in official sources. We do know, however, that he was a ward secretary in Sofia in 1941, and by 1942 at the latest was again on the Sofia district committee, to which he had first been elected in 1934. He was a partisan organiser in 1943–4, and participated in the September 1944 coup. His first task following this was to organise a people's militia. His skills and dedication were soon recognised, and he was elected a candidate member of the Central Committee in 1945; full membership came in 1948. For the next two years he occupied the top local-government and Party posts in Sofia. In January 1950 he was appointed Secretary to the Central Committee, and by the end of that year was a candidate member of the Political Bureau; he became a full member in 1951.

In 1954, Zhivkov succeeded Chervenkov as First Secretary – a post he has thus held for the past twenty-five years. Nevertheless, his power and position as leader were not really consolidated until he had removed first Chervenkov (1961) and then Yugov (1962). From 1962 to 1971, Zhivkov headed the Council of Ministers; he relinquished this post in 1971 in order to assume the presidency of the newly-created State Council. Although his leadership does not appear to have been accepted unquestionably in the past (see the earlier in this chapter), his position at present would appear to be as secure as any communist leader's; at sixty-seven years of age, he could lead Bulgaria for some time to come. He has been a member of the National Assembly since 1945 and of the National Council of the Fatherland Front since 1962.

Stanko Todorov, Bulgaria's Chairman was born in a village south of Sofia in September 1920. His family were working class and members of the Orthodox Church. After an elementary education, Todorov became a tailor. He joined the communist youth organisation in 1935 and was rapidly promoted within it. He was drafted into the military in 1940, but deserted in 1943 and joined the communists. He was arrested in 1944, but escaped and worked under cover for the Party, helping to prepare for the September coup. From late 1944 to 1950 he worked in the Youth League, and from 1950 to 1952 was secretary to first the Sofia then the Burgas district committee of the BCP. He was Minister of Agriculture from 1952 to 1957, when he became a Central Committee secretary; he had been elected a member of the Central Committee in 1954. Todorov was promoted to candidate membership of the Political Bureau in 1959, and lost his secretaryship to become the head of the State Planning Commission and Chairman. In November 1961 he became a full member of the Political Bureau, and shortly afterwards (1962) re-linquished his position as chief planner to concentrate on his role as Deputy Chairman; this post had become more important following the creation of an 'inner cabinet' of the Council of Ministers (the Bureau) at that time. Virtually simultaneously, Todorov was appointed Bulgaria's permanent representative to Comecon. In 1966 he was again appointed secretary to the Central Committee, and gave up his deputy Chairmanship. He retained this secretaryship until July 1971, when he relinquished it to take up his present post of Chairman.

BASIC FACTS ABOUT BULGARIA

Official name: People's Republic of Bulgaria (Narodna Republika Bulgaria).
Area: 110,912 sq. km. (42,796 sq. miles).
Population (end 1977): 8, 825,000
Population density: 79 per sq. km.
Population distribution (1976): 58 per cent urban, 42 per cent rural.
Membership of the BCP (Bulgarska Komunisticheska Partiya) in Jan 1978: 817,000.
Other parties: Bulgarian Agrarian Union (membership 120,000 in 1971).

Administrative division: 27 districts (*okruzi*), plus the city commune of Sofia.

Ethnic nationalities: Bulgarians, 85·5 per cent; Turks, 8·6 per cent; Gypsies, 2·6 per cent; Macedonians, 2·5 per cent; others, 0·8 per cent. (The Bulgarians do not now recognise separate ethnic groups, so that no figures appear on these in the 1975 census. The last detailed official breakdown appeared in 1956, and it is these outdated figures which are given here.)

Population of major towns (1975): Sofia (the capital), 965,728; Plovdiv, 300,242; Varna, 231,654; Ruse, 160,351; Burgas, 144,449.

Main natural resources: crude lignite, coking coal, copper, lead, zinc, iron, manganese, timber.

Foreign trade (1976): exports, 5199·8 million leva ($5382·4 million); imports, 5436·0 million leva ($5626·1 million); total, 10,635·8 million leva ($11,008·5 million).

Main trading partners: USSR, GDR, Poland, FRG, Czechoslovakia, Romania.

National income by sector (1976): industry 51 per cent; agriculture and forestry 22·1 per cent; construction 8·8 per cent; transportation and communications 8·2 per cent; retail and wholesale trade 7·8 per cent; other sectors 2·1 per cent.

Rail networks (1976): 6217 km.

Road network (1976): 37,740 km.

Universities (1976): (1) Sofia University 'Kliment Ohridsky' (12,616 students); (2) Plovdiv University 'Paissij Hilendarskii' (3893 students); (3) Veliko Tarnovski University 'Kirill i Metodii' (5046 students).

Foreign relations: diplomatic relations with 98 states (1977); member of Comecon since 1949, and of the UN and WTO since 1955.

Main religions: Bulgarian (Eastern) Orthodox; Moslem; Catholic.

NOTES

1. The most useful books on Bulgarian communism in the pre-1944 period are J. Rothschild's *The Communist Party of Bulgaria: Origins and Development 1883–1936* (1959), and N. Oren's *Bulgarian Communism — The Road to Power* (1971).
2. Figures from N. Oren, *Bulgarian Communism*, pp. 66–7, 109, 167, 200, 257.
3. According to official sources, 10,897 people had by March 1945 been tried as war criminals. Of these, 1940 received twenty-year prison sentences and 2138 were executed. See R. L. Wolff, *The Balkans in Our Time* (1956) p. 293.

4. For details of the Petkov affair, see M. Padev, *Dimitrov Wastes No Bullets: Nikola Petkov, the Test Case* (1948).
5. See Table 6.3; also J. F. Brown, *Bulgaria under Communist Rule* (1970) p. 12, and N. Oren, *Revolution Administered: Agrarianism and Communism in Bulgaria* (1973) pp. 94–102.
6. For details, see Wolff, *The Balkans in Our Time*, pp. 93, 100, 143–7 and 242–67.
7. On the suppression of the communists, see Rothschild, *The Communist Party of Bulgaria, passim* and esp. pp. 144–8, 269–79.
8. This figure is from K. Vassilev (ed.), *A Short History of the Bulgarian Communist Party* (1977) p. 248.
9. Ibid., pp. 265–6, 270, 272, 280.
10. Ibid., p. 276.
11. Figures on the distribution of land in the pre-communist period can be found in Brown, *Bulgaria under Communist Rule*, pp. 196–7.
12. Bulgaria has a very good record within Eastern Europe for introducing progressive social-welfare legislation. For instance, it was the first communist state to guarantee old-age pensions to the collective farmers.
13. The word 'natural' is in inverted commas because some commentators have cast doubt on the official explanation of Dimitrov's death.
14. Vassilev, *A Short History*, p. 285.
15. In addition, Georgi Chankov was ousted from the Political Bureau; however, the main reason for this was probably his excessive ambitiousness.
16. A useful study of the economy until the 1970s is B. Dobrin, *Bulgarian Economic Development since World War II* (1973).
17. For details on the reform and its aftermath, see H. Vogel, 'Bulgaria', in H. H. Höhmann, M. Kaser and K. C. Thalheim (eds), *The New Economic Systems of Eastern Europe* (1975) pp. 199–222.
18. Two concise overviews of political events in the 1960s are F. Stephen Larrabee's 'Bulgaria's Politics of Conformity', *Problems of Communism*, XXI (July–Aug 1972) 42–52, and M. Costello's 'Bulgaria', in A. Bromke and T. Rakowska-Harmstone (eds), *The Communist States in Disarray 1965–1971* (1972) pp. 135–57. On Velchev's ouster see J. L. Kerr, *Radio Free Europe—Research Background Report/74 (Bulgaria)*, 18 Apr 1978, and L. A. D. Dellin, 'Bulgaria', in R. F. Staar (ed.), *Yearbook on International Communist Affairs — 1978* (1978) p. 11.
19. Details are from *Ustav Na Bulgarskata Komunisticheska Partiya* (Sofia: 1969).
20. For an interesting general discussion of democratic centralism see K. von Beyme, 'A Comparative View of Democratic Centralism', *Government and Opposition*, X (1975) 259–77.
21. Of course, a higher-ranking party body (e.g. the Central Committee Secretariat) does have such rights of control.
22. Since 1944, congresses have taken place as follows: Fifth Congress, Dec 1948, Sixth Congress, Feb–Mar 1954, Seventh Congress, June 1958, Eighth Congress, Nov 1962, Ninth Congress, Nov 1966, Tenth Congress, Apr 1971, Eleventh Congress, Mar–Apr 1976.
23. The other was held in March 1974, and was concerned with problems of labour productivity.

24. Generally speaking, moves towards more democracy (in the sense of greater political participation) in communist states have been within the State machinery and the society at large rather than the Party.

25. Until 1966, the process was further complicated by the fact that applicants had to serve a probationary period (candidacy) before obtaining full membership; this practice was dropped after the Ninth Congress. The present details are from *Ustav* . . . , pp. 18–21.

26. It was announced in December 1977 that such an exchange is to be implemented in the period 1978–80.

27. Figures for 1922, 1944, and 1948–66 are taken from Brown, *Bulgaria under Communist Rule*, p. 318; those for 1945 and 1976, from Vassilev, *A Short History*, pp. 223 and 362; those for 1971, from M. Pundeff, 'Bulgaria', in R. F. Staar (ed.), *Yearbook on International Communist Affairs – 1972* (1972) p. 10; and those for 1978, from BBC, *Summary of World Broadcasts*, EE/5802/B/1, 2 May 1978.

28. Figures are from the same sources as given in note 27, except that the 1976 figures are from Dellin, 'Bulgaria', in Staar (ed.), *Yearbook 1978*, p. 10.

29. The first constitution can be found in A. J. Peaslee (ed.), *Constitutions of Nations*, vol. III (1974) pp. 93–110, and J. F. Triska (ed.), *Constitutions of the Communist Party States* (1968) pp. 151–79. The new constitution is available in an official translation (Sofia, 1971).

30. Figures are from *Keesing's Contemporary Archives* for the respective years.

31. These appointments are usually ratifications of proposals from other State bodies.

32. Thus, Zhivkov proposed such a body at the July 1968 plenum of the Central Committee.

33. This type of council is not exclusive to Bulgaria. For instance, Romania and the GDR have had similar organs since the beginning of the 1960s.

34. Oren, *Revolution Administered*, pp. 162–3.

35. Brown, *Bulgaria under Communist Rule*, pp. 215–6.

36. Vassilev, *A Short History*, p. 355. For the reader interested in developments in the relationship between the churches and the State in Bulgaria, a useful source is the journal *Religion in Communist-dominated Areas*.

37. Such products include non-ferrous metal products (e.g. cables), electric vehicles and good-quality tobacco.

38. On this see R. R. King, *Minorities under Communism: Nationalities as a Source of Tension among Balkan Communist States* (1973) pp. 187–219. For a more informal discussion of both the Macedonian issue and the relationship between Bulgaria and the USSR, see P. Lendvai, *Eagles in Cobwebs: Nationalism and Communism in the Balkans* (1969) pp. 207–61. See also Costello, 'Bulgaria', in Bromke and Rakowska-Harmstone, *The Communist States in Disarray* pp. 140–8. For recent Bulgarian and Yugoslav documents regarding the Macedonian question see B. Szajkowski, (ed.) *Documents in Communist Affairs–1979*, pp. 357–85.

BIBLIOGRAPHY

Beyme, K. von, 'A Comparative View of Democratic Centralism', *Government and Opposition*, X (1975), 259–77.

Brown, J. F., *Bulgaria under Communist Rule* (London: Pall Mall, 1970).
——, *Constitution of the People's Republic of Bulgaria* (Sofia, 1971).
Costello, M., 'Bulgaria', in A. Bromke and T. Rakowska-Harmstone (eds), *The Communist States in Disarray 1965–1971* (Minneapolis: University of Minnesota Press, 1972) pp. 135–57.
Dellin, L. A. D., 'Bulgaria', in R. F. Staar (ed.), *Yearbook on International Communist Affairs – 1978*.
——, (ed.), *Bulgaria* (New York: Praeger, 1957).
Dobrin, B., *Bulgarian Economic Development since World War II* (New York: Praeger, 1973).
Kerr, J. L., *Radio Free Europe – Research Background Report/74 (Bulgaria)*, 18 Apr 1978.
King, R. R., *Minorities under Communism: Nationalities as a Source of Tension among Balkan Communist States* (Cambridge, Mass.: Harvard University Press, 1973).
Larrabee, F. S., 'Bulgaria's Politics of Conformity', *Problems of Communism*, XXI (July–Aug 1972) pp. 42–52.
Lendvai, P., *Eagles in Cobwebs: Nationalism and Communism in the Balkans* (London: Macdonald, 1969).
Oren, N., *Bulgarian Communism – The Road to Power 1934–1944* (New York: Columbia University Press, 1971).
Oren, N., *Revolution Administered: Agrarianism and Communism in Bulgaria* (Baltimore: Johns Hopkins University Press, 1973).
Padev, M., *Dimitrov Wastes No Bullets: Nikola Petkov, the Test Case* (London: Eyre and Spottiswoode, 1948).
Peaslee, A. J., (ed.), *Constitutions of Nations*, vol. III (The Hague: Martinus Nijhoff, 1974).
Pundeff, M., 'Bulgaria', in R. F. Staar (ed.), *Yearbook on International Communist Affairs – 1972*.
Rothschild, J., *The Communist Party of Bulgaria – Origins and Development 1883–1936* (New York: Columbia University Press, 1959).
Staar, R. F. (ed.), *Yearbook on International Communist Affairs* (Stanford, Calif.: Hoover Institution Publications, annual).
Szajkowski, B. (ed.), *Documents in Communist Affairs – 1979* (annual: 1977–9, Cardiff: University College Cardiff Press; 1980– , London: Macmillan).
Triska, J. F. (ed.), *Constitutions of the Communist Party States* (Stanford, Calif.: Hoover Institution Publications, 1968).
Ustav Na Bulgarakata Komunisticheska Partiya (Sofia, 1969).
Vassilev, K. (ed.), *A Short History of the Bulgarian Communist Party* (Sofia: Sofia Press, 1977).
Vogel, H., 'Bulgaria' in H. H. Höhmann, M. Kaser and K. C. Thalheim (eds), *The New Economic Systems of Eastern Europe* (Berkeley and Los Angeles, Calif.: University of California Press, 1975).
Woolf, R. L., *The Balkans in Our Time* (Cambridge, Mass.: Harvard University Press, 1956)

7 People's Republic of China

BILL BRUGGER

HISTORY[1]

It is not the intention here to discuss the first twenty years (1921–41) of the Communist Party of China (CPC) which included the establishment of a Soviet Republic in Central China (1931–4) and the epoch-making Long March (1934–5).[2] It is sufficient to note that these years were characterised by consistently bad advice from the Comintern in Moscow,[3] intensive debates about the nature of the united front which the Party maintained with the Kuomintang (1922–7 and 1937–41)[4] and arguments concerning the degree to which an urban base should be maintained or recaptured.

As the newly elected Chairman of the Political Bureau, Mao Tse-tung collected his forces together in the Yenan region after the Long March and a new united front was forged to resist Japan, it was clear that Soviet advice would no longer be accepted uncritically. By that time, Mao Tse-tung's strategy of People's War seemed to have been vindicated.[5] This was expressed as the slogan 'The enemy advances, we retreat; the enemy camps, we harass; the enemy tires, we attack; the enemy retreats, we pursue.' Avoiding war along fixed fronts, large bodies of troops were concentrated to pick off enemy units one by one in a protracted war in the Chinese countryside. Likening the Army to 'fish' in a 'sea' of rural people, Mao felt time to be on the side of the troops which maintained close relations with the peasants.

The Yenan regime confronted enormous difficulties.[6] Plagued by mutual hostility, the united front ceased to be effective after early 1941 and a sustained Japanese offensive inflicted great damage on areas controlled by the Communist Party. At the same time, an embargo on goods transported from areas held by the Kuomintang and the

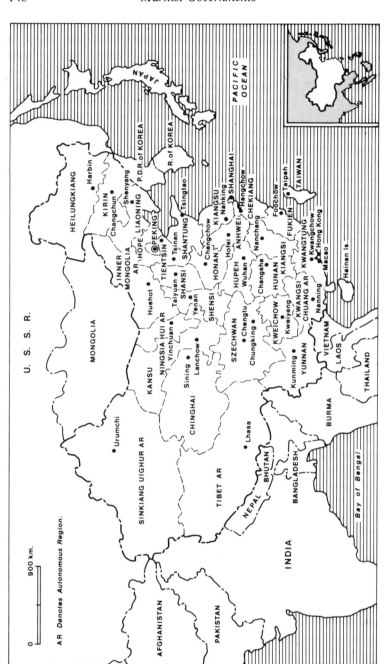

China: provincial and autonomous region boundaries

curtailment of subsidies from Chungking (the Kuomintang wartime capital) resulted in crippling taxes and a loss of morale. Many leaders, recruited in earlier periods of nationalist fervour, had little idea about Communist Party policies, much less a commitment to Marxism, and had been slotted into an inflexible bureaucratic structure. A new, flexible approach was required, and in 1942–3 the Party worked out a set of policies which radically changed the situation and laid the basis for what later became known as a distinctly Chinese approach to development.

Although the united front of the Kuomintang and the CPC had broken down by 1942, the united-front formula was still used by the latter in its treatment of the various classes in Chinese society. The revolution being undertaken was seen not as socialist but as 'new democratic'.[7] Policy was to unite all groups which opposed the Japanese, including rural landlords. Thus, the former policy of radical land reform, in abeyance since 1936, was replaced by a series of rent-reduction campaigns, which required a new political apparatus in the countryside. Attempts by work teams, however, to build such an apparatus were effective for only a short period, since peasants were suspicious of agencies of government sent down from above. The method adopted in the reforms of 1942–3 was to form peasant associations, which were given the tasks of checking up on the process of rent reduction and forming agricultural producer co-operatives. Mindful perhaps of the disastrous collectivisation campaign of the Soviet Union in the late 1920s when it had been attempted to impose forms of organisation on the peasants from *without*, a new approach sought to transform traditional structures from within existing organisations.

To do this effectively a new form of leadership had to be trained – the cadre. To effect change from *within*, the cadre was expected to operate within a network of *human* solidarity (between human beings or groups of human beings) rather than *technological* solidarity (between roles and structures), as did the modern bureaucrat and manager. The cadre's commitment was first to 'virtue' (self-awareness of action and motive, later known as 'redness') rather than 'ability' (knowing how to do things and having the talent to do them, later known as 'expertise'). In this he shared a pattern of commitment with the traditional bureaucrat who had ruled China for centuries. There was, however, one crucial difference: whereas the traditional bureaucrat was committed to the preservation of a landholding elite, the cadre was ideally committed to Marxist-Leninist values and the service of poorer peasants; in short, he was committed to change.[8]

To preserve this commitment and to prevent him from becoming more like the traditional bureaucrat, the CPC prescribed a policy known as 'the mass line'.[9] This required each cadre at each level of organisation to explain policy to those he operated amongst and to collect their opinions to form the basis of future policy. He was to steer a middle course between 'commandism' (relying too much on central directives) and 'tailism' (just doing what the masses wanted, without regard to central policy). He was required to submit himself to 'criticism' and to undertake periodic 'self-criticism', and the results of this process were to be recorded in a dossier. Scrutiny of these dossiers by higher-level Party organisations was periodically combined with an intensive study programme, for which the cadre would be summoned to Yenan or some central location. This was known as 'rectification'.

To facilitate the operation of the mass line, a distinction was made between Party policy and cadre operations. Policy was kept general, to allow for flexible implementation and modification according to mass demands. At the same time, cadres engaged in office work were regularly sent to the countryside to integrate with ordinary people. They could thus act as transmitters of central policy and mass demands, familiarise themselves with the day-to-day problems of the villages, help create Party branches and participate in a mass education movement.

The mass education movement of 1943 was based on the assumption that a literate and highly motivated work force was more important than the production of an educated elite.[10] Rather than concentrate simply on building more schools and training more teachers, a programme was launched of 'people-run' education, whereby as many people as possible were to participate in the educational process either as teachers or as students. The peasant associations could help housing, co-operatives might provide students' clothing, and the schools could set up their own productive enterprises. The idea here was to effect the closest possible merger between schools and society.

The above was part of a much wider policy of attempting to prevent rigidity in the social division of labour. Other features of this included the integration of regular army units with guerrilla forces and the village militia, and an ambitious attempt to ensure that regular army units achieved a degree of self-sufficiency by participating in land reclamation and other farming tasks. It was also part of a policy of radical decentralisation whereby decision-making power in administration and production was progressively handed down to local areas. Thus, administrative and productive units were responsible not not only to branches of central government but also to local Party committees, which were instructed to organise the various campaigns to effect rent reduction, promote co-operativisation, and so on. It was on this basis of *dual rule*, that the campaign style of politics, so characteristic of the CPC, rested.[11]

Much of the above-described Yenan model grew out of a response to economic blockade, the exigencies of guerrilla war and what the CPC felt to be the low level of political consciousness of urban intellectuals who had come to Yenan merely out of nationalist motives. It was also, however, an imaginative attempt to deal with ideological and organisational problems inherent in Soviet forms of organisation implemented in part in the old Soviet Republic and in the early days of Yenan. Cadre leadership, the mass line and rectification were all aimed at preventing the growth of a Soviet-type bureaucratic or managerial leadership. The emphasis on combating 'dogmatism' in the rectification documents of 1942 was directly aimed at those who brought to China prepacked models of revolution from the Soviet Union. The separation of policy and operations and the decentralisation of administration were designed to overcome structural rigidity, already apparent in the Soviet Union. Yet, for all that, it was not at all clear to what extent such policies needed to be modified once the war was over, the composition of the united front had changed and the problems of urban administration had to be faced.

The Japanese surrender in 1945 and the resumption of civil war in 1946 did in fact change the nature of the united front.[12] A new, radical land-reform programme sought to confiscate the land of both landlords and rich peasants. As troops began to move over great distances, it became very difficult for them to maintain close relations with civilians, much less to pursue agricultural work. Since there was little time to consolidate peasant associations in newly occupied areas, much of the initiative in land reform was taken by work teams sent down from above, and ineffective control led occasionally to the slaughter of landlords and the violation of the land-law provisions.[13] As towns began to be occupied for the first time, industrial plant was destroyed to prevent it from falling into the hands of the enemy. Even as towns began to be occupied permanently, after 1948, cadres were confused as how to organise city government, and 'ultra-leftist' experiments in worker control were said to have sometimes resulted in the cessation of production.[14]

The situation became so confused in 1948 that, at the height of the fighting, the Party felt constrained to order a rectification campaign to moderate what it felt to be excessive 'ultra-leftism'. Such rectification, however, was to be much more difficult than that of 1942, owing to the sheer expansion in the number of cadres and the often complete lack of Party organisations in newly liberated areas. Control over the Army itself took on awesome proportions as its ranks became swollen with raw recruits and Kuomintang defectors. By the end of the Civil War the Army had expanded to 5 million, of whom two-fifths were defectors from the enemy.[15]

The problems which beset the CPC in 1949 were no doubt aggravated by the fact that no one had foreseen just how quickly the Kuomintang regime would collapse. As cities were taken over in the wake of retreating enemy forces, there was no recourse but to government by military control commissions and *ad hoc* committees. It was a question not of working out a new and streamlined administrative structure but of attempting to preserve any structure which would prevent chaos.

The establishment of the Chinese People's Republic 1949–50

As the Civil War drew to a close, an attempt was made to formalise the new united front. As in the early 1940s, the CPC defined its revolution as 'new democratic' rather than socialist. Under this formula workers were defined as 'masters' but were joined in their dictatorship over landlords and 'bureaucratic capitalists' (those with ties with the Kuomintang government or foreign countries) by peasants, petty bourgeoisie and 'national' capitalists.[16] This four-class bloc, collectively known as 'the people', was a somewhat wider concept than Lenin's 'democratic dictatorship of workers and peasants'. The new democratic revolution was seen as a process rather than an act, the act whereby power was transferred being known as 'liberation'.

The principles of 'new democracy' were formally embodied in a series of documents promulgated in 1949 by a body known as the Chinese People's Political Consultative Conference.[17] The government structure established in these documents is illustrated in Figure 7.1.

Until 1954, the powers of these central-government organs were limited by those of six large administrative regions which were set up by the various field armies which operated in the final stages of the Civil

War.[18] Below these came the traditional administrative divisions: province (or directly administered city); special district; *xian*, county (or *shi*, urban municipality); *xiang*, township (or *zhen*, market town); and village. (See Table 7.1 near end of chapter.) At each of these levels government was at first in the hands of military control commissions, which were entrusted with restoring order and making an inventory of

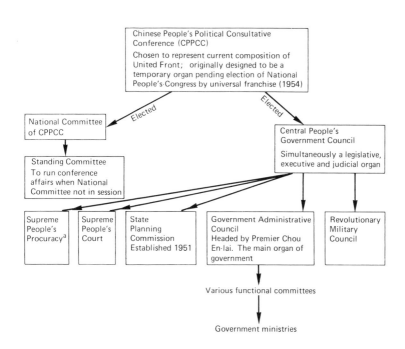

FIGURE 7.1 Chinese government organs in the early 1950s

all property. These commissions then handed over power to local people's governments, consisting of a triple combination of local CPC activists, members of the People's Liberation Army (which often formed the nucleus of Party branches) and personnel retained from the old regime.

The composition of the new people's governments varied from level to level and from place to place. Regions liberated earlier had few retained personnel, but those liberated during 1949 retained for a while many old Kuomintang officials and the former police system.[19] There were two main reasons for this. First, there were fewer people to be retained in the north-east and north, since former Kuomintang officials had at first accompanied the retreating army. Secondly, those areas liberated after 1948 were subject to a new and more conservative policy, dictated by the confusion of 1948 and the need to restore the economy as quickly as possible.

The new conservatism was reflected not only in the policy towards retained cadres but also in rural policy. In 1950 land reform was halted in all areas unless it could be assured that production would not suffer. Nothing was to be done without authorisation from above and initiative rested with work teams rather than peasant associations.[20] In the industrial sector, attempts were made to establish factory-management committees on the triple-alliance formula (old managers, Army–Party representatives, and elected workers), but these were made subject to managerial veto and the more active workers on them were often promoted into management or Party jobs.[21]

In many fields, however, policy could only be *ad hoc*. Committees, of varying composition, were established to register the population, control vagrancy, supervise inter-enterprise contracts, regulate the activities of private schools, and promote a new Marriage Law.[22] Pending the establishment of a rural taxation system, work teams were sent to the countryside to requisition grain (often against peasant opposition). At the same time, campaigns to mop up 'bandits' and to counter Kuomintang air attacks continued.[23]

The gradualist policies of 1949–50 bear a striking resemblance to those of Russia from 1917–18, prior to the beginning of the Civil War. As in Russia they were to give rise to serious problems. Faced with the task of supervising the establishment of a new administrative machinery, local Party branches often confused their functions with that of the formal bureaucracy and management. Many Party cadres were just too busy with administrative detail to worry about overall questions of policy and others were content to rest upon their laurels following the cessation of major hostilities.[24] As the focus of Party recruitment switched to the cities, a lot of people of questionable political reliability were taken into the Party because of their technical skill or administrative position; these occasionally included gang bosses and secret-society elements who had in the past managed to join any political party which became dominant.[25] The newly formed labour unions were weak and ineffective. They not only confused their functions with management in the State sector, but also often disregarded Party policy by siding with management in the private sector. There were problems, too, concerning how to subordinate the private sector of the economy to the State. The takeover of industry and commerce designated as 'bureaucratic capitalist' had been relatively easy, since much of it was already State-owned before 1949, but the sector designated as 'national capitalist' could not be left to its own devices if anything like a national planning system was to be created.

The mass movements of 1950–2

A new period of radicalism was launched early in June 1950 and took the form of an attempt to eradicate gang bosses and secret-society elements within industry and to reform Party and union branches. It was not very effective, owing in part to ineffective leadership. Indeed, early attempts to impart more vigour into the labour unions often resulted in their ceasing to be 'tails of management' only to demand immediate economic benefits at the expense of other sectors of society.[26]

By late June the situation seemed more urgent, as hostilities broke out in Korea. There can be no doubt that the Chinese government was taken by surprise, since orders had been issued for the post-Civil War demobilisation of part of the People's Liberation Army the day before hostilities commenced.[27] By that time, military expenditure constituted 39 per cent of the official draft budget for 1950 (though, because of disguised items, this might have been nearer 60 per cent).[28] The cancellation of the demobilisation order was a bitter blow. An even more bitter blow was the sealing of the Taiwan Straits by the United States Seventh Fleet, which postponed indefinitely the impending Taiwan campaign. The effect of this action on foreign policy was incalculable. Despite the fact that US–China relations had soured after 1944, that the United States had provided considerable aid to Chiang Kai-shek up until 1948, that China was mortally afraid of the possible remilitarisation of Japan, and that a decision had already been taken to 'lean to the side of the Soviet Union' in foreign policy,[29] many analysts believe that US–China relations might have been established on at least the partial basis that they were with Britain soon after liberation. The US action in June 1950, however, cemented relations with the Soviet Union, and Stalin's distrust of Mao was no longer evident.[30] Within five months, as American troops pressed close to the Chinese border, China actively intervened in the Korean War at tremendous cost in terms of troops, munitions and (as regards the Soviet Union) freedom of action.[31]

The immediate domestic effect of the outbreak of the Korean War was consolidation of control over Tibet (though the existing government of the Dalai Lama remained in office), an intensification of land reform, a ruthless campaign to suppress counter-revolutionaries, a movement for the ideological reform of intellectuals, a major drive to reform the labour unions, and a renewed attempt to end the power of gang bosses and secret societies in the cities.[32]

The urban campaigns enjoyed only limited success and when the problem was identified as weak and ineffective Party leadership, a major movement was launched known as the 'Three Anti' campaign, to wipe out graft, waste and bureaucratism. By the end of this campaign, in 1952, it was reported that 4·5 per cent of all State officials in China had received some form of punishment.[33] Concurrently, the Three Anti campaign was joined by another movement, focusing on the private sector and known as the 'Five Anti' (aimed at bribery, tax evasion, theft of State property, cheating on government contracts and stealing State economic information). By the end of that movement, 'national capitalists' had surrendered much of their former independence. The movement greatly strengthened organisations specifically designed to maintain control over them and a large corps of urban activists had been created which might in future be mobilised to press further the socialisation of industry and commerce.[34]

In the second half of 1952 the movements wound down. Pressure on national capitalists abated. Caution was expressed about implementing too rapidly the provisions of the Marriage Law. Land reform in southern China stopped, and attempts to speed up the process of co-operativisation were suspended. A period of consolidation had begun in which a form of administration was adopted in direct emulation of the Soviet Union. The mass movements of 1950–2 undoubtedly prepared the way for the adoption of this Soviet model, and some of them, such as the Campaign for the Suppression of Counter-revolutionaries, which was imposed from above without much mass mobilisation, were similar to Soviet campaigns. In general, though, the extent to which activism had been fostered by local Party committes and other bodies in the major movements of 1951–2 was reminiscent of the Yenan campaign style. The mood in late 1952 and 1953 was to be very different.

The Soviet model of administration, 1953–5[35]

The new period of consolidation coincided with improved relations between China and the Soviet Union. Although the Sino-Soviet Treaty of 1950[36] had resulted in Soviet aid and loans, and although the Korean War had brought China and the Soviet Union closer together, there remained some tension between the two countries, stemming perhaps from delays in the supply of Soviet military equipment for Korea, the continued Soviet occupation of the Chinese ports of Lushun and Talien and control over railways in the north-east. By 1952, however, Soviet military supplies were more forthcoming and an agreement was concluded on the railway issue. Following the death of Stalin in March 1953, new aid agreements were concluded, and Lushun and Talien were eventually handed back to China.

The bulk of Soviet assistance took the form of the importation of key industrial plants, which were to form the backbone of China's first five-year plan (1953–7). With the plants came Soviet advisers and planners, who played a key role in launching China's industrialisation drive following the Korean armistice. They were instrumental too in establishing a State Planning Commission. This was headed by Kao Kang, the Party leader in north-eastern China, the centre of China's heavy industry and the area in which the Soviet model was most enthusiastically implemented.

As in the Soviet Union, priority was given to heavy industry over light industry, and industry in general over agriculture. This is not surprising, since the main reason why the Chinese adopted a model, which in so many ways contradicted the Yenan experience, was probably the need to strengthen defence. The new slogan was 'regularise, systematise, rationalise and centralise'. In such a situation, 'cadre' leadership gave way to managerial leadership or (amongst the more sluggish) bureaucratic leadership. Commitment was more to 'ability' than to 'virtue', and the latter was increasingly interpreted in terms of the former. As vertically organised chains of ministerial command were established, Party branches often became no more than ancillary staff in a system where line management was supreme. Control was exercised not so much by local Party organisations (as in the old dual-rule scheme), but by an external Ministry of State Control and the People's Procuracy.

The mass line, therefore, could not but atrophy. Workers participated less in planning; they were more educated in how to fulfil centrally determined plans. The former collectivist orientation gave way to a system of individual responsibility and individual material incentive which reached an extreme form in the Soviet managerial system known as 'one-person management'. The stress on expertise, with the engineer as the new culture hero, gave rise to a technocratic education system which was geared more to selecting an elite than to creating the conditions for mass participation. The Army increasingly developed a professional orientation and less and less was said about the theory of People's War. Military academies were set up and ranks introduced, whilst the militia system gave way to a reserve system brought about by the introduction of conscription.[37]

In the countryside, the new stress on 'rationalisation' resulted in the transformation of the former peasant associations into organs of administration. As such they, became bureaucratised, the more so because a shortage of cadres made the *xiang* rather than the natural village the basic unit of government.[38] Perhaps the major problem in the countryside, however, was that the earlier attempt to follow up land reform with a programme of co-operativisation was abandoned; indeed, many co-operatives were actually dissolved. The result was that many peasants with uneconomical parcels of land were forced to mortgage their land to richer peasants and were occasionally rendered landless when bad harvests occurred.[39] At the same time, their hardship was exacerbated by a national policy which demanded that the peasants pay the cost of rapid industrialisation. By 1954 the burden of State grain purchases at low prices was quite severe.

In the cities 'rationalisation' abolished the *ad hoc* committees which had been set up following liberation, and replaced them with a hierarchy of street offices and street committees. Though this system undoubtedly extended popular participation in local urban government, it led to a separation in administration between organisations based on the workplace (largely male-dominated) and those based on units of residence (often female-dominated). Such a situation could only make the system work more in the interests of social control than of integrated mass participation.[40]

The establishment of a permanent government structure, 1954

The culmination of the Soviet model was to be the establishment of a new government structure. The Electoral Law of February 1953 prepared the way for the convocation of a National People's Congress.[41] Significantly, it made no mention of the large administrative regions into which China had been divided since liberation. The abolition of these regions, however, was said to have been opposed by some powerful figures in the Communist Party, notably Kao Kang and Jao Shu-shih, the leaders of the two most significant regions, northeastern China and eastern China, who were subsequently charged with attempting to create 'independent kingdoms'.[42]

The attack on Kao Kang was somewhat paradoxical. The logic of the Soviet model demanded greater centralisation, and Kao himself, an admirer of Stalin, was perhaps the arch-exponent of the Soviet model in his own particular 'independent kingdom'. Thus, moves to strengthen part of the Soviet model (greater national centralisation) resulted in much less importance being given to the major area in which the model as a whole had been implemented. One is presented here with the possibility that opponents of the Soviet model advocated greater centralisation in order to prepare for future decentralisation.[43] The above is somewhat speculative, for scholars are divided in their estimates as to the extent that the Soviet model was a major issue in the arguments over Kao Kang.[44] Suffice it to say that the removal of Kao in 1954 led immediately to the promulgation of a new State structure (see Figure 7.2).

The generalisation of the Yenan heritage, 1955–6[47]

The initial response to problems stemming from the adoption of the Soviet model was fully consonant with the model itself. In contrast to Mao's metaphor of 'curing the sickness to save the patient', Stalin preferred to 'amputate the diseased limb'. According to this latter principle, a campaign was launched in 1955 known as *Sufan*, aimed at the eradication of counter-revolutionaries.[48] It was run in a bureaucratic way with fixed quotas of targets being singled out for investigation. Scholars disagree in their evaluation of the movement. Though I am sure that it was largely a response to problems of the Soviet model, some have argued that it was a device to get opponents of the socialist transformation of industry and commerce out of the way. Whatever the intention, the latter was indeed a major consequence.

The most pressing problem in 1955 was the deteriorating rural situation. The imposition of a State monopoly on the trade in grain in 1953 had removed the power of unscrupulous merchants only to facilitate the imposition of inordinately high grain quotas by the State.

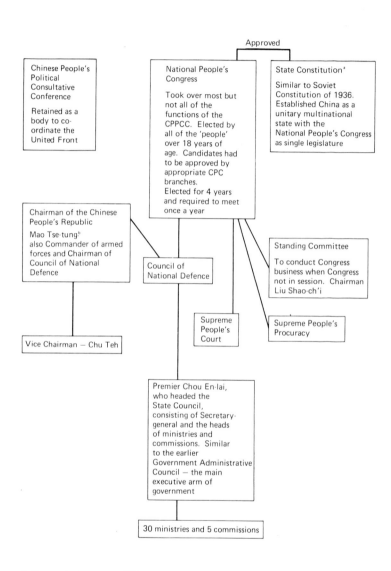

Approved

Chinese People's
Political
Consultative
Conference

Retained as a
body to co-
ordinate the
United Front

National People's
Congress

Took over most but
not all of the
functions of the
CPPCC. Elected by
all of the 'people'
over 18 years of
age. Candidates had
to be approved by
appropriate CPC
branches.
Elected for 4 years
and required to meet
once a year

State Constitution ͣ

Similar to Soviet
Constitution of 1936.
Established China as a
unitary multinational
state with the
National People's Congress
as single legislature

Chairman of the Chinese
People's Republic

Mao Tse-tung ᵇ
also Commander of armed
forces and Chairman of
Council of National
Defence

Council of
National Defence

Standing Committee

To conduct Congress
business when Congress
not in session. Chairman
Liu Shao-ch'i

Supreme
People's
Court

Supreme People's
Procuracy

Vice Chairman — Chu Teh

Premier Chou En-lai,
who headed the
State Council,
consisting of Secretary-
general and the heads
of ministries and
commissions. Similar
to the earlier
Government Administrative
Council — the main
executive arm of
government

30 ministries and 5 commissions

ͣ See note 45 on p. 199.
ᵇ See note 46 on p. 199.

FIGURE 7.2 Chinese government organs in 1954

These were often assigned bureaucratically without any regard for the productivity of various regions. In March 1955, therefore, a campaign was launched to re-assign grain quotas on a household basis. As a result, the former 'commandist' attitude often switched to one that was more 'tailist', and some quotas were felt to be set too low. In such a situation, the Party considered that the situation could only be improved by a radical strengthening of leadership in the villages.[49]

The improvement of local Party leadership was felt to be urgent, because the pace of rural co-operativisation had been extremely slow. Indeed the main form of rural co-operation consisted only in the formation of mutual-aid teams of a few households. Now that the main focus in Party recruitment was the countryside, attempts were made to establish at least one agricultural producers' co-operative in every *xiang*.

The initial co-ops (subsequently referred to as 'lower-stage co-ops') consisted of some two to three dozen households, which pooled most machinery, draught animals and all but about 5 per cent of their land. Payment was made at harvest time, after taxes had been paid and compulsory grain purchases concluded. They were felt to be 'co-operative' in form rather than 'socialist', in that this payment was based not only on the amount of labour contributed but also on the resources pooled. Needless to say, richer peasants, who could put in greater resources, did much better out of the arrangement than poorer peasants did, but, despite this, many rich peasants were unwilling to contribute anything at all.

The speed of rural co-operativisation was affected not only by the attitude of richer peasants but also by the opposition to too-rapid development by part of the highest Party leadership, which felt that co-operativisation should wait upon adequate mechanisation. In this situation, Mao Tse-tung himself directly intervened in July 1955, calling for the establishment of 1·3 million co-ops by the autumn of 1956, so that there might be at least one co-op in each of the 200,000-odd *xiang*.[50] In Mao's view, the complete 'socialist transformation' was to take some two or three five-year plans before it could be completed. He thus drafted a twelve-year plan for agriculture, which set some quite spectacular targets. Grain production, for example, was to increase from 175 million tonnes in 1955 to 300 million tonnes in 1967–8, and cotton was to increase from 1·5 million to 6 million tonnes.[51] If these targets were to be fulfilled, a 'great leap' in agriculture would take place, the first step in which would be the rapid co-operativisation of agriculture.

Throughout the second half of 1955, a massive propaganda campaign was launched and the pace of co-operativisation increased even beyond Mao's targets. In this atmosphere of euphoria a new form of co-op began to appear, known as the 'higher-stage co-op'. This was similar to the Soviet *kolkhoz* (collective farm) and ranged in size from a few of the original lower-stage co-ops to collectives as big as a whole *xiang*. They were similar to the lower-stage co-ops in that all land, draught animals and major tools were pooled, but payment was now exclusively according to work, rather than resources originally pooled, though some compensation was made for loss of property.[52] It seemed that nothing could stop the momentum. By the end of 1956, 83 per cent of all rural households' were co-op members, rising to 97 per cent in the summer of 1957. Despite the speed, there is general agreement that the movement was a success. There was some slaughter of livestock and some coercion was applied to rich peasants, but in general the Yenan principle of transformation from within seems to have been adhered to. In marked contrast to the Soviet collectivisation campaign in the late 1920s, a major reorganisation of the Chinese countryside was achieved without any major loss of production.[53]

The rural co-operativisation movement coincided with another major movement to complete the socialisation of industry and commerce. Ever since the Five Anti Campaign, the possibility of State takeover of the private sector of industry and commerce had been ever-present and businessmen had been unwilling to invest large sums in their concerns. To remedy this situation, the State occassionally made loans to the private sector and accorded private businessmen favourable treatment. With the radicalisation of 1955, however, this changed. Large numbers of activists pressed for the establishment of joint public and private concerns in which the State took over the ownership of private business, paying the former owners between 1 and 5 per cent per annum on the estimated value of the enterprise. The owners were then usually re-employed as managers on a State salary and persuaded to invest their fixed interest in government bonds.[54]

A third aspect of the radicalisation of 1955–6 concerned the People's Liberation Army. Criticisms were directed at excessive professionalism and plans were made for the Army to participate once again in agricultural production in support of Mao's twelve-year plan for agriculture. Political training was also stressed but little attention was paid to the militia organisation, which had played such a major part in the Yenan tradition.[55]

China's response to the Twentieth Congress of the CPSU, 1956–7

Attempts were made in early 1956 to slow down the pace of radicalisation, though the rural and urban movements had acquired such a momentum that little was done. Undoubtedly, a major reason for caution was Khrushchev's speech, to the CPSU Congress in March, denouncing the excesses of Stalin. Although the CPC went part of the way with Khrushchev in the period immediately after the Congress, Mao felt one could not explain away 'contradictions' in Soviet society merely in terms of the aberration of Stalin.[56] He certainly had no love for the former Soviet leader, and in unpublished speeches was quite critical of Stalin's leadership.[57] After all, the Chinese were currently dismantling a Soviet model which owed its inspiration to Stalin. By 1956, one-person management was virtually defunct[58] and the un-Stalinist policies of dual rule and the mass line had been given a new lease of life. To concentrate merely on Stalin's errors, however, would, Mao felt, gloss over the causes of present troubles and play into the hands of Western powers.

Mao's solution was not to criticise Stalin but to publish a series of articles analysing the 'contradictions' in Chinese society and calling for a major movement amongst intellectuals, minor political parties and labour unions to criticise cases whereby power was abused. Such was the genesis of a policy known as 'let a hundred flowers bloom, let a hundred schools of thought contend'.[59] In this way, Mao thought, one could avoid the disturbances which were occurring in Eastern Europe as a result of the Khrushchev revelations.

In 1956, however, the movement did not get off the ground. Intellectuals were unwilling to criticise the Party, fearing reprisals, and Party cadres were often loath to encourage them. In the meantime, the Party machine sought to consolidate the situation following collectivisation, specifying model regulations for collectives, warning against further change and restoring some of the free markets.[60] In industry, an across-the-board wage rise for workers was implemented, and the Party itself prepared for its first national congress since 1945. Although the Eighth Party Congress of September 1956 ratified the partial dismantling of the Soviet model which had taken place over the past year, the general impression was that China had entered a long period of stability.[61] The implications of Khrushchev's secret speech and Mao's analysis of contradictions, however, were just too profound. Many Chinese leaders were not prepared to follow Khrushchev's formula of 'peaceful co-existence' and 'peaceful competition' with the

United States. Such a formula was all right for relations with newly independent states and had been enshrined in the Bandung spirit of 1955.[62] They could not accept, however, that the disposition of the United States had changed just because there was a danger of nuclear war. They were resentful of the Soviet Union's lukewarm support during the Taiwan Straits crisis of 1954,[63] when, it is alleged, the United States did employ the nuclear threat. From 1956, Chinese and Soviet foreign policies diverged, though there were still one or two periods of relative amity.

The 'Hundred Flowers' and Anti-rightist movements, 1957[64]

The Chinese response to the tension between the Soviet Union and the East European states in 1956 was one of a conciliator. The Hungarian uprising, however, which the Chinese Government felt might endanger the whole socialist camp, saw China actively support Soviet military action. In the aftermath, Chinese analyses stressed that, unless further moves were taken to dismantle the repressive Soviet model, the same kind of thing might happen in China. To prevent the growth of organisations such as the Petöfi Club, which had played a major role in Hungary, Mao once again insisted on the movement to 'let a hundred flowers bloom and a hundred schools of thought contend'. Progress, as he saw it, was dependent on the stimulation and resolution of contradictions. Any attempt to suppress them resulted in their becoming antagonistic.[65]

This time his call was answered, though there were many powerful figures who were wary of trusting intellectuals to criticise the Party. As the movement developed, senior union officials became uneasy as criticism revealed both the ineffectiveness of unions and the apathy and 'economism' of union members.[66] In the Army a lively debate on the relative importance of military training and political study may have contributed to the view of some senior military cadres that people outside the Party were not qualified to criticise it. The greatest furore, however, was in the elite universities, where some senior academics began to oppose the socialist system itself.

The Party machine was not slow to react. In June the 'blooming and contending' was called off and the movement turned into an Anti-rightist movement in which some of the earlier critics were themselves accused of rightist deviation and sent to the countryside. Mao's role in this switch of policy is obscure though there is some evidence that he was not pleased with the decision to terminate the 'blooming and contending'.[67] He was, however, before long to embrace the Anti-rightist movement as it expanded beyond the original (early 1957) criticisms to denounce 'economism' in the labour unions, a 'purely military viewpoint' in the Army, and the tendency to relax in the countryside following the consolidation of the new higher-stage agricultural producer co-operatives.

As an increasing number of peasants spent more and more time on their private plots and were not dissuaded from so doing by local Party cadres, the Anti-rightist movement grew into a Socialist Education movement designed to prevent any backsliding in agriculture. To implement this, hundreds and thousands of cadres were sent down from their offices to work for a time in the rural sector.[68]

The renewed radicalism in agriculture soon gave rise to a debate about general economic strategy. The key problem was how to increase agricultural output to pay for industrialisation. Facing an acute investment crisis, radicals among the Chinese leadership recommended a further reorganisation of agriculture. As Mao's twelve-year plan for agriculture was resurrected, decisions were taken to decentralise operational authority over large sectors of industry to provincial level, the more easily to integrate agricultural and industrial activity.[69] A huge water-conservancy campaign was launched which removed peasants for periods of time from the villages they had always lived in and raised the possibility of creating units larger than the agricultural producer co-operatives. At the same time a new major rectification campaign got under way, with the specific aim of improving the quality of rural leadership.

The Great Leap Forward, 1958–9

Most of the features of the old Yenan model were re-stressed in early 1958. Rectification, the downward transfer of cadres, a reaffirmation of the mass line, radical decentralisation and cadre leadership were all given prominence. As the militia was revitalised in the face of a new Taiwan Straits crisis, a military dimension was added to the process of mass mobilisation. As war against natural obstacles was declared, nothing seemed impossible. Production targets were constantly revised upwards, to the point where they became quite unrealistic.[70] The mechanisms for reporting statistics broke down, so that no one was quite sure what had been produced. Yet everyone was sure that all production records had been broken and one cannot help feeling that a good many were, particularly since the 1958 harvests were, by all accounts, excellent.

Most significant, however, was the attempt to foster the development of small-scale industry in the countryside. In each *xiang*, plants were established to process food, manufacture or repair tools and produce fertiliser. The mistakes, such as the attempt to produce steel in *xian*-level factories, were on a grand scale, but then so were the successes. But how was one to evaluate relative success or failure?

By March 1958, it became apparent that the central government was losing control of the situation. In a new session of the Eighth Party Congress, attempts were made to moderate the fervour,[71] but the radicals, led by Mao, pressed for the extensive implementation of experiences in mass mobilisation in the model province of Honan.[72] Here a number of agricultural producers co-operatives had merged, forming the nucleus of what were to become people's communes. The communes were much more than amalgamated co-operatives. They became, in the summer of 1958, basic organs of local government replacing the *xiang*. They were charged with organising rural industry and were given control over State agencies responsible for mechanisation (tractor stations) and commerce. They also organised their own schools and became units of local defence.

The regulations, introduced in August 1958 to govern the establishment of people's communes[73] were cautious, yet the enthusiasm at local levels was such that caution was thrown to the winds. Private plots were abolished, communal child-care centres and old-people's homes were set up, and in some places cadres even contemplated the establishment of a partial free-supply system, according to the 'communist' principle of 'to each according to his needs'. As co-operatives amalgamated, there seemed no end to the process. The initial communes grew bigger and bigger, often embracing the *qu* (the intermediate level between *xiang* and *xian*), and, in at least one case, embracing a whole *xian*. In general in late 1958, communes contained some 30,000–60,000 people and had grown too big too quickly; it is possible, therefore, that these new organisations may have cut across traditional marketing areas and contributed to rural dislocation.[74] A further problem lay in the fact that what had started as a do-it-yourself exercise in organisation sometimes invited a 'commandist' mentality on the part of cadres obsessed with economies of scale. At the same time, over-optimism in the face of faulty statistics and an excellent harvest resulted in a reduction in the area sown in grain, which was to cause great problems in later less abundant years.[75] For all the shortcomings, however, a form of organisation had been established in the countryside aimed explicitly at closing the gap between town and country.

Communisation was not confined to the countryside. In the cities, attempts were made to set up urban communes.[76] Some of these were formed around core factories and included all commercial and educational establishments in the surrounding area. On occasion they even included a suburban rural component. The most successful were able to set up satellite factories to employ the dependants of workers in the core factories, but urban topography imposed limits on what was possible. A more common type of urban commune, therefore, was simply an urban residential unit charged with the task of integrating street industries and generating employment. But the urban-commune experiment was short-lived. First, it proved impossible in the short run to develop a unified system of remuneration which embraced both industrial workers and suburban peasants. Whereas workers were paid national wage rates, peasants (as in the rural communes) were awarded work points, which formed the basis for dividing the harvest, and subsidiary workers in satellite factories were paid whatever commune funds would allow, regardless of national standards. Secondly, the urban sprawl, inherited from the past, meant that little industrial reorganisation could be effected without colossal expense. After 1960, urban communes existed only in name, but the idea of integrating productive activity and residence in urban areas remained a long-term goal.

Opposition to the Great Leap Forward, 1959–60

As the Central Committee of the Communist Party met in plenary session in December 1958, there was general agreement that the Great Leap Forward had given rise to serious problems.[77] The 'communist' method of remuneration was criticised and the basic unit of account in the countryside (the unit at which distribution of income occurred) was transferred down from commune to brigade level (a commune sub-division corresponding at that stage to two or three of the old higher-stage co-ops). At this meeting Mao decided to retire as State Chairman, though he retained his post as Chairman of the CPC. It is possible, though in my view unlikely, that he was forced out of office by conservatives who wished to bring the Great Leap Forward to a close and restore the badly damaged planning machinery.

There can be no doubt, however, that, in the aftermath of the December 1958 plenum, Mao was dissatisfied with what did in fact look like an abandonment of the Great Leap. In early 1959, Party authority in the communes was restricted in favour of commune management committees, some free markets were opened to cope with the dislocation of the supply and marketing network, and, once again, calls went out to postpone any further strengthening of the communes until adequate mechanisation had been achieved. In this situation, Mao concentrated on reviving the Great Leap in the face of conservative opposition. This is not to say that Mao had a dogmatic faith in the commune. He noted that the bulk of economic activity was in fact run at brigade level and supported the idea of a federal commune structure.[78] He probably supported the decentralisation of the unit of account to brigade level, though this was at a time when communes consisted of some 5000 households.[79]

The reversal of Great Leap policy in late 1958 and early 1959 was very welcome to the Soviet leadership. The Twenty-first Congress of the CPSU maintained that all socialist states would attain communism simultaneously, which was no different from the Chinese position (though some extremists in 1958 may have dissented). The Khrushchevian assertion, however, that communes were no better than the Soviet *kolkhoz* was perhaps most unwelcome to the more radical of the Chinese leadership. In the meantime, however, Minister of Defence P'eng Teh-huai was sent on a tour of Warsaw Pact countries, where he was greeted with the utmost cordiality.[80]

Particularly galling to radical leadership in China was the meeting between P'eng and Khrushchev in Albania, which might have been interpreted as Chinese endorsement for the Soviet attempts to bring the recalcitrant Albania to heel. Their dissatisfaction was increased even further when, less than one week after P'eng's return to China, in June 1959, the Soviet Union unilaterally cancelled a nuclear sharing agreement concluded in 1957. This, was perhaps a *quid pro quo* for an American undertaking not to provide West Germany with nuclear weapons.

P'eng's position in the Chinese leadership had already been weakened before his return to China. Perhaps to retrieve his position and mobilise conservative support, he published on 14 July a letter attacking the Great Leap Forward.[81] Four days later he was joined in his denunciations by Nikita Khrushchev himself, who explicitly attacked the whole idea of people's communes. Seeing P'eng's action as a Soviet attempt to undermine the Chinese leadership, Mao mobilised support for a confrontation with the conservatives and, at a plenum of the Central Committee at Lushan, succeeded in defending the Great Leap

Forward and having P'eng Teh-huai replaced as Minister of Defence by Lin Piao.

The revival of the Great Leap and the worsening Sino-Soviet dispute, 1959–60

The revival of radicalism in late 1959 coincided with a drive to carry out reforms in Tibet, following an unsuccessful rising there earlier in the year.[82] In part the rising had been due to reactions against the Great Leap, but American, as well as Chinese, sources reveal an important foreign influence. As changes were set in motion in Tibet, cautious attempts were made elsewhere to revive the Great Leap. The principle of commune decentralisation was endorsed. Free markets were restricted but not abolished, and only sporadic moves were made to restrict private plots. Perhaps the main reason for this caution was that over 30 per cent of the land under cultivation in 1959 was hit by bad weather and morale was low.

The most important consequence of the revival of the Great Leap was a sudden deterioration in Sino-Soviet relations. The P'eng Teh-huai issue had already soured relations, and, when Khrushchev arrived in China on 30 September flushed with the 'spirit of Camp David'[83] and the possibility of Soviet–US detente, the Chinese leaders were unimpressed. In a speech to the Supreme Soviet on 31 October, Khrushchev suggested that the Chinese line on Taiwan was similar to that of Trotsky at Brest Litovsk. The Chinese response in early 1960 was to publish a series of articles in praise of Lenin to the effect that the Soviet Union had abandoned Lenin's theory of imperialism.[84] After that the polemics in international communist circles escalated to the point where the Soviet leadership unilaterally withdrew all aid, technicians and blueprints.[85] Coinciding with China's second year of bad harvests, this was a severe blow and many construction projects remained unfinished for several years. A final attempt was made to reach an agreement in Moscow in the autumn of 1960, though the resulting document was no more than a collation of views which could be interpreted in a number of different ways.[86] It implied that greater independence should be enjoyed by individual communist parties, and the Albanian leader, Enver Hoxha, was quick to respond.[87]

The years of natural calamities, 1959–61

From 1959 to 1961, China suffered the worst natural calamities it had known for several decades. Since statistics were inflated for the Great Leap and non-existent thereafter, we can only guess at how serious the situation was. The official figure for grain production for 1957 was 185 million tonnes, and this figure is generally accepted as accurate. In 1958 production was about 200 million tonnes (though official figures give over 250 million). In 1959 (despite an official claim of 270 million tonnes) production dropped to about 170 million, falling yet again to about 160 million in 1960. Despite a slight rise in 1961, the figure remained very low.[88]

The major problem, then, was how to feed the population. Communes and production brigades had little surplus to distribute to the peasants. Once the grain set aside for animal fodder was consumed by humans, animals were killed and the supply of animal fertiliser reduced: thus, crop output was further lowered. To keep up the supply of food, the area sown in industrial crops was reduced and light industrial enterprises went short of materials. These industries were then forced to scour the countryside for materials in disregard of planning directives. When they were successful, the free market was strengthened and, when they failed, the spectre of unemployment loomed, exacerbated no doubt by the cessation of Soviet aid projects. Faced with the problem of feeding the cities, the authorities tried first to put new life into the urban communes[89] and, when this failed, were forced to transfer large numbers of people back to the rural areas from whence they and their relatives had come.[90]

To restore control in the rural areas, a new campaign of transferring cadres to the villages was undertaken, but the problems were often beyond the abilities of the retrenched cadres. They, moreover, lacked the enthusiasm that had accompanied the downward transfer of 1957. This is not surprising considering that they had been criticised for being *too* enthusiastic about the Great Leap Forward.

There was much argument in 1960–1 about how to interpret the Great Leap. A common attitude among Western economists was that the dislocations of the Great Leap prevented all of the 1958 harvest from being gathered. Over-confidence had let to a reduction in the area sown in grain and the resulting food shortage was exacerbated by the subsequent bad harvests. Fewer material incentives had led to a loss in peasant confidence, and the economic boom of 1958 had encouraged rather than reversed the drift of peasants into the cities. Thus, the main cause of the troubles of 1960–1 was the Great Leap itself.[91] A contrary view, however, maintained that the primary cause was flood and drought and that it was precisely the commune organisations, created during the Great Leap, which caused the hardships to be equitably shared and prevented mass starvation; there was no evidence that peasants were dissatisfied by the incentive policy of 1958, and a loss of morale was to be expected once crops failed.[92]

This latter view was that of the radical Chinese leadership, in eclipse after 1960. We cannot be so clear as to the view of the more conservative Party leadership, under Liu Shao-ch'i, which dominated policy-making during those years. Liu is on record as saying, however, that only 30 per cent of the difficulties in production were owing to natural calamities and that the other 70 per cent were man-made factors. He suggested also that it might have been better had the communes not been formed.[93]

Whatever their assessment of the Great Leap, the conservative leadership was unwilling to see any renewal of radicalism. In late 1960, decisions were taken to transfer the unit of account down to the level of the production team (corresponding to the old lower-stage co-op), communes were reduced in size to about 2000 households, and 5 per cent of agricultural land was set aside for private cultivation.[94] Rural markets were encouraged, subject in theory to Government control, though often quite free. Many rural industrial enterprises were closed down as unproductive. Local production brigades or teams were allowed to establish contracts with urban industrial enterprises, thus strengthening market relationships. 'People-run' schools in poorer areas were often closed, on the grounds that they required too much public expenditure. 'Politics' ceased to be 'in command' in industrial enterprises (despite the provisions of a constitution endorsed by Mao for the mammoth Anshan Iron and Steel Corporation)[95] and industrial managers enjoyed an unprecedented degree of economic independence.

In this, the most unradical period in China since liberation, the former hard foreign policy line began to soften. There was even talk of the return of Soviet experts. The new (June 1961) programme of the CPSU, which defined communism in largely economic terms and which was later to be denounced as 'goulash communism', was passed over almost in silence. Khrushchev's attacks on Albania at the Twenty-second Congress of the CPSU, in 1961, did see a brief renewal of polemics, but they were much softer in tone than the unpublished statements of Mao, which spoke of a 'revisionist usurpation' and an impending revolutionary change in the Soviet Union. One might also argue that the Chinese line on Laos was more conciliatory in 1961–2 than it had been two years before. There were, however, two areas in which the Chinese position was unyielding. The third Taiwan Straits crisis (1962) and the Sino-Indian border war were hardly examples of the 'capitulationist policy' which was later said to characterise this period.

As conservative policies prevailed, a series of discussions was published in the Chinese press on the question of 'redness' and 'expertise' (the old 'virtue' and 'ability') with the former being interpreted increasingly in terms of the latter. At the same time, a determined effort was made by Party conservatives to rehabilitate P'eng Teh-huai and discredit the Great Leap Forward. In this connection, it is said that Liu Shao-ch'i's book *On Self Cultivation* (better known in English as *How to Be a Good Communist*) was republished, since one of its major themes was the need to combat 'ultra-leftism'. But perhaps the most famous publication in defence of P'eng was a play written by the Deputy Mayor of Peking, Wu Han, who cast P'eng as a Ming dynasty official who sought to give land back to the peasants after it had been stolen from them. He was eventually dismissed by a senile emperor badly advised by corrupt officials.[96] The senile emperor was clearly meant to be Mao, but it was four years before the issue was debated openly. More outspoken even than Wu Han was Teng T'o, the one time editor of the Party Central Committee newspaper *Renmin Ribao*, who implied that Mao had been misled by flattery, that he suffered from amnesia and that he was cut off from reality.[97]

During this period of enforced retirement, Mao felt that he was 'like an ancestor attending his own funeral'. His only cause for satisfaction was the repoliticisation of the Army under Lin Piao in the wake of the P'eng Teh-huai case.[98] Mao's writings of the time reveal a tentative reassessment of the theory of socialist transition. He urged that class struggle in socialist society must be directed not only against residues of the past (the Soviet view) but also against newly formed class groupings.[99] Unless this were done, China would revert to capitalism, a process already under way in the Soviet Union. The implications here are profound. The notion of 'new democracy' had been seen as a protracted process, but it was widely held that the socialisation of industry and commerce and the co-operativisation of agriculture had somehow created a socialist society; socialism, therefore, was not a process but an ideal type of social formation which rested on a 'socialist mode of production'. Such had been Stalin's view of the Soviet Union in 1936. Mao was now implying that there was no such thing as a socialist mode of production, that socialism was merely the transition from capitalism to communism, and that it was a reversible process. The extent to which the capitalist mode of production was negated in the process of its reproduction depended in the first instance on political action.[100]

The Socialist Education Movement, 1962–5

To promote that political action, Mao returned in 1962 to what he called the 'front line'. At the Tenth Plenum of the Eighth Central Committee, in September, he established as the main policy of the Party the continuation of class struggle and the need to combat 'revisionism'.[101] He launched a Socialist Education Movement in the countryside, which, like its namesake in 1957, prepared the ground for a restoration of some of the Great Leap policies. At the same time, a campaign in literature and the arts was initiated, aimed at reversing what Mao felt to be the retrogression of 1960–2.

As the Socialist Education Movement got under way in early 1963, attention was focused on how to clean up corruption in the countryside and halt the drift towards capitalist practices. The conservatives favoured the continued use of work teams sent down from above, whilst the radicals sought to combine this approach with the formation of peasant associations in the old Yenan tradition. To promote the latter, a set of instructions was issued by Mao in May 1963,[102] but they were negated in spirit by the operational instructions governing their implementation.[103] One of the functions of the peasant associations was to supervise local Party cadres, and yet the associations themselves were often placed under the leadership of the very bodies they were to supervise and criticise. As central directives were transmitted down the Party hierarchy, they were modified in such a way that the Party machine was able to preserve its position and halt any moves towards radicalisation.

The propaganda organs which most actively promoted the radical approach to the Socialist Education Movement were those of the Army. The Army promoted the use of the book of quotations from Mao Tse-tung (the 'little red book' soon to be famous);[104] it put forward models for emulation and, in its capacity as organiser of the militia, actually sent cadres down to the countryside to help in the formation of peasant associations. By February 1964, a nationwide campaign was launched to learn from the Army, and more and more military cadres were transferred to civilian duties. As political departments were set up in various branches of the economy, the Army sought to create channels of communication which might bypass the conservative Party machine and so overcome resistance by an entrenched Party organisation.

Though radical policies did not fare too well at the grass-roots level in 1962–4, the radicalisation of policy at the Centre had a direct bearing on Sino-Soviet relations. Khrushchev's hostile 'neutrality' during the Sino-

Indian border war of 1962, his alleged 'adventurism' and 'capitula-tionism' during the Cuban missile crisis, and the criticism of China during the various communist party congresses in Eastern Europe in 1962–3 all contributed to a hostility engendered by the implicit criticism of the Soviet Union in China's new drive to combat 'revisionism'. Attempts were made by other communist parties in 1963 to heal the breach, but this merely gave rise to the publication in 1963–4 of a series of open polemics, which became quite bitter.[105] Finally, with the partial test-ban treaty, which was seen by the Chinese as an example of great-power collusion aimed at, amongst other things, preventing the development of an independent Chinese nuclear deterrent, the point of no return was reached. This led to a new effort to develop Chinese atomic weapons, the first of which was tested in October 1964.

By 1963 the Sino-Soviet breach was beyond repair, and the initial response to the disintegration of the international communist move-ment was an attempt to foster the development of communist parties (Marxist–Leninist) in a number of countries, with the eventual aim of forming a new international organisation.[106] At the same time, increasing attention was paid to establishing state to state relations not only with newly independent Third World countries but also with countries in the 'second intermediate zone' (non great powers and non-Third World).

The campaign in literature and the arts was launched in 1963 and intensified in the following year. It consisted of an attempt by Chiang Ch'ing to reform traditional Peking opera, with Army support and the formation of a committee under P'eng Chen to work out more general plans.[107] At the same time a campaign to 'cultivate revolutionary successors' amongst the young began, and this led to a crisis in the Communist Youth League. Furious debates occurred in philosophical circles about the Marxist theory of progress[108] and different opinions were exchanged on economic strategy. Radical models of self-reliance were propagated in a far from radical climate. Libermanist economic policies[109] had been entertained in the early 1960s and, although these had been shelved after the radicalisation of 1962, market relations in the economy were still strong. In 1963 a conservative wage rise had been announced which intensified the gap between rural and urban stan-dards of living. Attempts were made to promote the mechanisation of agriculture by huge vertically integrated 'trusts', responsible for their own profits and losses and subject to a minimum of Party control.[110] At the same time, much of industry depended on contract labour from the countryside, paid at low wages. Such may have helped to close the urban–rural gap, but it also led to sharp intra-urban differentials, which remained a source of profound tension.

The overwhelming impression one gets of developments between 1962 and 1965 is of the continued frustration of radical policies by a Party machine which feared for its own position and was anxious that renewed confusion might lead to a loss in production. It was all right to criticise the Soviet Union for 'revisionism' but not to explore the consequences of that criticism for Chinese society. In July 1964 Mao made these consequences quite explicit[111] and in early 1965 called for the criticism of 'top persons in authority taking the capitalist road'.[112] The stage was set for a decisive confrontation.

The temporary deradicalisation of 1965

Mao's call was intended to promote further radicalisation. It achieved the opposite. As the focus of criticism shifted to the Party centre, local cadres could breathe more easily and the central leadership was just too strong for Mao's injunction to have any effect. In any case, whatever happened to the domestic movements in China would be determined by the outcome of a growing tension in international politics.

The attempts of 1963 to promote a new international communist movement had yielded little fruit. Most communist parties (Marxist-Leninist) remained small and ineffective. At the same time, China's attempts to foster Third World opposition to the United States collapsed as a series of right-wing coups took place in Africa, Asia and Latin America. Undoubtedly the key area of Chinese concern was Vietnam.[113] The bombing of targets near to the Chinese border in May led to a debate about strategy in which the major protagonists were Chief of Staff Lo Jui-ch'ing and Minister of Defence Lin Piao. Commemorating the twentieth anniversary of Victory in Europe, Lo suggested that, if China were invaded, the best tactic would be to implement the mobile and positional strategy characteristic of the Soviet defence against Germany in 1941.[114] For this to be effective, Soviet support was necessary. Indeed, following the removal of Khrushchev, it seemed for a time that Sino-Soviet relations might improve. By the time of Lo's speech, however, they had begun to sour again – amongst other things, because of the failure to reach agreement on joint action over Vietnam. There is some evidence to suggest that radicals among the leadership rejected Lo's position in the summer of 1965 as revealing a positional mentality out of keeping with the principles of People's War and involving sacrifices of independence of action with regard to the

Soviet Union. Significantly, it was Lin Piao who delivered the address commemorating the twentieth anniversary of victory over Japan, and in this speech he suggested that the response to any American attack should be the same as the response to Japanese attacks twenty-five years previously.[115] In such a situation, external support was not vital and one need not fear internal radicalisation. But Lin's analysis did not stop there. He generalised China's People's War experience as the basis for foreign policy. As he saw it, the world's countryside (the Third World) was surrounding the world's cities (the United States) and China need only remain a bastion of revolution waiting for the world's countryside to do its work. As such, Lin's international formula was a recipe for verbal rhetoric and political passivity.

In the domestic sphere, however, the publication of Lin's address heralded the end of any caution the Chinese may have felt about continuing the radical policies of the previous period. As Lin himself acquired prestige and power second only to Mao, the stage was set for the Cultural Revolution.

The Cultural Revolution, 1965–9[116]

Mao's strategy for promoting the Cultural Revolution was threefold. First, he initiated a campaign to criticise those writers who had attacked the Great Leap Forward in the early 1960s. Secondly, he promoted a rectification movement in the Army, to remove the influence of Lo Jui-ch'ing and the military technocrats. Thirdly, he lent his support to students pressing for educational reform.

The result of the first strategy was acute embarrassment for the Party machine. When it was seen that P'eng Chen, the very person placed in charge of literary reform, was attempting to sidetrack the criticism, he was dismissed and the Peking Party committee reorganised. Since the Peking Party committee had close ties with a number of senior academic administrators in Peking, this strengthened the organisation of critical student groups. Though a Cultural Revolution Group was formed in Peking to direct the movement, effective power in the capital rested with Liu Shao-ch'i and Teng Hsiao-p'ing's Party machine, which responded in a time-honoured way to the crisis by sending down work teams into the universities to make certain that the criticism did not get out of hand. They were almost successful. In July 1966, however, Mao Tse-tung, signalling to the whole country that he was in good health and about to take personal charge of the movement, went for a marathon swim in the Yangtze. Returning to Peking, he gave his full support to students who remained critical in defiance of Party instructions and gave legitimacy to groups they had organised.

These groups were to become the Red Guards. At a rally in August, Mao himself donned a red armband, and from then on Red-Guard groups fanned out from the capital denouncing anything they saw fit, be it in education, in the factories or in government. They linked up with groups which had formed in other towns and before long were joined by factory-based Red Rebels. In this early period of Red-Guard activity, almost anyone could find a Red-Guard group to join and the degree of spontaneity was such that factionalism was bound to occur.[117]

At first local Party committees clung to power. This was not difficult so long as criticisms were directed towards old customs, habits and ideology, but, when they became directed to the abuse of power in the Party machine, decisive confrontations took place. Occasionally Party authorities formed groups of Red Guards to counter the activities of Red Guards who had criticised them. Occasionally Party committees lent logistic support to the less radical Guard, whilst the Central Cultural Revolution Group provided the radicals with incriminating information from official archives. It was a very confusing situation, made more so by the movement of large bodies of Red Guards over the whole country to exchange revolutionary experiences, by clashes between university-based Red Guards and factory-based Red Rebels and by the vain attempts of various Party officials to 'ride the tiger'. Yet, for all that, the atmosphere of late 1966 was one of profound excitement. As Red Guards and Red Rebels were encouraged in early 1967 to seize power, anything seemed possible. Government offices and factories were taken over, and in a few places attempts were made to set up organisations based on the Paris Commune of 1871, which involved an implicit denial of Party leadership.[118]

But the problem of factionalism was immense. Since anyone could criticise anything, Red-Guard and Red-Rebel groups polarised around conflicting policy programmes and occasionally different groups seized power from each other several times without being able to agree on any stable structure. At other times Party officials arranged bogus seizures of power in which they still controlled the group which ostensibly replaced them. In some places strikes occurred and production was seriously affected. Nevertheless, millions of ordinary people were participating in administration for the first time and discussing general developmental problems.

By late January 1967, the situation was so chaotic that the Army was ordered to intervene and persuade warring Red-Guard groups to form alliances. Persuasion was sometimes used, but more often than not the Army responded with too heavy a hand and imposed order from above. The new organisational formula, which replaced the Paris Commune and other types of organisation, was known as the 'triple alliance' (consisting of Red Guards and rebels, old cadres and the Army). But at first it was the Army component which was decisive, just as it had been in an earlier version of the triple alliance, in 1949.

Fearing that the Cultural Revolution had been stifled in mid course, the radical leadership in Peking in April 1967 began to criticise Army action in the previous two months and a new period of radical fervour began. This time Red-Guard groups began to denounce the Army itself, for authoritarian behaviour. By the summer of 1967, these attacks had caused such frustration that one major military unit mutinied in the city of Wuhan and had to be put down by armed force. For the rest of the year the Army again played a major role in reconstructing the new order.

Throughout the second half of 1967, revolutionary committees were formed and consolidated. New orders for the Army to maintain control but not stifle debate meant that progress was very slow, and the whole situation was bedevilled by groups called 'ultra-leftist' who felt that the Army and the 'red bourgeoisie' headed by Chou En-lai had betrayed the Cultural Revolution. They considered that the revolution would logically end only with the construction of 'soviets' governed by 'the people in arms'.[119]

The spring of 1968 saw a recrudescence of 'ultra-leftist' agitation and a certain amount of localised fighting. By this time it was felt that, although the Army might hold the ring as reforms were carried out in civil administration and in the countryside (and, indeed, some felt the Army itself should carry out the reforms), it was worker propaganda teams who should go and restore peace in the universities. They were remarkably successful.[120] Earlier 'ultra-left' demands for the abolition of universities were dismissed, but the policy of integrating education with productive labour was readopted, together with a new policy of recruiting people only after they had spent time in the regular work force. A new downward transfer of youth facilitated the development of 'people-run' education and a general policy of integrating schools with the rest of society was pursued.

In the cities worker propaganda teams (with some Army support) supervised the establishment of revolutionary committees in the streets and the decentralisation of services.[121] Of these, the most spectacular was the provision of medical services by the use of paramedical workers trained in both traditional and modern medicine. In the countryside, where the impact of the Cultural Revolution had been much less, administration was regularised under Army supervision and revolutionary committees were formed. In the factories, new revolutionary committees stressed, once again, the participation of workers in management and managers in manual labour.

Yet there still remained enormous problems. The structure of the CPC had been dismantled and in the short run could be rebuilt only by the rehabilitation of old cadres (one of the components of the revolutionary committees). Which cadres should be rehabilitated, and what was their relationship to be with people who had achieved leadership positions in the Cultural Revolution? What was to be done with the countless Red Guards, who had played such an active part in the last few years and who now might be unwilling to remain quietly in the countryside? How was the Army to be phased out of administration? How many resentments would be harboured about harsh and maybe unjust treatment in the Cultural Revolution? The events of the 1970s were to show that these problems were not easily solved.

Perhaps more important still was the basic problem of theoretical orientation. In the early 1960s Mao had begun to develop the notion that new classes might be generated in a society undergoing socialist transition and had come to view socialism as a process rather than a social state (resting on a socialist mode of production). There had been much discussion in the Cultural Revolution about developmental strategy, but the overwhelming majority of analyses focused merely on the old Soviet notion that problems might be explained in terms of the persistence of old ideas.[122] Would one see any development of Mao's perspective?

The reconstruction of the CPC, 1969–70

The Twelfth Plenum of the Eight Central Committee of the CPC met in September 1968 and formally expelled Liu Shao-ch'i from the Party as well as (unconstitutionally) dismissing him from all State posts.[123] The way was clear for the convocation of a new Party congress. The Ninth Congress, which met in April 1969, nominated Lin Piao as Mao's 'successor'[124] and gave considerable stress to the role of the military (though perhaps less stress than the draft documents submitted to the Twelfth Plenum.) Half of the new Central Committee came from the Army, whilst the percentage of cadres in State administration went down from 60 per cent (in 1956) to 31 per cent. Thus, the proportion of mass representatives went up, but, significantly, did not include many prominent Red-Guard leaders.[125] Congress abolished the Party Secretariat and the Party control structure and endorsed a new policy known as 'open Party building', whereby candidates for Party membership had to be accepted not only by the appropriate Party branch, but also by the people with whom they worked.

Herein lay many problems. The intention was clearly to phase the Army out of administration and civilian Party work, but the principle of 'open Party building' from the bottom up encouraged the continuance of factionalism and the need for the Army to resolve conflicts.[126] Indeed, not long after the Congress, a renewed bout of 'ultra-leftism' occurred, resulting in violence and loss of life. In such a situation the principle of 'open Party building' seems to have been honoured more in the breach than in the observance, and, by the autumn of 1969, decisions were taken to concentrate on building the Party at middle levels (*xian*), rather than from the bottom up. When this also proved to be too slow, provincial Party committees were hastily set up and the Party built from the top down. Before long it was obvious that the same kind of structure was appearing as had existed before the Cultural Revolution.

In the economic sphere the Great Leap spirit was reinvoked, in the form of a 'flying leap'. The decision-making power of the provinces was enhanced and more power transferred down to *xian*. Indeed, a spectacular effort was directed towards developing integrated agro-industrial systems in each *xian*, as the industrialisation of the country-side proceeded.[127] The production team remained as the basic economic accounting unit, though occasionally efforts were made to raise the unit of account to brigade level (subsequently denounced as 'ultra-leftist'). The Tachai model of a self-reliant production brigade was advocated, though in a situation where free markets continued to exist. One gets the impression in 1969–70 of an attempt to reinvigorate the Great Leap, shorn of some of its excesses, though, to be sure, there were still cases of excessive coercion and the arbitrary confiscation of private plots.

In the field of foreign policy, the Lin Piao global perspective had failed to materialise and there had been no repetitions of the Vietnam War. After the Tet offensive of 1968, it seemed that United States power in Asia was in decline, whilst Soviet power was growing. The Sino-Soviet border crisis of early 1969, in the wake of the Czechoslovak invasion, was ample proof of that. As the Chinese began to see it, the two super-powers vied for 'hegemony' over the world and would eventually wage war with each other. In the meantime they would occasionally collude with each other when their joint hegemony was threatened. In such a situation China should attempt to forge links with whatever country it could in the Third World and 'second intermediate zone', in order to isolate the super-powers (now lumped together in a new version of the 'First World').[128] Furthermore, in a choice between the super-powers, China would lean to the side of the declining power, which was considered to be the United States. The result of this policy was eventually to be a partial normalisation of relations with the United States, and the virtual isolation of Taiwan. In the meantime it occasioned some opposition within China.

The Lin Piao crisis, 1970–1 [129]

Foreign policy was one of the minor issues which began to divide Lin Piao from other members of the Chinese leadership in 1970. There has been much speculation about what were the main issues in the Lin Piao crisis at that time. It has been suggested that Lin resented the intention to play down the role of the Army after the Ninth Congress, and that he felt that the Cultural Revolution had not gone far enough. Official explanations, however, focus on his personal ambition. It is argued that, since the dismissal of Liu Shao-ch'i as Head of State in 1968, Lin sought to replace him, in opposition to Mao, who wished to abolish the post. As Mao saw it, Lin had been responsible for a Mao cult which had replaced serious discussion by book-waving and slogan-chanting and had greatly inhibited Mao's freedom of action.[130]

At the Second Plenum of the Ninth Central Committee, in August 1970, a confrontation occurred. Fearing for the loyalty of part of the Army, which might rally to Lin Piao against the Party centre if things deteriorated, Mao immediately pressed for the reorganisation of the Peking Military Region. When this was completed, in January 1971, a group of people coalesced around Lin Piao – it is alleged, to plan a military coup. The document of these people known as the '571 Engineering Outline' noted that, if power were not seized immediately, they would be dismissed by Mao.[131] The document then went on to list objections to a string of current policies, revealing an odd amalgam of conservative and 'ultra-leftist' views. It was claimed that the Red Guards had been deceived. The downward transfer of cadres was criticised on the grounds that it was tantamount to labour reform. The retraining of old cadres in special schools was considered a form of unemployment and demands were made that the current wage freeze should be ended.

Lin Piao's followers noted that they had considerable power within the Air Force and that the Soviet Union might look sympathetically upon any group which ousted Mao Tse-tung. They were uncertain about the loyalty of regional military commanders, but felt that these could be won over if they were promised greater local independence. They proposed to set up a training group, to infiltrate doubtful military units with trusties, to promise to rehabilitate old cadres who felt aggrieved by their treatment in recent years and to establish Shanghai as the take-off point for a protracted guerilla war in Chekiang province if resistance proved to be great.

By the summer of 1971, as pamphlets and articles were circulated extolling the virtues of Lin Piao,[132] the possibility of a coup caused Mao to undermine Lin's position by attempting to secure the loyalty of regional military cadres. Mao was remarkably successful. Allegedly surviving some assassination attempts, Mao gained the support of the military regions as the crisis came to a head in September 1971. Caught off guard, Lin Piao fled in the direction of the Soviet Union, but his aircraft crashed in Inner Mongolia. Immediately Lin's trusties were rounded up and moves were taken to set up a new central military leadership.

The consolidation of 1971–3

The Second Plenum of August 1970 brought to an end the 'flying leap' which had begun in 1969. Policies were now more cautious than hitherto and varied in their degree of radicalism from sector to sector. The least radical sector was industry.[133] Rules and regulations began to be stressed, a twenty-four grade salary scale for cadres was reintroduced and a national wage rise of about 10 per cent on average took place (though with a higher percentage for veteran workers on low wages). Piecework was still prohibited, and managers were still required to participate in manual labour, though voices were raised that such a policy was not cost-effective. At the same time, decisions were taken to import a number of complete plants from overseas, and this caused problems in implementing the radical policy of agro-industrial integration.

In general, though, policies concerning agro-industrial integration remained quite radical. The establishment of *xian*-level industrial systems proceeded, and the Tach'ing oil field was vigorously promoted as a model of integration. The Tachai model of self-reliant development[134] was also stressed, though cadres were warned about applying prematurely all of its features (such as a democratic method of work-point allocation which took account of political attitude). Reforms were closely geared to productivity.

In education, the 'people-run' principle was maintained, as were the Cultural Revolution reforms concerning admission procedures. As worker propaganda teams handed over more power to school and college revolutionary committees, educational administration remained more representative and broadly based than before the Cultural Revolution. There was, however, a partial restoration of examinations and senior academics began to complain that standards had suffered because of the over-politicisation of the education system.[135]

In foreign policy, the detente with the United States gathered momentum as a huge programme of civil defence and tunnel-digging prepared for the possibility of a future Soviet attack. The policy of establishing good relations with Third World countries led occasionally to perhaps too great a show of warmth for rather authoritarian and repressive regimes. It is possible also that China's support for some national liberation movements slackened, and that policy in this regard was dictated too much by the attitude of the Soviet Union to those movements.

In the field of art and literature, the Cultural Revolution and its aftermath had not been very creative, in marked contrast to that earlier period of mass radicalism – the Great Leap Forward. The attempt by Chiang Ch'ing to reform Peking Opera resulted in the publication of a number of model Peking operas, which were constantly revised as their political content was scrutinised. This may have raised the level of political debate, but it did not lead to an adventurous attitude in the arts. By 1973, as publishing activity was stepped up again and as foreign artistic delegations and orchestras began to tour China, a debate began which, like so many such artistic debates in the past, led to a new period of radicalism.

The leftist campaigns of 1973–6[136]

In the moderately conservative climate of 1972, criticism of Lin Piao (as yet unnamed in publically released documents) focused on his 'ultra-leftism'. Articles denounced his belief in individual heroism and an idealist faith in human action divorced from socio-economic constraints. Following the official condemnation of Lin Piao at the Tenth Party Congress in 1973, however, he began increasingly to be portrayed as an 'ultra-rightist'. In retrospect, it is evident that this change indicated that, more often than not, references to 'Lin Piao and his ilk' referred to

Premier Chou En-lai, who, in the eyes of some radicals, represented a gradual curtailment of 'the socialist new things' produced in the Cultural Revolution. This group was later identified as the 'Gang of Four' (Chang Ch'un-ch'iao, Yao Wen-yüan, Wang Hung-wen and Chiang Ch'ing) though it is uncertain whether all of them shared the same view as early as 1973. They wished apparently to revive the spirit of the Cultural Revolution in accordance with Mao's injunction in 1967 that a number of cultural revolutions would be necessary before really significant changes could be achieved.

Following the Tenth Congress, in late 1973, the movement to denounce Lin Piao was joined by a parallel movement to criticise Confucius. The academic criticism of Confucius had begun in December 1972 and a lively debate concentrated on whether Confucius had sought to restore slave society in the fifth century BC or was the harbinger of the more progressive 'feudal' society.[137] It was not, however, a merely academic debate. A similar debate in the early 1960s had turned upon the Great Leap Forward and those who wished to restore the pre-1958 situation. It clearly focused on an interpretation of the Cultural Revolution, and, as far as some people were concerned, was aimed at the 'Confucian' behaviour of Chou En-lai, cast as the Duke of Chou, a paragon of Confucian virtue in a society of general slavery.

The explicit goals of the movement caused little contention — opposition to reverence for the past, particularistic loyalty, ritualism, filial piety and 'righteousness' (transcending classes). Such had been the case with the Socialist Education movement of 1962–6. We saw, however, that the earlier movement had masked very profound disagreements concerning its particular targets and the institutional arrangements necessary for carrying it out. We saw also that in 1963–5 the focus of attack was constantly deflected by the Party machine away from the Party and State structure. A similar process was to occur in 1974. Both sides seemed enthusiastically to enter the battle by historical analogy, to the point where the sheer volume of new historical interpretations rendered only the very skilled detective able to work out who was attacking whom. By late 1974, however, it was clear that the masses had not been significantly affected, since the movement had degenerated into historical obscurantism. A slight decline in production had been experienced in the earlier, more radical phase, but by November 1974, when the movement was officially summarised, it appeared that the industrial machine was working as smoothly as ever and that a new round of the Cultural Revolution was not going to occur. This is not to say, however, that the Anti-Confucius movement was without impact. Reinvigorated worker propaganda teams carried forward the revolution in education; criticism of particularistic loyalties continued; and the issue of equality between the sexes achieved a new prominence.

The criticism of Confucius continued into 1976 though the movement proper was over by the end of 1974. The Fourth National People's Congress in January 1975 stressed unity, and the major speeches of Chou En-lai and Chang Ch'un-ch'iao were both moderate in tone. Whilst stressing the need to make China into a modern socialist state by the year 2000, Chou also paid attention to immediate political tasks and Chang, whilst stressing class struggle, also paid attention to the guarantees embodied in a new State constitution.[138]

Some three weeks after the Congress, however, this unity was shattered in a campaign to 'study the theory of the dictatorship of the proletariat'. Setting the tone for the movement, two members of the 'Gang of Four' (Chang Ch'un-ch'iao and Yao Wen-yüan) called attention to Marx's *Critique of the Gotha Programme*. They noted that a society undergoing socialist transition would be characterised by 'bourgeois right', under which equal rights were granted to people made unequal by the economic system, and payment was made on the criterion of work for which people were unequally endowed. The generation of new classes in socialist society, they felt, stemmed from the failure to restrict this 'bourgeois right'.[139] Echoing Mao's analysis in the early 1960s, they seemed once again to call for a new round of the Cultural Revolution.

We are not sure of Chou En-lai's response to the above analysis. By 1975 he was suffering from terminal cancer and the major protagonist for Chou's modernisation call was the newly rehabilitated Teng Hsiao-p'ing, who had reportedly worked with Chou on a new ten-year plan for the development of the national economy. Condemning his opponents as 'ultra-leftist', Teng put forward a series of documents affirming the de-emphasis on political activity, the strengthening of the responsibility system, centralism, the importation of foreign technology and the conclusion of credit arrangements with foreign powers.[140]

In the autumn of 1975, a new attempt was made to push forward the educational revolution, with particular emphasis given to 'open-door' schooling, whereby students and teachers spent periods of time as ordinary workers, and workers and peasants were invited to help run the schools. As an intense debate began at Tsinghua University in Peking, Mao himself was asked to mediate. He refused to do so, sending a set of contentious documents back to the university for the comment of the masses. This move was taken by the radical critics to signify that Mao supported the criticisms, and soon the Minister of Education Chou Jung-hsin came under attack. By the new year the atmosphere was explosive.

The dominant New Year slogan for 1976 was 'Take the class struggle as the key link.' One week after it was put forward, Premier Chou En-lai died, leaving the State Council in the hands of a man who had very different ideas. Almost immediately, Teng came under attack in wall posters and was bypassed as acting Premier by Hua Kuo-feng, who was presumably a compromise candidate. In April, an attempt to remove wreathes laid in honour of Chou En-lai in Peking's Tien An Men Square resulted in violence, for which Teng was accused. The denunciation of Teng Hsiao-p'ing thereupon became a nationwide movement, as Hua Kuo-feng was appointed substantive Premier.

During the next few months the campaign against Teng unfolded, but it was a rather lifeless affair, either because the Party machine tried to dampen it down or (as the current leadership claims) because it did not have mass support. During this period, numerous rumours were spread, with allegations of perfidious conduct and forgery of documents. The death of the former Commander in Chief of the Army,Chu Teh, in July removed one of the rumoured architects of the compromise leadership, and the massive Tangshan earthquake strengthened the arm of those who feared for the consequences of a mass movement on production. Then, on 9 September, Mao Tse-tung died. Within one month, the 'Gang of Four' were arrested and Hua Kuo-feng became Chairman of the Party as well as Premier. All thought of an impending Cultural Revolution was quickly forgotten.

The campaign against the 'Gang of Four', and the new course, 1976–8

Accusations against the 'Gang of Four' were many and varied. They were said to have plotted to seize power with the aid of the Shanghai militia. They were accused of maintaining secret relations with foreign countries, calling for the dismissal of many senior cadres from key roles in the economy, sabotaging production and foreign trade, dominating the media, throttling artistic creation and undermining the armed forces. In a general sense, some of this may have been true. In retrospect, it does seem that much of the behaviour of the 'Gang' was unduly 'commandist', often naïve and occasionally thoughtless. For example, much has been made of their incompetence as politicians and their failure to carry through analysis of 'bourgeois right' into policies which would not violate the mass line. The ease with which they were disposed of does not testify to much support for their policies, but, in the short run, people are often motivated more by a reaction to unpleasant behaviour than consideration of a political line.

It is significant, therefore, that, in the first few months after the downfall of the 'Gang', the new leadership stressed behavioural rather than developmental questions of more substance. The new leadership made much of the difference between the position of the 'Gang' and that of Mao, but the Mao they cited was the Mao of the 1950s (as exhibited in the newly published fifth volume of Mao Tse-tung's *Selected Works*), not the Mao who had begun to develop a generative theory of class, nor the Mao of the Cultural Revolution.

Though some hostility continued to be shown towards Teng Hsiao-p'ing in the months following the arrest of the 'Gang of Four', his rehabilitation in July 1977 signalled the widespread adoption of his policies for national development; though only a vice-premier, Teng in effect took over the State Council. From the Eleventh Congress of the CPC, in August 1977, through to the Fifth National People's Congress, in February and March 1978, a new strategy for economic development was laid out, culminating in the publication of the details of the ten-year plan of 1975.[141]

In many ways the new plan is similar to Mao Tse-tung's twelve-year-plan of the mid 1950s, on which some of the policies of the Great Leap drew. Once again, increased consumer spending is combined with a very high investment target.[142] There is to be a dramatic increase in agricultural output,[143] and the simultaneous development of agriculture and heavy and light industry is stressed. It is hoped that by the end of the century, the output per unit of major agricultural products will reach or outstrip advanced world levels. The same kind of claims are made for industry, which is to serve and be closely integrated with agriculture.[144] The aim is to establish and strengthen fourteen local industrial bases, subject to central planning but still dependent upon local resources.

At this point, however, the parallel with the Great Leap ends. A key aspect of 1958 policies was the mass mobilisation of peasants to increase production and accumulation, with the incentive of finding a political solution to the urban rural gap. Such a policy is not likely to find favour with a leadership which holds that social change is to follow economic growth rather than accompany it. In many ways, current economic policy is perhaps more like that of the early 1960s. Once again, there is talk of the positive role of the profit motive, 'socialist market relations', control via the banking system, reliance on inter-unit contracts and vertically-integrated trusts.[145] In industry, there is stress on rules and regulations, individual responsibility and incentive, and strict work norms. There has even been a discussion of the possibility of reintroducing piecework.

In my view, the above policy offers no solution to Mao's 'three major differences' (between town and country, worker and peasant, and mental and manual labour). It may exacerbate another contradiction often stressed by Mao: that between leaders and led. The 'Gang of Four' have been criticised for equating this contradiction with 'class struggle'. They may indeed have had such a crude view, but one suspects that the current leadership's criticism is an attempt to gloss over Mao's theory of continuous revolution; this implied that differences in status and power might provide the basis for *class* differences (defined, in a Marxist sense, in relation to the means of production). Already there is a far more elitist approach to education and a partial undoing of the integration of schools and society, promoted on the grounds that academic and scientific standards had suffered. In addition, the CPC has been increasingly centralised, with an emphasis on discipline enforced by re-established control committees.

One may speculate on the impact of the above changes on the 35 million strong CPC (of which half has been recruited since the Cultural Revolution). It is likely that its intellectual component (and intellectuals in general) applaud the new policies, especially since they are accompanied by a freedom of discussion reminiscent of the 'Hundred Flowers' movement of 1957. Some intellectuals have been quite ready to trace back to Mao himself the origins of some of the policies of the 'Gang of Four', and have criticised the late Chairman in 'big character posters' — the medium which he pioneered. This criticism seems, in part, to be backed by Teng Hsiao-p'ing, and we may expect a re-evaluation of Mao's role since the Great Leap. It is very unlikely, however, that we shall see a Chinese-style de-Stalinisation.

We may expect also a heated debate amongst the top Chinese leadership. Ever since the second rehabilitation of Teng Hsiao-p'ing, in mid 1977, there appears to have been a difference of opinion between those who wished to widen the campaign to criticise the 'Gang of Four' and those who wished to terminate it. Significantly, the recently dismissed mayor of Peking, Wu Teh, was associated with the latter, and Lin Hu-chia, who replaced him, was responsible for 'taking the lid off the struggle' in Tientsin. What is at stake here is not just the re-evaluation of Mao, not just the fate of Chairman Hua Kuo-feng, who owes his position to the final campaign launched by the 'Gang of Four', but all that is distinctive about the Chinese approach to socialist development.

The Chinese approach to development, initiated in Yenan, generalised in the mid 1950s and confirmed after the Cultural Revolution, was a strategy of 'self-reliance'. During 1978, a number of decisions have been taken which challenge that approach. If the high investment target is not to be met by imposing harsh burdens on the peasants, nor by a renewed Great Leap, it can only be met by a strategy of export-led growth. The new modernisation programme, it seems, is to be financed by the export of vast amounts of oil and coal. To exploit these resources quickly enough, a large amount of capital equipment must be imported. Capital imports into China during the years 1973–7 amounted to about $2800 million. In the first half of 1978, China committed more than $5000 million, and by 1985 the total will probably exceed $20,000 million. Part of this is to be paid for by straight international barter agreements and disguised loans, but it seems inevitable that, before long, China will conclude direct government-to-government loans. It is possible also that China may enter into agreements with foreign multinational corporations for the joint exploitation of resources. Such a radical departure cannot but provoke intense debate. It is, after all, a major gamble. We are not sure just what China's oil resources are or, in the event of joint operations, whether it would be possible to agree on what is commercially exploitable. The speed with which capital might be generated by resource exploitation or the effectiveness with which loans might be repaid will depend on what happens to world prices and exchange rates. World inflation may thus have a significant effect on China. At the same time, the importation of complete plants from overseas must weaken the policy of 'walking on two legs' (integrating the modern and the traditional, the urban and the rural, the small-scale and the large).

How one evaluates China's new course depends upon one's own perspective. I have no doubt that Mao would have been disturbed, since, for him, economic modernisation and development of the 'productive forces' was no guarantee of socialist transition. From a Third World perspective, the economic strategy of 1978 still offers something far superior to what usually constitutes a development programme. But is it recognisable as *socialist*?

PARTY AND STATE – CONSTITUTIONAL STRUCTURE

The Communist Party of China

There have been eleven congresses of the CPC since its foundation in 1921. Of these, four have taken place during the period of the People's Republic (1956–8, 1969, 1973 and 1977). Some mention of them has already been made in the historical outline. The following is a summary of the Party constitution of 1977.[146]

The constitution of the CPC takes as its guiding ideology 'Marxism–Leninism–Mao Tse-tung Thought'. This is similar to the Ninth and Tenth Congress constitutions but dissimilar to that of the Eighth Congress, which dropped all reference to Mao Tse-tung Thought. The constitution stresses the need to maintain 'the dictatorship of the proletariat', though one can be sure that this term will be interpreted in a sense different from that used in the campaign of 1975. It stresses also unity with 'genuine' Marxist-Leninist parties, though one should note that these do not figure as large in Chinese calculations as they did in 1963. The Cultural Revolution and Mao's theory of continuous revolution are positively evaluated, and the constitution envisages more political revolutions like the Cultural Revolution, though these are hardly likely to occur in the immediate future.

Eight criteria are laid down for Party membership. If these are met, a Party branch must solicit the opinions about a candidate from both inside and outside the Party before admitting him to probationary membership (normally for one year). This is an echo of the 'open Party building' of 1969, though it is unlikely to be interpreted as it was just after the Cultural Revolution. Provisions are also laid down for disciplining or expelling Party members.

Party committees at all levels are charged with maintaining 'democratic centralism', the principle of 'combining collective leadership with individual responsibility' (the post-Stalin formula) and maintaining 'the mass line'. Party committees are required to report regularly to the appropriate level of Party congress, and individual members have the right to bypass immediate leadership and present appeals and complaints to higher bodies – right up to the Chairman of the Central Committee (a change introduced after the Cultural Revolution). One pre-Cultural Revolution feature which has been introduced, however, is the establishment of Party control commissions to maintain discipline.

As in earlier constitutions, the National Congress is established as the highest organ in the Party. It is stipulated that it should be re-elected every five years (though provision is made for the time limits to be waived). The Congress elects the Central Committee, which in 1977 consisted of 201 full members and 132 alternates.[147] Local Party organs are structured in a similar way to central organs, though provision is made for congresses to be elected every three years. Local bodies are headed by secretaries and standing committees. Primary organs of the Party are set up in factories, mines and other enterprises, people's communes, offices, schools, shops, neighbourhoods and companies of the People's Liberation Army. Provision here is made for annual elections. Party sub-branches may be set up below the level designated as 'primary', though they are not considered as independent Party organs.

Government

We have noted three State constitutions since the People's Republic was set up (1954, 1975 and 1978). The most recent constitution[148] is more like the 1954 document than that introduced by Chang Ch'un-ch'iao in 1975. It defines the People's Republic as a unitary multinational state and as a 'socialist state of the dictatorship of the proletariat led by the working class based on the alliance of workers and peasants'. The constitution specifies the leading role of the CPC and appoints the Chairman of the Party as Commander-in-Chief of the Armed Forces. As in the Party constitution, the guiding ideology is defined as 'Marxism–Leninism–Mao Tse-tung Thought'.

State power is vested in the National People's Congress and local people's congresses, which are required to practise 'democratic centralism'. These bodies are elected by all of the 'people' over the age of eighteen (thus it excludes 'landlords, rich peasants and capitalists who have not yet reformed'). The congresses are responsible for the appointment of State organs, which, in turn, are required to practise 'socialist democracy', allow for mass participation and arrange personnel in accordance with the (Cultural Revolution) principle of combining 'the old, the middle-aged and the young'. These State organs are pledged to develop science, education and culture.

Individual citizens are permitted to maintain their own homes and peasants are guaranteed private plots of land. In general, though, two main forms of ownership are recognised. The dominant form is State ownership and the subsidiary form collective ownership. Within the collectively owned people's communes, a three-level system of ownership is prescribed (commune, brigade and team): in general the team is the basic unit of account, though in some cases the brigade may be so designated.

National minorities are granted a special degree of autonomy, but not the right of separation. Individual citizens of all nationalities are granted a number of basic rights, including the right to strike. The Constitution also specifies certain duties, such as the duty to work and participate in national defence. Equality of the sexes is constitutionally guaranteed.

As in earlier constitutions, the National People's Congress is defined as the highest organ of State power. It is elected by local people's congresses and units of the People's Liberation Army for a period of five years and is normally to meet once a year. Provision is made, however, for these time limits to be altered. It has the power to amend the constitution, make laws and supervise enforcement, decide on the appointment of the Premier (on CPC recommendation) and other members of the State Council (on the recommendation of the Premier). It elects the President of the Supreme People's Court and the Chief Procurator of the Supreme People's Procuracy. It examines and approves State plans and budgets and changes of administrative boundaries. It also decides on questions of war and peace.

The National People's Congress appoints a standing committee, which carries out Congress business when it is not in session. The Chairman of this standing committee (currently Yeh Chien-ying) exercises many of the ceremonial duties formally carried out by the Chairman of the People's Republic before that post was abolished during the Lin Piao crisis.

The State Council remains the highest organ of government. It consists of the Premier plus a number of vice-premiers, ministers and heads of commissions.[49] (For chart showing local organs of state administration see Figure 7.3 on p. 197.)

The Supreme People's Court remains the highest judicial organ. It supervises local courts. It is not charged with interpreting the constitution, for such is the function of the National People's Congress, to which the Supreme People's Court is responsible. The President of the Court is Chiang Hua.

The Supreme People's Procuracy, in abeyance during the radical days of the 1960s and early 1970s, was revived in 1978. Its function is to ensure observance of the law by all State officials. It supervises lower-level procuratorial organs. Its president is Huang Huo-ch'ing.

The Chinese Academy of Sciences, once the scene of much radical criticism, was recently reorganised under the presidency of the veteran scholar Kuo Mo-jo[50] and has been joined by a new body, the Academy of Social Sciences, headed by Hu Ch'iao-mu.

Of particular interest in the new State structure is the revival of the Chinese People's Political Consultative Conference. This body once played a role similar to the National People's Congress until the formation of that body in 1954. After that, it retained a minor presence right up to the Cultural Revolution. It was brought back in 1978 to fulfil the same function as it exercised in the mid 1950s: that of providing a forum for the participation in administration of various secondary components of the united front (mass organisations, non-communist political parties, religious groups, and so on).[151]

MILITARY ORGANISATION[152]

The People's Liberation Army is 3–4 million strong. Current defence expenditure has been estimated at $23,000–28,000 million (probably under 10 per cent of gross national product). Recent decisions to modernise the armed forces and import military technology may be expected to raise this figure significantly.

The Army is divided into main force and local units. Both are administered by eleven military regions (subdivided into military districts), though the former might be transferred for service in any part of the country. Their relative strengths are as follows (in divisions).[153]

Military regions	Main force	Local force
Shenyang and Peking	55	25
Lanchow and Sinkiang	20	8
Tsinan, Nanking		
Foochow and Kwangchow	28	18
Wuhan	15	11
Chengtu and Kunming	18	8

The Navy is deployed in three fleets as follows: North Sea Fleet, about 200 vessels; East Sea Fleet, about 500 vessels; South Sea Fleet, about 200 vessels. There are about 300,000 in the Navy including 30,000 in the naval air force and 38,000 marines. There are twenty-two major combat ships, sixty-seven submarines and about 1200 other vessels (including 300 small coastal and river vessels). The naval air force has about 700 aircraft. The Air Force has about 5200 combat aircraft and is about

500,000 strong. Nuclear testing has gone on since 1964, there having been twenty-one tests. A nuclear strike force is operational and consists largely of medium-range ballistic missiles (range 600–700 miles). These missiles are gradually being replaced with intermediate-range ballistic missiles (range 1500–1750 miles), and an intercontinental ballistic missile has been tested (1976) but is not yet operational.

BIOGRAPHIES

Hua Kuo-feng, Chairman of the CPC, was born in 1920 in Shansi province. In the 1940s he served in Liuling mountain guerrilla base. In 1947 he became Yangchu *xian* Party secretary and political officer of local troops (ultimately under the command of Liu Po-ch'eng and Teng Hsiao-p'ing's Second Field Army). In 1949 he went from Shansi to Hunan and became Party secretary and political commisar of *xian* armed forces in Hsiangyin, where he became active in agrarian reform work. In 1951 he became *xian* Party secretary of Hsiangt'an (Mao Tse-tung's home *xian*), in 1952 head of Hsiangt'an special district government office, and in 1955 Hsiangt'an special district secretary, in which capacity he took the lead in the local co-operativisation campaign. In 1956 he became head of the Culture and Education Office of the Hunan provincial government. In 1957, as head of the Hunan United Front Work Department, he may have played a major role in the Anti-rightist movement. In 1958 he went on to head the Hunan Party Committee Small Group in charge of Economic Affairs (troubleshooter role) and became provincial Vice-governor. During 1958–9 he emerged as a major figure in solving the economic problems of the Great Leap in Hunan. In 1959, following the dismissal of provincial first secretary Chou Hsiao-chou (associated with P'eng Teh-huai), he became a provincial Party secretary on the personal recommendation of Mao Tse-tung. That same year, during the revival of the Great Leap, he led criticism of rightists. In the early 1960s, concerned with economic rehabilitation, he returned to Hsiangt'an (though he retained his provincial post) and was responsible for promoting Maoti'en district as a model agricultural area (earning Mao's praise). In 1962–3 he may have assisted Mao in providing materials supportive of the radical position in the Socialist Education movement. In 1964 he returned to full-time work in Changsha; in addition to his economic work, he was active in developing the militia during the escalation of the Vietnam War (in which he probably made close contact with Yeh Chien-ying). In 1967 he was one of two people to establish the Hunan Preparatory Group of the provincial revolutionary committee. In 1968 he came under severe 'ultra-leftist' attack and was branded a member of the 'red bourgeoisie', but he survived this attack to become, in 1968, Vice-chairman of the Hunan revolutionary committee. In 1969 he was a member of the Ninth Central Committee, and in 1969– 70, after a contest with leading military figures in Hunan, became the most important leader in the province. In 1970 he was appointed first secretary of the newly established Hunan Party committee. In 1971 he transferred to Peking to serve in the Staff Office of State Council under Chou En-lai. In 1972–3 he was involved in investigating the Lin Piao affair in both Peking and Hunan. In 1973 he became a member of the Political Bureau, and in 1974 he survived a brief attack in the Anti-Confucius movement. During 1974–5 he was involved in public security and agricultural affairs. In 1975 he was appointed Vice-premier and Minister of Public Security; he gave the keynote address to the Conference on Learning from Tachai. In 1976 he became in turn acting Premier, substantive Premier, First Vice-chairman of the CPC, and, then, following the death of Mao Tse-tung, Chairman.

Teng Hsiao-p'ing, Vice-chairman of the CPC and Chief of Staff of the Army, was born in 1904. From the 1920s to the 1940s he served as a military commander, and political commissar of the Second Field Army. From 1949 to 1954 he was a member of the Central People's Government Council and People's Revolutionary Military Council. In 1950 he became Vice-chairman of the South-west Military and Administrative Committee and Chairman of its Finance and Economics Committee. In 1952 he was appointed Vice-premier of the Government Administrative Council and a member of the State Planning Commission. In 1953 he became Minister of Finance, and in 1954 Vice-premier of the State Council. From 1954 to 1956 he was Secretary-general of the CPC Central Committee, becoming a member of the Political Bureau in 1955. In 1956 he became General Secretary of the CPC Central Committee (a new post, signifying a promotion). In 1966– 7 he was denounced in the Cultural Revolution as 'number-two person taking the capitalist road' (Liu Shao-ch'i was number one), but in 1973 he was reinstated as Vice-premier and re-elected to the CPC Central Committee. In 1975 he went on to become Vice-chairman of the Party and Chief of Staff of the People's Liberation Army. In 1976 he was dismissed from all posts but allowed to retain Party membership; then in 1977 he was reinstated in all posts. He is currently the second most powerful man in China (some might argue, the most powerful).

TABLE 7.1 Administrative divisions of China, 1974

Large administrative region		North					North-east			East							Central South					North-west					South-west				Totals
		Peking municipality	Tientsin municipality	Hopei	Shansi	Inner Mongolian autonomous region	Heilungkiang	Kirin	Liaoning	Shantung	Shanghai municipality	Kiangsu	Anhui	Chekiang	Kiangsi	Fukien	Honan	Hupei	Hunan	Kwangtung	Kwangsi Zhuang autonomous region	Shensi	Ninghsia Hui autonomous region	Kansu	Tsinghai	Sinkiang Uighur autonomous region	Szechwan	Kweichow	Yunnan	Tibet autonomous region	
Large administrative region	6																														
Provincial																															
Provinces	21																														
Autonomous regions (national minority)	5																														
Directly administered Municipalities	3																														
Population in millions (est. 1977)	850	8	7	40	23	8	32	23	33	68	10	55	45	35	28	20	60	40	40	54	31	26	3	18	3	10	80	24	28	2	

Provincial capital		Shihchiachuang	Taiyuan	Huchot	Harbin	Changchun	Shenyang	Tsinan	Nanking	Hofei	Hangchow	Nanchang	Foochow	Chengchow	Wuhan	Changsha	Kwangchow (Canton)	Nanning	Sian	Yinchuan	Lanchow	Sining	Urumchi	Chengtu	Kweiyang	Kunming	Lhasa
District																											
Districts	174	10	7		8	3	4	9	7	9	8	6	7	10	8	9	7	8	7	3	8		6	12	6	7	5
Administrative district	1																1[a]										
Autonomous *zhou* (national minority)	29					1									1	1					2	6	5	3	2	8	
Leagues (national minority)	7			4	1	1	1																				
Municipalities																											
Administered by provinces	178	9[b]	5	8	12	10	11	9	11	8	3	8	6	14	6	8	10	6	5	2	4	1	4	9	4	4	1
County																											
Xian (county)	2012	137	101	16	63	39	44	106	64	70	65	80	60	110	73	85	94	72	93	16	66	32	74	181	70	106	71
Autonomous *xian* (national minority)	66				1	2	2									4	3	8			6	5	6	3	9	15	
Banners (national minority)	53			27		7	7														2						
Autonomous Banners (national minority)	3				3															1							
Zhen (market town)	1																1										

[a] Hainan Island.

[b] Only the rural parts of directly administered municipalities are divided into *xian*. The urban parts of all municipalities are divided into *qu* (wards) which, in turn are divided into neighbourhoods (streets) each, until 1979, headed by a revolutionary committee. *Xian* are divided into people's communes. These are divided into production brigades which, in turn are divided into production teams. Before 1958, *xian* were divided into *qu*, which in turn were divided into *xiang* (townships) and *zhen* (market towns).

BASIC FACTS ABOUT CHINA

Official name: People's Republic of China (Zhonghua Renmin Gongheguo).

Area: 9·6 million sq. km. (3·8 million sq. miles).

Population: official figures (including Taiwan) is 975,230,000.[154] The provincial estimates in Table 7.1 give a figure of about 850 million.

Population distribution: 15 per cent urban, 85 per cent rural.

Membership of the CPC (1979): 37 million[155] (4 per cent of population).

Ethnic nationalities: there are over 50 officially recognised national minorities, which together constitute 6 per cent of the population. The most numerous are the Chuang, Hui, Uighur, Yi, Tibetan, Miao, Manchu, Mongolian, Puyi and Korean.

Rail network (1978): 50,000 km.

Road network (1978): 890,000 km.

Foreign relations: diplomatic relations with over 118 countries; member of the UN (between 1949 and 1971 the Chinese seat at the UN was occupied by Taiwan).

The economy[156]

Natural calamities and the policies of the 'Gang of Four' are said to have resulted in a poor production record in 1976. Since that time scholars have debated the possible impact of these factors and have come up with varying estimates. The following are official (1979) figures.[157]

	1977	1978	Plan[158]
Grain (million tonnes)	283	305	400 by 1985
Agricultural growth	4% (est.)	9%	4·5% p.a. to 1985
Coal (million tonnes)	550	618	
Steel (million tonnes)	24	32	60 by 1985
Crude oil (million tonnes)	94	104	
Industrial growth	11–12% (est.)	14%	10% p.a. to 1985

GNP (est. 1978) $300–400 thousand million
GNP per capita (est. 1978) $300–400
Trade balance: 1974–$1230 million deficit
             1975– $835 million deficit
             1976– $696 million surplus
             1977–$1000 million surplus
             1978–$1300 million deficit

For a discussion of changes in economic strategy, together with details of the current plan, see earlier.

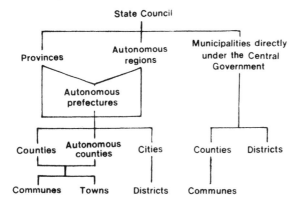

FIGURE 7.3 Local organs of state administration, 1979.

NOTES

1. The following is based on B. Brugger, *Contemporary China* (1977).
2. A number of good introductory histories exist for the period 1921–42. On the career of Mao Tse-tung, see S. Schram, *Mao Tse-tung* (1966); J. Ch'en, *Mao and the Chinese Revolution* (1965); B. Schwartz, *Chinese Communism and the Rise of Mao* (1966); E. Snow, *Red Star Over China* (1961). On the early years of the Party, see J. Guillermaz, *A History of the Chinese Communist Party 1921–1949* (1972); M. Meisner, *Li Ta-chao and the Origins of Chinese Marxism* (1967); and Schwartz, *Chinese Communism.* On the Kiangsi Soviet, see J. Rue, *Mao Tse-tung in Opposition 1927–1935* (1966); S. Swarup, *A Study of the Chinese Communist Movement* (1966); D. Waller, *The Kiangsi Soviet Republic: Mao and the National Congresses of 1931 and 1934* (1973). A useful collection of excerpts from various writings is H. F. Schurmann and O. Schell, *China Readings 2, Republican China* (1968).
3. See R. North, *Moscow and Chinese Communists* (1963), and H. Isaacs, *The Tragedy of the Chinese Revolution* (1966).
4. For a historical survey of the united front from the 1920s to the 1950s, see L. Van Slyke, *Enemies and Friends: The United Front in Chinese Communist History* (1967).
5. On Mao's theories of People's War, see Mao Tse-tung, *Selected Military Writings* (1966); M. Elliott Bateman, *Defeat in the East: The Mark of Mao Tse-tung on War* (1967); J. Girling, *People's War* (1969) pp. 49–109; and Lin Piao, *Long Live the Victory of People's War* (1965).
6. The description of Yenan given here is taken from M. Selden, *The Yenan Way in Revolutionary China* (1971).

7. See Mao Tse-tung, Jan 1940, in *Selected Works*, vol. II (1965) pp. 339–84.
8. H. F. Schurmann, *Ideology and Organization in Communist China* (1966) p. 236. This is the best work on leadership and organisation in contemporary China.
9. For a concise definition, see Mao Tse-tung, 1 June 1943, in *Selected Works*, vol. III (1965) p. 119.
10. P. Seybolt, 'The Yenan Revolution in Mass Education', *China Quarterly*, no. 48 (1971) 641–69.
11. Schurmann, *Ideology and Organization*, pp. 188–94.
12. As of 1946, landlords and rich peasants were classified as 'the enemy'.
13. For a gripping account of land reform, see W. Hinton, *Fanshen: A Documentary of Revolution in a Chinese Village* (1966).
14. K. Lieberthal, 'Mao versus Liu? Policy towards Industry and Commerce' *China Quarterly*, no. 47 (1971) 509–12.
15. J. Gittings, *The Role of the Chinese Army* (1967) p. 19.
16. Mao Tse-tung, *Selected Works*, vol. IV (1961) pp. 411–24.
17. These documents are discussed in D. Waller, *The Government and Politics of Communist China* (1970) pp. 81–4. The most important document, 'The Common Programme', may be found in *Current Background*, no. 9 (21 Sep 1950).
18. For a discussion of the continuing role of these field armies, see W. Whitson, 'The Field Army in Chinese Communist Military Politics', *China Quarterly*, no. 37 (1969) 1–30.
19. It was said that as many as 90 per cent of the old administrative personnel were retained in Shanghai. On the process of takeover, see A. Barnett, *China on the Eve of Communist Takeover* (1963) p. 340; W. Brugger, *Democracy and Organisation in the Chinese Industrial Enterprise 1948–1953* (1976) pp. 74–5; E. Vogel, *Canton under Communism: Programs and Politics in a Provincial Capital 1949–1968* (1971) pp. 47–55; and Schurmann, *Ideology and Organization*, pp. 371–2.
20. See Liu Shao-ch'i, *Collected Works* (1969) vol. II, pp. 215–33.
21. See Brugger, *Democracy and Organisation*, pp. 217–52.
22. *The Marriage Law of the People's Republic of China* (1950).
23. See Vogel, *Canton under Communism* pp. 61–2.
24. Brugger, *Contemporary China*, pp. 61–2.
25. Brugger, *Democracy and Organisation*, pp. 92–5.
26. See p. Harper, 'The Party and the Unions in Communist China', *China Quarterly*, no. 37 (1969) 89–99.
27. Gittings, *The Role of the Chinese Army*, p. 27. On China's perception of events in Korea, see E. Friedman, 'Problems of Dealing with an Irrational Power: America Declares War on China', in E. Friedman and M. Selden (eds), *America's Asia: Dissenting Essays on Asian–American Relations* (1971) pp. 207–52.
28. Gittings, *The Role of the Chinese Army*, pp. 26–7.
29. Mao Tse-tung, *Selected Works*, vol. IV, p. 415.
30. Stalin apparently thought of Mao as another Tito until the Korean War. See Mao Tse-tung, in S. Schram (ed.), *Mao Tse-tung Unrehearsed* (1974) p. 191.
31. On China's decision to intervene in Korea, see A. Whiting, *China Crosses*

the Yalu: The Decision to Enter the Korean War (1968).
32. Discussed in Brugger, *Contemporary China*, pp. 73–82.
33. Ibid., pp. 84–6.
34. See. J. Gardner, 'The Wu-fan Campaign in Shanghai: A Study in the Consolidation of Urban Control', in A. Barnett (ed.), *Chinese Communist Politics in Action* (1969) pp. 477–539.
35. For accounts of the Soviet model, see Schrumann, *Ideology and Organization*, and Brugger *Democracy and Organisation*.
36. Text of treaty in *Current Background*, no. 62 (5 Mar 1951).
37. Gittings, *The Role of the Chinese Army*, pp. 117–18, on the Soviet model in the Army.
38. Schurmann, *Ideology and Organization*, pp. 438–9.
39. Ibid., pp. 444–5.
40. Ibid., pp. 374–80.
41. *The Electoral Law of the People's Republic of China* (1953).
42. See W. Chai, *Essential Works of Chinese Communism* (1970) pp. 343–5.
43. For an interesting discussion of this problem, see Schurmann, *Ideology and Organization*, pp. 327–35.
44. Current work in progress by F. Teiwes challenges Schrumann's interpretation.
45. See *Constitution of the People's Republic of China* [20 Sep 1954] (1961).
46. The Chairman could, when necessary, convene a Supreme State Conference consisting of the Vice-chairman, the Chairman of the Standing Committee of the National People's Congress and the Premier.
47. This term was coined by Benjamin Schwartz.
48. Discussed in Vogel, *Canton under Communism*, pp. 135–8, and Brugger, *Contemporary China*, pp. 111–13.
49. See T. Bernstein, 'Cadre and Peasant Behaviour under Conditions of Insecurity and Deprivation: The Grain Supply Crisis of the Spring of 1955', in Barnett, *Chinese Communist Politics in Action*, pp. 365–99.
50. Mao Tse-tung, 31 July 1955, in *Selected Works*, vol. v (1977) pp. 184–207.
51. See *A Miscellany of Mao Tsetung Thought* (20 Feb 1974) p. 16.
52. Schurmann, *Ideology and Organization*, pp. 453–5.
53. For a comparison of the two campaigns, see T. Bernstein, 'Leadership and Mass Mobilisation in the Soviet and Chinese Collectivisation Campaigns of 1929–30 and 1955–56: A Comparison', *China Quarterly*, no. 31 (1967) 1–47.
54. A good survey of the socialisation of industry and commerce may be found in Vogel, *Canton under Communism*, pp. 156–73.
55. Gittings, *The Role of the Chinese Army*, pp. 158–75.
56. See R. Bowie and J. Fairbank, *Communist China 1955–1959: Policy Documents with Analysis* (1965) pp. 144–51.
57. See, for example, Mao Tse-tung, 8 Dec 1956, in Schram, *Mao Unrehearsed*, p. 40, and Jan 1957, ibid., pp. 49–50.
58. It was officially abolished at the Eighth Party Congress. See Li Hsüeh-feng, in *Eighth National Congress of the Communist Party of China* (1956) vol. II, p. 306.
59. Mao's original call for 'blooming and contending' was put forward in

April 1956. See *A Miscellany of Mao Thought*, p. 33. The slogan dates from the early 1950s, though at that time it applied only to literature.

60. See Schurmann, *Ideology and Organization*, pp. 457–64.
61. See *Eighth National Congress*.
62. At the Afro-Asian Conference of heads of government held in Bandung, Indonesia, in April 1955, Premier Chou En-lai played a major role in forging 'five principles of peaceful co-existence', which became the theoretical basis of China's policy towards non-imperialist states. They were: (1) mutual respect for sovereignty and territorial integrity; (2) mutual non-aggression; (3) non-interference in each other's internal affairs; (4) equality and mutual benefit; and (5) peaceful co-existence. China's future disagreement with the Soviet Union rested on the perception that the Soviet government was applying the principle of peaceful co-existence to imperialist states.
63. On the possibility of war between the mainland and Taiwan in 1954, see H. Hinton, *Communist China in World Politics* (1966) pp. 260–2.
64. The best summary of the 'Hundred Flowers' movement may be found in R. Solomon, *Mao's Revolution and the Chinese Political Culture* (1971) pp. 268–329.
65. See Mao Tse-tung, 27 Feb 1957, in *Selected Works*, vol. V, pp. 384–421. The version here is somewhat watered down and was not published until after the 'Hundred Flowers' movement had been brought to an end. The original is unavailable.
66. Harper, in *China Quarterly*, no. 37, pp. 99–114.
67. Solomon, *Mao's Revolution*, pp. 319–22.
68. See R. Lee, 'The Hsia Fang System: Marxism and Modernisation', *China Quarterly*, no. 28 (1966) pp. 40–62.
69. This was coupled with the decentralisation of decision-making power *within* economic units. See S. Andors, 'Revolution and Modernization: Man and Machine in Industrializing Society, the Chinese Case', in Friedman and Selden, *America's Asia*, pp. 393–444.
70. See, for example, Vogel, *Canton under Communism*, pp. 233–5.
71. See, for example, Liu Shao-ch'i, in *Collected Works*, vol. II, p. 36.
72. Mao Tse-tung, 20 Mar 1958, in Schram, *Mao Unrehearsed*, p. 104.
73. The formal resolution governing the formation of communes (29 Aug 1958) may be found in *Documents of Chinese Communist Party Central Committee* (1971) pp. 299–304.

    The defence aspect covered the transformation of communes into large militia units under the slogan 'everyone a soldier'. The rebuilding of the militia began with the onset of a new Taiwan Straits crisis in 1958. It was increased when Soviet support for the Chinese position appeared only lukewarm. Sino-Soviet relations had deteriorated since the conclusion of a nuclear-sharing agreement in 1957. A Soviet request for the establishment of a joint naval command (under Soviet direction) was rejected and calls were made for institutions to be created capable of waging 'People's War'.
74. This is the view of W. Skinner, 'Marketing and Social Structure in Rural China: Pt III, *Journal of Asian Studies*, XXIV, no. 3 (May 1965) 363–99.
75. K. Walker, 'Organization of Agricultural Production', in A. Eckstein, W.

Galenson and Liu Ta-chung, *Economic Trends in Communist China* (1968) pp. 444–5.

76. See J. Salaff, 'The Urban Communes and Anti-City Experiment in Communist China', *China Quarterly*, no. 29 (1967) 82–109.

77. See Mao Tse-tung, 19 Dec 1958, in *A Miscellany of Mao Thought*, pp. 140–8, and the public resolution in *Documents of CPC Central Committee*, pp. 123–48.

78. Mao Tse-tung, 21 Feb 1959, in *A Miscellany of Mao Thought*, p. 161.

79. Before long, communes, brigades and teams were reduced in size, to roughly that of, respectively, the old *xiang*, the old higher-stage co-operative and the old lower-stage co-operative.

80. On the case of P'eng Teh-huai, see J. Simmonds, 'P'eng Te-huai: A Chronological Re-examination', *China Quarterly*, no. 37 (1969) pp. 120–38; and *The Case of P'eng Teh-huai* (1968) – a documentary collection.

81. Ibid., pp. 7–13.

82. The literature on the Tibetan rising is extremely partisan. For conflicting views, see A. Strong, *When Serfs Stood up in Tibet* (Peking: New World Press, 1965); and *Tibet and the Chinese People's Republic: A Report to the International Commission of Jurists by its Legal Inquiry Committee on Tibet* (1960).

83. After the replacement of US Secretary of State Dulles by Christian Herter in April 1959, Khrushchev moved once again towards detente with the United States, forgetting an earlier ultimatum on Berlin. The meeting between Khrushchev and Eisenhower at Camp David was felt to herald a new era of peaceful co-existence.

84. *Long Live Leninism* (1960).

85. The most famous clash was at the Third Congress of the Communist Party of Romania in late June. The withdrawal of aid was designed to bring China to heel. See J. Gittings, *Survey of the Sino-Soviet Dispute: A Commentary and Extracts from the Recent Polemics 1963–67* (1968) pp. 129–43.

86. See the discussion in *The Polemic on the General Line of the International Communist Movement* (1965) pp. 83–9; and D. Zagoria, *The Sino-Soviet Conflict 1956–61* (1966) pp. 367–8.

87. Significantly, in the months which followed, the Soviet press referred to 'Albania' when it meant China, and the Chinese press, for its part, referred to 'Yugoslavia' when it meant the Soviet Union.

88. A. Eckstein, 'Economic Growth and Change in China: A Twenty Year Perspective', *China Quarterly*, no. 54 (1973) 216.

89. See Vogel, *Canton under Communism*, pp. 266–8.

90. See Schurmann, *Ideology and Organization*, pp. 399–402.

91. This is the view of Walker, in Eckstein *et al.*, *Economic Trends*, pp. 444–5.

92. See J. Robinson, *The Cultural Revolution in China* (1969), p. 35.

93. *Selections from China Mainland Magazines*, no. 652 (28 Apr 1969) pp. 25 and 27.

94. Peasants were officially allowed to derive 20 per cent of their income from this source, though the actual figure was often higher.

95. For Mao's note, see *Peking Review*, 1 Apr 1977, pp. 3–4. For details, see *Peking Review*, 3 Apr 1970, p. 11, and 17 Apr 1970, p. 3.

96. Discussed in J. Pusey, *Wu Han: Attacking the Present through the Past* (1969).
97. See M. Goldman, 'The Unique "Blooming and Contending" of 1961–62', *China Quarterly*, no. 37 (1969) 54–83.
98. Discussed in Gittings, *The Role of the Chinese Army*, pp. 248–9.
99. Mao Tse-tung, 30 Jan 1962, in Schram, *Mao Unrehearsed*, p. 168. See the discussion in G. Young and D. Woodward, 'From Contradictions among the People to Class Struggle: The Theorie of Uninterrupted Revolution and Continuous Revolution', *Asian Survey*, Sep 1978, 912–33.
100. Mao's remarks in the early 1960s are somewhat contradictory, and I may have read too much into them. Suffice it to say that it was this rethink of 1960–2 which led Mao to seek to return to the 'front line' once the economy had improved and to propagate the idea of carrying out class struggle.
101. Mao Tse-tung, 24 Sep 1962, in Schram, *Mao Unrehearsed*, pp. 188–96.
102. Text in R. Baum and F. Teiwes, *Ssu-Ch'ing: The Socialist Education Movement of 1962–1966* (1968) pp. 58–71.
103. Text ibid., pp. 72–94.
104. Mao Tse-tung, *Quotations from Chairman Mao Tse-tung* (1966).
105. This provides the substance of *The Polemic on the General Line of the International Communist Movement*.
106. For an interesting account of the different theoretical perspectives on Chinese foreign policy, see J. Peck, 'Why China "Turned West" ', *Socialist Register*, 1972, pp. 289–306.
107. As Mayor of Peking, P'eng Chen had been implicated in the satirisation of the Great Leap in the early 1960s and there has been much speculation as to why he was chosen for the post. Was this the conservative response to Mao's radical programme or was P'eng being set up for future denunciation? Whatever the reason for his appointment, little was achieved.
108. See D. Munro, 'The Yang Hsien-chen Affair', *China Quarterly*, no. 22 (1965) 75–82.
109. I. e. policies based on a theory of socialist market relations. These were heavily criticised during the Cultural Revolution.
110. See the discussion by J. Gray, 'The Two Roads: Alternative Strategies of Social Change and Economic Growth in China', in S. Schram (ed.), *Authority, Participation and Cultural Change in China* (1973) p. 145.
111. *Polemic*, pp. 417–80. This essay has been attributed to Mao.
112. See Baum and Teiwes, *Ssu-Ch'ing*, pp. 118–26; also attributed to Mao.
113. For an interesting discussion of the strategic debate, see M. Yahuda, 'Kremlinology and the Chinese Strategic Debate 1965–6', *China Quarterly*, no. 49 (1972) 32–75.
114. Lo Jui-ch'ing, *Peking Review*, 14 May 1965, pp. 7–15.
115. Lin Piao, *Peking Review*, 3 Sep 1965, pp. 9–30.
116. For a survey of the Cultural Revolution, see J. Esmein, *The Chinese Cultural Revolution* (1973). See also J. Daubier, *A History of the Chinese Cultural Revolution* (1974); D. and N. Milton, *The Wind Will Not Subside*, (1976); J. Robinson, *Cultural Revolution*; T. Robinson (ed.), *The Cultural Revolution in China* (1971); G. Bennett and R. Montaperto, *Red Guard:*

The Political Biography of Dai Hsiao-ai (1971) and N. Hunter, *Shanghai Journal* (1969).

117. See the account in Bennett and Montaperto, *Red Guard*, pp. 74–88.
118. See J. Starr, 'Revolution in Retrospect: The Paris Commune through Chinese Eyes', *China Quarterly*, no. 49 (1972) 106–25.
119. See K. Mehnert, *Peking and the New Left: At Home and Abroad* (1969).
120. See W. Hinton, *Hundred Day War: The Cultural Revolution at Tsinghua University* (1972).
121. See J. Salaff, 'Urban Residential Communities in the Wake of the Cultural Revolution', in J. Lewis (ed.), *The City in Communist China* (1971) pp. 289–323.
122. This view is reflected by J. Robinson (in *Cultural Revolution*). R. Rossanda challenges her but perhaps reads more into the Cultural Revolution material than is actually there; for all that, Rossanda's analysis is quite stimulating. See R. Rossanda, 'Mao's Marxism', *Socialist Register*, 1971, pp. 53–80.
123. *Peking Review*, 1 Nov 1968, supplement.
124. *Peking Review*, 30 Apr 1969, pp. 36–9.
125. See J. Domes, *The Internal Politics of China 1949–1972* (1973).
126. See G. Young, 'Party Building and the Search for Unity', in B. Brugger (ed.), *China: The Impact of the Cultural Revolution* (1978) pp. 35–70.
127. See J. Sigurdson, 'Rural Industry and the Internal Transfer of Technology', in Schram, *Authority, Participation*, pp. 199–232.
128. See G. O'Leary, 'Chinese Foreign Policy – From "Anti-imperialism" to "Anti-hegemonism"', in Brugger, *China: Impact*, pp. 203–52.
129. See J. van Ginnekan, *The Rise and Fall of Lin Piao* (1976); D. Woodward, 'Political Power and Gun Barrels – the Role of the PLA', in Brugger, *China: Impact*; W. Burchett, 'Lin Piao's Plot – the Full Story', *Far Eastern Economic Review*, 20 Aug 1973; R. Powell, 'The Military and the Struggle for Power in China', *Current History*, LXIII, no. 373 (Sep 1972); P. Bridgham, 'The Fall of Lin Piao', *China Quarterly*, no. 55 (1973) pp. 427–49.
130. For Mao's views on the cult in December 1970, see E. Snow, *The Long Revolution* (1972) pp. 169–70.
131. The '571 Engineering Outline' may be found in *Issues and Studies*, VIII, no. 5 (May 1972) pp. 78–83. Here Mao was referred to by the codename 'B-52' because of his alleged fondness for dropping bombs.
132. The most remarkable example of this genre which I have seen has been translated in *Current Background*, no. 894 (27 Oct 1969). This extravagant praise extended into 1971; see Bridgham, in *China Quarterly*, no. 55, p. 437.
133. See A. Watson, 'Industrial Management – Experiments in Mass Participation', in Brugger, *China: Impact*, pp. 171–202.
134. See M. Meisner, 'Dazhai: The Mass Line in Practice', *Modern China*, IV, no. 1 (Jan 1978) 27–62.
135. See S. Chan, 'Revolution in Higher Education', in Brugger, *China: Impact*, pp. 95–125.
136. See Brugger, ibid., pp. 256–76.
137. See *Selected Articles Criticizing Lin Piao and Confucius* (1974); R. Price (ed.), *The Anti Confucius Campaign in China* (1977); M. Goldman, 'China's

Anti-Confucian Campaign 1973–74', *China Quarterly*, no. 63 (1975) 435–62.

138. Chang Ch'un-ch'iao, 13 Jan 1975, in *Peking Review*, 24 Jan 1975, pp. 18–20. For the Constitution, see ibid, pp. 12–17.
139. Yao Wen-yüan, in *Peking Review*, 7 Mar 1975, pp. 5–10; Chang Ch'un-ch'iao, in *Peking Review*, 4 Apr 1975, pp. 5–11.
140. For a summary of these, see J. Gittings, 'New Material on Teng Hsiao-p'ing', *China Quarterly*, no. 67 (1976) 489–93. For full texts of three of these (the 'three poisonous weeds'), see *Issues and Studies*, XIII, no. 7 (July 1977) 90–113, and comment in no. 9 (Sep 1977) 77–9; no. 8 (Aug 1977) 77–99; and no. 9 (Sep 1977) 63–70.
141. See section on the economy, preceding these notes.
142. Hua Kuo-feng, 26 Feb 1978, in Peking Foreign Languages Press, *Documents of the First Session of the Fifth National People's Congress of the People's Republic of China* (1978) p. 39.
143. Twelve key areas for grain production have been designated and it is estimated that 85 per cent of the whole rural area will be mechanised by 1985 (though we do not know the degree of mechanisation implied by this figure). By the end of the ten-year plan, it is anticipated that, for each member of the rural population there will be one *mu* (one-fifteenth of a hectare) of farmland, with guaranteed high stable yields, irrespective of flood or drought.
144. 120 large-scale projects are planned, including ten iron and steel complexes, nine non-ferrous metal complexes, eight coal mines, ten oil and gas fields, thirty power stations, six trunk railways and five major harbours.
145. Hu Ch'iao-mu, *Peking Review*, 10 Nov 1978, pp. 7–12; 17 Nov 1978, pp. 15–23; 24 Nov 1978.
146. Text in B. Szajkowski (ed.), *Documents in Communist Affairs – 1979* (1979) pp. 99–113.
147. The First Plenum of the Central Committee elected a Chairman, Vice-chairmen and a Political Bureau. Hua Kuo-feng was elected Chairman, and the vice-chairmen elected were Yeh Chien-ying, Teng Hsiao-p'ing, Li Hsien-nien and Wang Tung-hsing. These together constituted the Political Bureau Standing Committee. Other members of the Political Bureau were Wei Kuo-ch'ing, Ulanfu, Fang Yi, Liu Po-ch'eng, Hsü Shih-yu, Chi Tengk'uei, Su Chen-hua, Li Hsien-nien, Li Teh-sheng, Wu Teh, Yü Ch'iu-li, Chang Ting-fa, Ch'en Yung-kuei, Ch'en Hsi-lien, Keng Piao, Nieh Jungchen, Ni Chih-fu, Hsü Hsiang-ch'ien and P'eng Ch'ung. There were three alternates: Ch'en Mu-hua (the only woman), Chao Tzu-yang and Saifudin.
148. Text in Szajkowski, *Documents – 1979*.
149. The following were the important posts (1978).

Premier: Hua Kuo-feng.
Vice-premiers: Teng Hsiao-p'ing, Li Hsien-nien, Hsu Hsiang-ch'ien, Chi Teng-k'uei, Yü Ch'iu-li, Ch'en Hsi-lien, Keng Piao, Ch'en Yung-kuei, Fang Yi, Wang Chen, Ku Mu, K'ang Shih-en, Ch'en Mu-hua.
Minister of Foreign Affairs: Huang Hua.
Minister of National Defence: Hsü Hsiang-ch'ien.

Minister in Charge of the State Planning Commission: Yü Ch'iu-li.
Minister in Charge of the State Economic Commission: K'ang Shih-en.
Minister in Charge of the State Capital Construction Commission: Ku
  Mu.
Minister in Charge of the State Scientific and Technological Commission:
  Fang Yi.
Minister in Charge of the State Nationalities Affairs Commission: Yang
  Ching-jen.
Minister of Public Security: Chao Ts'ang-pi.
Minister of Civil Affairs: Ch'eng Tzu-hua.
Minister of Foreign Trade: Li Ch'iang.
Minister of Economic Relations with Foreign Countries: Ch'en Mu-hua.
Minister of Agriculture and Forestry: Yang Li-kung.
Minister of Metallurgical Industry: T'ang K'e.
Minister of First Ministry of Machine Building: Chou Tzu-chien.
Ministry of Second Ministry of Machine Building: Liu Wei.
Ministry of Third Ministry of Machine Building: Lü Tung.
Ministry of Fourth Ministry of Machine Building: Wang Cheng.
Ministry of Fifth Ministry of Machine Building: Chang Chen.
Ministry of Sixth Ministry of Machine Building: Ch'ai Shu-fan.
Ministry of Seventh Ministry of Machine Building: Sung Jen-ch'iung.
Ministry of Coal Industry: Hsiao Han.
Minister of Petroleum Ministry: Sung Chen-ming.
Minister of Chemical Industry: Sun Ching-wen.
Minister of Water Conservancy and Power: Ch'ien Cheng-ying.
Minister of Textile Industry: Ch'ien Chih-kuang.
Minister of Light Industry: Liang Ling-kuang.
Minister of Railways: Tuan Chun-yi.
Minister of Communications: Yeh Fei.
Minister of Posts and Telecommunications: Chung Fu-hsiang.
Minister of Finance: Chang Ching-fu.
President of the People's Bank of China: Li Pao-hua.
Minister of Commerce: Wang Lei.
Director of the All China Federation of Supply and Marketing Co-
  operatives: Ch'en Kuo-tung.
Minister of Culture: Huang Chen.
Minister of Education: Liu Hsi-yao.
Minister of Public Health: Chiang Yi-chen.
Minister in Charge of the State Physical Culture and Sports Commission:
  Wang Meng.

150. Kuo died in 1978.
151. Mass organisations include such bodies as the Communist Youth League,
  the All China Federation of Trade Unions and the All China Women's
  Federation. On the reactivation of these bodies, see *Peking Review*, 19 May
  1978, pp. 10–13. In the 1950s, a number of minor political parties which
  had supported the Communist Party in the Civil War continued to exist,
  but not much was heard about them after the Cultural Revolution.
  Attempts were also made after 1949 to form national religious bodies

(Buddhist, Christian, and so on). Both the minor parties and the religious bodies were revived in 1979 and participated in the revived Chinese People's Political Consultative Conference.

152. Data from International Institute for Strategic Studies, *The Military Balance 1977–78* (London, 1977) pp. 52–4.

153. Divisions are grouped into some forty armies (usually consisting of three infantry divisions, three regiments of artillery and sometimes three armoured regiments).

154. 1978 official figure. For a recent discussion of estimates of China's population, see L. Orleans, 'China's Population Growth: Another Perspective', *Current Scene*, XVI, nos 2–3 (Jan–Mar 1978) 1–24.

155. Figures presented at the Eleventh National Congress of the Party. Press communiqué, 18 Aug 1977, in *The Eleventh National Congress of the CPC (Documents)* (1977) p. 200.

156. Introductions to the Chinese economy include A. Eckstein. *China's Economic Revolution* (1977), and E. Wheelwright and B. McFarlane, *The Chinese Road to Socialism* (1970).

157. Based on official statistics, presented by Yü Chiu-li to the Second Session of the Fifth National People's Congress, June 1979. See State Statistical Bureau 'Communique on Fulfillment of China's 1978 National Economic Plan', 27 June 1979.

158. Outlined by Hua Kuo-feng, 26 Feb 1978, in *Documents of the First Session of the Fifth National People's Congress of the People's Republic of China* (1978) pp. 38–9.

BIBLIOGRAPHY

Andors, S., *China's Industrial Revolution, Politics, Planning and Management, 1949 to the Present* (New York: Pantheon, 1977).

Barnett, A., *China on the Eve of Communist Takeover* (New York: Praeger, 1963).

—— (ed.), *Chinese Communist Politics in Action* (Seattle: University of Washington Press, 1969).

Bateman M. Elliot, *Defeat in the East: The Mark of Mao Tse-tung on War* (London: Oxford University Press, 1967).

Baum, R., *Prelude to Revolution: Mao, the Party and the Peasant Question* (New York: Columbia University Press, 1975).

Baum, R. and Teiwes, F., *Ssu-Ch'ing: The Socialist Education Movement of 1962–1966* (Berkeley, Calif.: University of California, Center for Chinese Studies, 1968).

Bennett, G. and Montaperto, R., *Red Guard: The Political Biography of Dai Hsiao-ai* (New York: Doubleday, 1971).

Bernstein, T., 'Leadership and Mass Mobilisation in the Soviet and Chinese Collectivisation Campaigns of 1929–30 and 1955–56: A Comparison', *China Quarterly*, no. 31 (1967) 1–47.

Bettelheim, C., *Cultural Revolution and Industrial Organization in China* (New York: Monthly Review Press, 1974).

Bowie, R. and Fairbank, J., *Communist China 1955–1959: Policy Documents with Analysis* (Cambridge Mass.: Harvard University Press, 1965).

Bridgham, P., 'The Fall of Lin Piao', *China Quarterly*, no. 55 (1973) 427–49.

Brugger, B., *Contemporary China* (London: Croom Helm, 1977).

——, *China: The Impact of the Cultural Revolution* (London: Croom Helm, 1978).

Brugger, W. (B.), *Democracy and Organisation in the Chinese Industrial Enterprise 1948–1953* (Cambridge: Cambridge University Press, 1976).

Burchett, W., 'Lin Piao's Plot – the Full Story', *Far Eastern Economic Review*, 20 Aug 1973.

The Case of P'eng Teh-huai (Hong Kong: Union Research Institute, 1968).

Chai, W., *Essential Works of Chinese Communism* (New York: Pica Press, 1970).

Chang, P., *Power and Policy in China* (London: The Pennsylvania State University Press, 1975).

Chao Kuo-chün, *Economic Planning and Organization in Mainland China: A Documentary Study (1949–1957)* (Cambridge, Mass.: Harvard University, East Asian Research Center, 1963) 2 vols.

Chen, C. and Ridley, C., *Rural People's Communes in Lien-chiang: Documents Concerning Communes in Lien-chiang County, Fukien Province 1962–1963* (Stanford, Calif.: Hoover Institution Press, 1969).

Ch'en, J., *Mao and the Chinese Revolution* (London: Oxford University Press, 1965).

Constitution of the People's Republic of China (Peking: Foreign Languages Press, 1961).

Daubier, J., *A History of the Chinese Cultural Revolution* (New York: Vintage Books, 1974).

Davin, D., *Women-work: Women and the Party in Revolutionary China* (Oxford: Clarendon Press, 1976).

Dittmer, L., *Liu Shao-ch'i and the Chinese Cultural Revolution: The Politics of Mass Criticism* (Berkeley, Calif.: University of California Press, 1974).

Documents of Chinese Communist Party Central Committee (Hong Kong: Union Research Institute, 1971).

Documents of the First Session of the Fifth National People's Congress of the People's Republic of China (Peking: Foreign Languages Press, 1978).

Domes, J., *The Internal Politics of China 1949–1972* (London: Hurst, 1973).

Donnithorne, A., *China's Economic System* (London: George Allen and Unwin, 1967).

Dreyer, J., *China's Forty Millions: Minority Nationalities and National Integration in the People's Republic of China* (Cambridge, Mass.: Harvard University Press, 1976).

Eckstein, A., 'Economic Growth and Change in China: A Twenty Year Perspective', *China Quarterly*, no. 54 (1973) 211–41.

——, *China's Economic Revolution* (Cambridge: Cambridge University Press, 1977).

Eckstein, A., Galenson, W. and Liu Ta-chung, *Economic Trends in Communist China* (Edinburgh: Edinburgh University Press, 1968).

Eighth National Congress of the Communist Party of China (Peking: Foreign Languages Press, 1956) 3 vols.

The Electoral Law of the People's Republic of China (Peking: Foreign Languages Press, 1953).

The Eleventh National Congress of the Communist Party of China (Documents) (Peking: Foreign Languages Press, 1977).

Esmein, J., *The Chinese Cultural Revolution* (New York: Anchor Books, 1973).

Friedman, E. and Selden, M., (eds), *America's Asia: Dissenting Essays on Asian–American Relations* (New York: Vintage Books, 1971).

Ginnekan, J. van, *The Rise and Fall of Lin Piao* (Harmondsworth: Penguin, 1976).

Girling, J., *People's War* (London: George Allen and Unwin, 1969).

Gittings, J., *The Role of the Chinese Army* (London: Oxford University Press, 1967).

——, *Survey of the Sino-Soviet Dispute: A Commentary and Extracts from the Recent Polemics 1963–1967* (London: Oxford University Press, 1968).

——, *The World and China 1922–1972* (London: Eyre Methuen, 1974).

——, 'New Material on Teng Hsiao-P'ing', *China Quarterly*, no. 67 (1976) 489–93.

Goldman, M., 'The Unique "Blooming and Contending" of 1961–2', *China Quarterly*, no. 37 (1969) 54–83.

——, *Literary Dissent in Communist China*, (New York: Atheneum, 1971).

——, 'China's Anti-Confucian Campaign 1973–74', *China Quarterly*, no. 63 (1975) 435–62.

Gray, J. (ed.), *Modern China's Search for a Political Form* (London: Oxford University Press, 1969).

Guillermaz, J., *A History of the Chinese Communist party 1921–1949* (London: Eyre Methuen, 1972).

——, *The Chinese Communist Party in Power* (Boulder, Col.: Westview Press, 1976).

Harper, P., 'The Party and the Unions in Communist China', *China Quarterly*, no. 37 (1969) 84–119.

Hinton, H., *Communist China in World Politics* (London: Macmillan, 1966).

Hinton, W., *Fanshen: A Documentary of Revolution in a Chinese Village* (New York: Vintage Books, 1966).

——, *Hundred Day War: The Cultural Revolution at Tsinghua University* (New York: Monthly Review Press, 1972).

Hoffman, C., *The Chinese Worker* (Albany, N.Y.: State University of New York Press, 1974).

Howe, C., *Employment and Economic Growth in Urban China 1949–1957* (Cambridge: Cambridge University Press, 1973).

——, *Wage Patterns and Wage Policy in Modern China 1919–72* (Cambridge: Cambridge University Press, 1973).

Hunter, N., *Shanghai Journal* (New York: Praeger, 1969).

Isaacs, H., *The Tragedy of the Chinese Revolution* (Stanford, Calif.: Stanford University Press, 1966).

Klein, D. and Clark, A., *Biographic Dictionary of Chinese Communism 1921–1965* (Cambridge, Mass.: Harvard University Press, 1971).

Lee, D., 'The Hsia Fang System: Marxism and Modernisation', *China Quarterly*, no. 28 (1966) 40–62.

Lewis, J., (ed.), *The City in Communist China* (Stanford, Calif.: Stanford University Press, 1971).

Lieberthal, K., 'Mao versus Liu? Policy towards Industry and Commerce', *China Quarterly*, no. 47 (1971) 494–520.

Lin Piao, *Long Live the Victory of People's War* (Peking: Foreign Languages Press, 1965).

Liu Shao-ch'i, *Collected Works* (Hong Kong: Union Research Institute, 1969) 3 vols.

Long Live Leninism (Peking: Foreign Languages Press, 1960).

Macciocchi, M., *Daily Life in Revolutionary China* (New York: Monthly Review Press, 1972).

MacDougall, C., 'The Chinese Economy in 1976', *China Quarterly*, no. 70 (1977) 355–70.

MacFarquhar, R., *Contradictions among the People, 1956–1957* (New York: Columbia University Press, 1974).

Maitan, L., *Party, Army and Masses in China* (London: New Left Books, 1976).

Mao Tse-tung *Quotations from Chairman Mao Tse-tung* (Peking: Foreign Languages Press, 1966).

——, *Selected Military Writings* (Peking: Foreign Languages Press, 1966).

——,*Selected Works* (Peking: Foreign Languages Press, 1965 [vols. I–III], 1961 [vol. IV] and 1977 [vol. V]) 5 vols.

The Marriage Law of the People's Republic of China (Peking: Foreign Languages Press, 1950).

Mehnert, K., *Peking and the New Left: At Home and Abroad* (Berkeley, Calif.: University of California, Center for Chinese Studies, 1969).

Meisner, M., *Li Ta-chao and the Origins of Chinese Marxism* (Cambridge, Mass., Harvard University Press, 1967).

Meisner, M., 'Dazhai: The Mass Line in Practice', *Modern China*, IV, no. 1 (Jan 1978) 27–62.

Milton, D. and N., *The Wind will Not Subside* (New York: Pantheon, 1976).

A Miscellany of Mao Tse-tung Thought, Joint Publications Research Service, no. 61269–1 (20 Feb 1974).

Moseley, G., *The Party and the National Question in China* (Cambridge, Mass.: MIT Press, 1966).

Munro, D., 'The Yang Hsien-chen Affair', *China Quarterly*, no. 22 (1965) 75–82.

Nee, V. and Peck J. (eds), *China's Uninterrupted Revolution* (New York: Pantheon, 1975).

North, R., *Moscow and Chinese Communists* (Stanford, Calif.: Stanford University Press, 1963).

Orleans, L., 'China's Population Growth: Another Perspective', *Current Scene*, XVI, nos 2–3 (Jan–Mar 1978) 1–24.

Peck, J., 'Why China "Turned West"', *Socialist Register*, 1972, pp. 289–306.

The Polemic on the General Line of the International Communist Movement (Peking: Foreign Languages Press, 1965).

Powell, R., 'The Military and the Struggle for Power in China', *Current History*, LXIII, no. 373 (Sep 1972).

Price, R., *Education in Communist China* (London: Routledge and Kegan Paul, 1970).

—— (ed.), *The Anti Confucius Campaign in China* (Melbourne: Latrobe University, 1977).

Pusey, J., *Wu Han: Attacking the Present through the Past* (Cambridge, Mass.: Harvard University Press, 1969).

Rice, E., *Mao's Way* (Berkeley, Calif.: University of California Press, 1972).

Richman, B., *Industrial Society in Communist China* (New York: Random House, 1969).

Robinson, J., *The Cultural Revolution in China* (Harmondsworth: Penguin, 1969).

Robinson, T. (ed.), *The Cultural Revolution in China* (Berkeley, Calif.: University of California Press, 1971).

Rossanda, R., 'Mao's Marxism', *Socialist Register*, 1971, pp. 53–80.

Rue, I., *Mao Tse-tung in Opposition 1927–1935* (Stanford, Calif.: Stanford University Press, 1966).

Salaff, J., 'The Urban Communes and Anti-City Experiment in Communist China', *China Quarterly*, no. 29 (1967) pp. 82–109.

Scalapino, R. (ed.), *Elites in the People's Republic of China* (Seattle: University of Washington Press, 1972).

Schram, S., *Mao Tse-tung* (Harmondsworth: Peking, 1966).

——, *The Political Thought of Mao Tse-tung* (New York: Praeger, 1969).

—— (ed.), *Authority, Participation and Cultural Change in China* (Cambridge: Cambridge University Press, 1973).

—— (ed.), *Mao Tse-tung Unrehearsed*, (Harmondsworth: Penguin, 1974).

Schurmann, H. F., *Ideology and Organization in Communist China* (Berkeley, Calif.: University of California Press, 1966).

Schumann, H. F. and Schell, O., *China Readings 2, Republican China* (Harmondsworth: Penguin, 1968)

Schwartz, B., *Chinese Communism and the Rise of Mao* (Cambridge, Mass.: Harvard University Press, 1966).

Selden, M., *The Yenan Way in Revolutionary China* (Cambridge, Mass.: Harvard University Press, 1971).

Selected Articles Criticizing Lin Piao and Confucius (Peking: Foreign Languages Press, 1974).

Seybolt, P., 'The Yenan Revolution in Mass Education', *China Quarterly*, no. 48 (1971) 641–69.

Simmonds, J., 'P'eng Te-huai: A Chronological Re-examination', *China Quarterly*, no. 37 (1969) 120–38.

Skinner, W., 'Marketing and Social Structure in Rural China: Pt III', *Journal of Asian Studies*, XXIV, no. 3 (May 1965) 363–99.

Slyke, L. van, *Enemies and Friends: The United Front in Chinese Communist History* (Stanford, Calif.: Stanford University Press, 1967).

Snow, E., *The Long Revolution* (New York: Random House, 1971).

Solomon, R., *Mao's Revolution and the Chinese Political Culture* (Berkeley, Calif.: University of California Press, 1971).

Starr, J., 'Revolution in Retrospect: The Paris Commune through Chinese Eyes', *China Quarterly*, no. 49 (1972) 106–25.

——, *Ideology and Culture* (New York: Harper and Row, 1973).

Stavis, B., *Making Green Revolution: The Politics of Agricultural Development in China* (Ithaca, N.Y.: Cornell University, Rural Development Committee, 1974).

Strong, A., *When Serfs Stood up in Tibet* (Peking: New World Press, 1965).

Swarup, S., *A Study of the Chinese Communist Movement* (Oxford: Clarendon Press, 1966).

Szajkowski, B. (ed.), *Documents in Communist Affairs – 1979* (annual: 1977–9, Cardiff: University College Cardiff Press; 1980– , London: Macmillan).

Tibet and the Chinese People's Republic: A Report to the International Commission of Jurists by its Legal Inquiry Committee on Tibet (Geneva, 1960).

Townsend, J., *Politics in China* (Boston, Mass.: Little, Brown, 1974).

Vogel, E., *Canton under Communism: Programs and Politics in a Provincial Capital 1949–1968* (New York: Harper and Row, 1971).

Waller, D., *The Government and Politics of Communist China* (London: Hutchinson, 1970).

——, *The Kiangsi Soviet Republic: Mao and the National Congresses of 1931 and 1934* (Berkeley, Calif.: University of California, Center for Chinese Studies, 1973).

Watson, A., *Living in China* (London: Batsford, 1975).

Wang Gungwu, *China and the World since 1949* (London: Macmillan, 1977).

Wheelwright E. and McFarlane, B., *The Chinese Road to Socialism* (New York: Monthly Review Press, 1970).

Whiting, A., *China Crosses the Yalu: The Decision to Enter the Korean War* (Stanford, Calif.: Stanford University Press, 1968).

Whitson, W., 'The Field Army in Chinese Communist Military Politics', *China Quarterly*, no. 47 (1969) 1–30.

—— (ed.), *The Military and Political Power in China in the 1970s* (New York: Praeger, 1972).

Wilson, D. (ed.), *Mao Tse-tung in the Scales of History* (Cambridge: Cambridge University Press, 1977).

Witke, R., *Comrade Chiang Ch'ing* (Boston, Mass.: Little, Brown, 1977).

Wong, J., *Land Reform in the People's Republic of China: Institutional Transformation of Agriculture* (New York: Praeger, 1973).

Yahuda, M., 'Kremlinology and the Chinese Strategic Debate 1965–6', *China Quarterly*, no. 49 (1972) 32–75.

Young, G. and Woodward, D., 'From Contradictions among the People to Class Struggle: The Theorie of Uninterrupted Revolution and Continuous Revolution', *Asian Survey*, (Sep 1978) 912–33.

Zagoria, D., *The Sino-Soviet Conflict 1956–1961* (New York: Atheneum, 1966).

——, *Vietnam Triangle: Moscow, Peking, Hanoi* (New York: Pegasus, 1968).

8 People's Republic of the Congo

SAMUEL DECALO

Congo occupies an irregularly shaped territory of 342,000 sq. km. that straddles the equator, with a narrow 160 km. Atlantic littoral and 1000 km. of its long border with Zaire delineated by the Congo River. The territory rises from a narrow sandy plain to the forested Mayombé escarpment (altitude 500–600 metres), which is notable for its hydroelectric potential.[1] In the foothills are found large potash deposits[2] and valuable, though dwindling, timber resources. Further to the east is the fertile Niari valley (approximately 245,000 hectares), the centre of Congolese agriculture. The valley slopes northwards to the Chaillu massif (near the Gabon border), to the east of which is the poorly settled and infertile Batéké plateau. The north-eastern part of the country is part of the Congo basin, a region of dense equatorial forests, swamps and rivers, virtually uninhabited except for small population centres at its rim.

Communications in Congo have been, until very recently, poor to non-existent, except in the more populous areas of the south. The Congo–Ocean railway links Brazzaville with the Atlantic Ocean (at Pointe Noire) and serves as the main commercial artery for landlocked Chad and the Central African Empire.

Congo's small population of less than 1·5 million people is mostly concentrated in the southern part of the country. An unusually harsh French colonial rule, forced conscription with corvée labour, and Brazzaville's status as the capital of the French Equatorial Africa federation all contributed to the development of a major rural–urban exodus and the proletarianisation and radicalisation of the urban masses. Fully 35 per cent of the population live in urban centres; over 15 per cent in Brazzaville alone. Their demands for financial security through a position in the administration, and thirst for educational and

The Congo: provincial boundaries

social services, have created inexorable fiscal pressures (and a bloated, underworked bureaucracy) contributing to Congo's political volatility.

The country's main ethnic groups include the Vili along the coast, the Kongo (divided into several clans and numbering fully 45 per cent of the entire population) in the south, and the Téké, M'bochi and Sangha in the central and northern plateaux. Mutually hostile in the past, inter-ethnic strife, tensions and competitions have been carried into the modern era to form the backdrop to all political conflicts in Congo. An added dimension of this ongoing struggle for supremacy is the affiliation of many clans in the south to syncretic religious cults,[3] which have at various times had a major political impact and have sometimes led to bloody inter-ethnic clashes.

Economically Congo is one of Africa's more developed countries. It possesses a variety of exploitable minerals and ores (including petroleum and potash), a valuable although overexploited timber industry, and a growing processing and industrial sector, all of which place it among the continent's more industrialised states, with (for Africa) a relatively high per capita income. The economy is largely based upon the country's extractive resources, the exploitation of which has traditionally been in the hands of large expatriate concessionary combines. Notwithstanding the declaration for Marxism-Leninism in 1963 and of a People's Republic in 1968, many of the most profitable segments of the economy are still under private expatriate control, and the country remains beholden to France and public aid from the West. The inconsistencies and contradictions between, on the one hand, Congo's ideological militancy and vehemently radical rhetoric and, on the other, the country's continuing dependence on France have polarised society on yet another plane, adding the ideological element to the political tug-of-war that has made Congo Africa's most praetorian political system.[4]

BACKGROUND TO THE 1963 REVOLUTION

Congo emerged at independence under the leadership of the arch-conservative defrocked priest Foulbert Youlou, who, utilising his religious background and ethnic origins to gain the electoral support of the largest Bakongo clans, emerged victorious over the political leaders of the coastal Vili and the northern Kouyou-Mbochi. The intensity of the political contest (which had religious overtones among the Bakongo) and the politicisation of residual inter-ethnic animosities resulted in several hundred deaths in the volatile southern urban centres.

Youlou's administration was noteworthy for its laissez-faire rudderless economic policy, corruption, autocracy and reactionary foreign policy.[5] Openly supported by the French expatriate community in Brazzaville, Youlou rapidly alienated many of the core Bakongo groups that had helped him come to power. Unwilling and unable to stem spiralling urban unemployment, Youlou's policies directly contributed to the creation of a large, volatile and progressively radicalised unemployed proletariat.[6]

Profligate expenditures on prestige projects (a television station for less than 300 sets in the entire country) at a time of acute economic stress, the free reign given to expatriate concessionary interests with a record of crass exploitation,[7] undisguised disdain for youth and an overt renunciation of interest in northern Congo[8] all added to the boiling cauldron of grievances that were eventually to explode in the upheaval of August 1963.

The three days of rioting and urban demonstrations that finally dislodged Youlou – 'les trois glorieuses' of the present national hymn of Congo – were neither a revolution, as the subsequent regime was to claim, nor a classic-type coup by the minuscule armed forces. Youlou's plans to impose a one-party system on Congo, and the centralisation of the union movement into one federation, triggered existing grievances, which rapidly built up into urban demonstrations for his resignation. When the armed forces refused to prop up the regime and France's General de Gaulle turned down a plea for military assistance, Youlou's fate was sealed, and the army presided over the handover of power to Alphonse Massemba-Debat, who promptly declared Congo/Brazzaville a Marxist-Leninist state.[9] Since the collapse of Youlou and the orientation of the successor regime were not acclaimed by all strata in society – especially in traditional Bakongo areas and in the southern bureaucracy – periodic plots and commando assaults have been mounted either to return Youlou to power or to reverse the tide of the revolution.

CONGO SINCE THE REVOLUTION

The 1963 upheaval ushered in a dual-executive government headed by President Massemba-Debat, the former moderate socialist schoolteacher turned Speaker of the National Assembly.[10] Within months Massemba-Debat had achieved what had tripped Youlou – a one-party system, and the unification of all ancillary structures. A Marxist-

Leninist party, the Mouvement National de la Révolution (MNR) was set up in 1964, and with it a militant youth wing, the JMNR, which rapidly became extremely powerful and a potent threat to both government and armed forces alike. The first five-year Plan (1964–8) introduced central planning, a new State sector was created, and official rhetoric called for the total nationalisation of the means of production and the expulsion of the overwhelming French economic presence in the country.

Notwithstanding the radicalisation of rhetoric in Brazzaville, or the erection of the outward trappings of a socialist state, the civilian phase of the Congolese revolution (1963–8) in reality changed little of the country's core infrastructure.[11] The economy remained firmly in expatriate hands; new private capital was offered investment conditions more favourable than in 'capitalist' Ivory Coast,[12] and the small State sector became to all intents and purposes the province of sinecures and sources of corruption, which were to be a perpetual drain on Congo's scarce financial resources.

The political structures of the new regime provided power bases for competitive loyalty pyramids within the ruling elite, while the turn to the left and the demise of Youlou added further planes of division to the cleavage-ridden society. The rise to power of youth (a 'political-age class'[13]) in armed paramilitary formations, unruly and regarding themselves as the true guardians of the revolution, antagonised many while constituting a corporate threat to the army. The tensions between the military and the JMNR were finally resolved in an armed confrontation that the army won (August 1968). The formations were disarmed and reorganised, under tight military control, into the Union de la Jeunesse Socialiste Congolaise (UJSC), while some of the most militant elements were co-opted into the military hierarchy. Massemba-Debat was overthrown the same month, after his attempt to reassert his authority over the various factions and ambitious leaders had failed, and an attempted purge (for the second time) of the popular Major Marien Ngouabi resulted in an army mutiny.

Ngouabi's administration (1968–77) accelerated Congo's outward development into a Marxist state but did little about Congo's economic dependence upon France; nor did it bring about a redistribution of economic power domestically or soothe domestic strife. For all its radical rhetoric and Ngouabi's stress on ideological militancy and purity,[14] only the superficial, trivial and structural aspects of Marxism were superimposed on Congo. A new revolutionary party – the Parti Congolais du Travail (PCT), or Congolese Labour Party – was erected, a new constitution and red flag were adopted, and Congo was declared a People's Republic. Youth was organised under tighter control, a 'people's' militia was set up on Chinese lines as the security arm of the PCT, while 'bourgeois' or reactionary structures (i.e. the gendarmerie and the police) were disbanded. But, although the regime dramatically expanded its diplomatic network and was able to secure foreign aid from an incredible array of donors, it was only in 1975, following a major though brief windfall of oil profits, that it moved to nationalise several sectors of the economy.[15] The acute deficits piled up by the new State sector ('organised bungling', according to Ngouabi himself[16]) in the long run only deepened Congo's dependence upon French fiscal largesse. By 1976 the country had 'no resources to cover immediate Treasury needs';[17] the State sector had become a gigantic financial disability, with industries nationalised promptly losing their efficiency and profitability;[18] and the blame for this turn of events was placed squarely on the revolutionary party, the PCT.

As in the economic field, the political evolution of socialism in Congo has been full of pitfalls. Plots, attempted coups and acute jostling for influence buffeted the administration with regularity, whilst ethnic resistance to the northern-led regime multiplied in the south. Bitter ideological clashes – or personal power struggles camouflaged as a competition over socialist rectitude – continued erupting, polarising and destroying the unity of the Party, ancillary structures and armed forces. The handpicked vanguard party was twice minutely purged. In 1972 it practically disappeared in all but name, as its Political Bureau was reduced to three members, its Central Committee to five, and total membership to 160.[19] In a second bout of purges, in 1976, Ngouabi strongly denounced the entire Party membership, claiming that there were only seventeen members of the fifty members of the Central Committee who, 'while not perfect', were at least capable of carrying on the revolution;[20] the bulk of the PCT used 'Marxist phraseology only out of political opportunism' and were more concerned with a 'frantic race for material advantages'.[21] It was in the aftermath of the subsequent purges and the extraordinary PCT meeting of November 1976 that one of the periodic assaults on Ngouabi succeeded: he was killed by a suicide squad on 18 March 1977. Shortly later Masseba-Debat was unconvincingly accused of complicity and summarily executed, as well as a number of other leaders; the assassination is still clouded with mystery, however, and there is speculation that the true engineers of the crime are part of the governing elite.

The successor regime of General Yhombi-Opango lasted until 8

February 1979. As the most senior officer in the Armed Forces – who had saved Ngouabi from almost certain defeat at the time of the Diawara attempted coup in 1972 – Yhombi-Opango was able to assert his primacy but only for a short while. A well-known *bon vivant* and pro-Western by inclination, he had constantly been criticised as a re-actionary by student and unionist groups in Brazzaville.[22] Since he assumed power – bypassing constitutional procedures for the succession – neither his personal department, political appointments nor policies were supported by the militant members of the party, while the deepening economic crisis in the country – that he was unable to alleviate – eroded his remaining sources of *de facto* authority. Internal factional rivalries that he was unable to juggle as adroitly as Ngouabi finally sealed his fate and he was purged on 8 February 1979. At the subsequent Special Congress of the party in March he was accused of 'treason', arrested, and had his not inconsiderable personal property confiscated. (Among which was a recent acquisition – a $80,000 luxury vibrating bed.) The Congress ratified Colonel N'Guesso's primacy as President of the Republic, and Chairman of the Central Committee of the party. A close associate of Ngouabi, N'Guesso's elevation to power signified both a return to Ngouabi-style 'orthodoxy' and a move away from the over-concentration of power in the hands of the military faction of the party so visible under Yhombi-Opango.

The Congolese Labour Party (Parti Congolais du Travail)

The PCT was established on 31 December 1969 as a successor of the Mouvement National de la Révolution (MNR). In structure, ideology, organisation and membership it is an elitist party tightly under the control of its executive – the Central Committee and its Political Bureau.

Since its inception the PCT has had a very checkered history. Total membership has never been higher than 1600, composed of the key political personalities, administrators and militants in the country, many of whom have been largely passive and opportunistic members. The Party has always been sharply divided into factions supporting either its military or its civilian wing, its radical or its conservative faction, and its top intellectuals and leaders have been linked to different ideological variants of Marxism and have been supported and financed by different 'friendly' embassies in Brazzaville.

The supreme organ of the PCT is its congress, which meets in ordinary session every five years. Its fifty-man Central Committee meets three times a year, while the executive organ of the Party is the Political Bureau. The PCT has been convened for two extraordinary congresses (April 1970 and December 1972) in connection with crises arising from plots against the regime. In 1975 its membership was 1423, of whom 32 per cent were farmers, 12 per cent soldiers, 22 per cent 'revolutionary intellectuals' and 34 per cent workers. The Party has two specialised ancilliary organisations: the Union Révolutionnaire des Femmes Congolaises (URFC) and the Union de la Jeunesse socialiste congolaise (UJSC). A Party school has also been set up, with aid from the USSR.

The multiplicity of conflicting allegiances to differing ideologies and ethnic camps, and the membership's lukewarm support for the goals of the revolution brought about on two occasions the virtual destruction of the Party. In 1971–2 the PCT was truncated by massive purges that cut Party membership to 160.[23] A Party congress scheduled for 1974 was convened nearly two years earlier, in order to infuse new blood into the skeleton party, yet the hand-picked membership was itself found wanting in 1975–6 in another massive purge. So monumental were the criticisms levelled against the Party that Ngouabi suspended its organs, establishing instead a special Revolutionary General Staff as the supreme theoretical and policy-making organs of the PCT. The November 1976 congress of the Party accepted the sincerity of the self-criticisms of numerous officials purged in 1971–2, and approved their re-integration at all levels of the Party and administration.

In the succession crisis following Ngouabi's assassination, neither the Republic's, nor the Party's constitution was adhered to. Alphonse Mouissou-Poaty (later rewarded with a cabinet seat) the President of the National Assembly and legitimate successor was shunted aside in favour of Yhombi-Opango. The latter emerged at the head of an inner informal elite called the Comité Militaire du Parti, made up of 11 military officers.[24]

Comité Militaire du Parti

Brigadier Yoachim Yhombi-Opango (President), Major Denis Sassou N'Guesso (First Vice-president), Major Louis Sylvain Goma (Second Vice-president), Major Felix Ebacka, Major François Xavier Katali, Major Pascal Bima, Major Marcel M'bia, Lt. Col. Raymond N'Gollo, Captain Nicholas Okongo, Captain Martin Siba and Lieutenant Pierre Anga.

On 8 February 1979, in a major shift in the balance of power in the party

Yhombi-Opango was purged in favour of N'Guesso. Two days later the Comité Militaire du Parti was disbanded. The latter development signified the ascendance of the civilian wing of the party over the military faction, albeit under the leadership of N'Guesso.

GOVERNMENT

The constitution

The current constitution of Congo is a brief 24-article Fundamental Law promulgated by General Yhombi-Opango on 5 April 1977, shortly after he succeeded the slain Colonel Marien Ngouabi in a manner contrary to the constitution then in force.[25]

The Fundamental Law is a temporary document pending the promulgation of a new constitution. The organs specifically dissolved by the Law include the National Assembly, the Council of the State and the local (i.e. regional, district and commune) assemblies.

Following the purge of Yhombi-Opango on 8 February 1979, his successor, Colonel N'Guesso, pledged a return to constitutional normality.

The executive

During the two-year Yhombi-Opango internegnum Congo had a dual exucutive composed of a Prime Minister in charge of the daily governance of the country, and a President who was also the key power-wielder. Following Yhombi-Opango's eclipse in February 1979, Colonel N'Guesso temporarily assumed both executive roles.

The Cabinet

The Cabinet includes 17 ministers (see Table 8.1) of whom four are military officers. The composition of the cabinet in April 1979 was as follows:

TABLE 8.1 Members of the Cabinet of the Congo

Colonel Louis Sylvain Goma	Prime Minister
Mr Pierre Nze*	Minister of Foreign Affairs and Co-operation
Major Francois Xavier Kitali*	Minister of the Interior

TABLE 8.1 (*Continued*)

Captain Florent Tsiba*	Minister of Information, Post and Telecommunications
Mr Henri Lopes	Minister of Finance
Mr Victor Tamba-Tamba	Minister of Labour and Justice and Keeper of Seals
Mr Moundele Ngolo	Minister of Land Improvement, Construction and Housing
Mr Jean Babtiste Taty-Loutard	Minister of Culture, Arts, Sports and Scientific Research
Mr Antoine Ndinga Oba	Minister of National Education
Mr Gabriel Oba Apounou	Minister for Youth
Mr Hilaire Mounthault	Minister of Transport and Civil Aviation
Mr Rodolphe Adada	Minister of Mines and Energy
Mr Marius Mouambenga	Minister of Industry and Tourism
Mr Jean Itadi	Minister of Rural Economy
Mr Pierre Moussa	Minister of Planning
Mr Joseph Elenga Ngaporo	Minister of Trade
Mr Pierre Daniel Boussoukou Boumba	Minister of Health and Social Affairs

* Denotes member of the Political Bureau of the Congolese Labour Party.
Note: President Colonel Denis Sassou N'Guesso* also holds the portfolio of Minister of Defence.

The legislature

The current Fundamental Law of 5 April 1977 abrogated the 1973 constitution and, pending a promised new basic law, dissolved the former 115-member National Assembly.

Local government

Congo is divided into nine regions plus the capital district of Brazzaville, and these divisions in turn are subdivided into districts and communes. The nine districts and their administrative headquarters are:

Region	Headquarters
Kouilou	Pointe Noire
Niari	Loubomo
Lékoumou	Sibiti
Bouenza	Madingou
Pool	Kinkala
Cuvctte	Owando
Plateaux	Djambala
Sangha	Ouesso
Likouala	Impfondo

All the provisions of the 1973 constitution with respect to elected local (regional) executive councils under political commissars were abolished with the assassination of President Ngouabi in 1977. In the interim the Fundamental Law provides for administrative decrees from the centre, including the power to appoint local administrative bodies.

OPPOSITION GROUPS

There are an inordinate number of sources of opposition to the regime in Brazzaville. Most opposition stems from within the armed forces (involving both personal ambitions and ideological and ethnic divisions) or the civil service (which is mostly southern and conservative), and is linked with exile groups, civilian or military (ideological or ethnic), in Zaire and Europe. These groups may be aided by foreign intelligence services seeking discreetly to topple the Marxist regime in Brazzaville. In the countryside, as has been evidenced by past experience, many groups will support any anti-Brazzaville attack by sheltering the assaulting force (prior to and after the attempt) and by not reporting its existence. This tacit support is at times based on ethnic affinity alone, as when the 'Maoist' Ange Diawara remained at large in the Brazzaville area for over a year after his 1972 attempted coup, despite a massive dragnet and manhunt.

There are also several exiled opposition 'parties' – though these tend to be quite small. One of the more recently established is the Democratic Front for Congolese Resistance (FDRCO), set up in November 1976 in Paris by former National Assembly Vice-president Alois Moudileno-Massengo.

MASS ORGANISATIONS

Trade unions

Until the 1963 upheaval, Congo's union movement was divided into three main branches (as in much of francophone Africa), either formally or informally affiliated with the French Socialist, Communist or Catholic union federations.[26] The Catholic had become the most powerful union in Congo, with a membership of around 40 per cent of the country's organised labour. Organised labour, however, has never encompassed a large percentage of Congo's wage-earners, and has had its power further diluted by the existence in the southern urban centres of large numbers of unemployed youth. The latter have stolen much of labour's political thunder, with the unions increasingly concerned with protecting their members' privileges and demanding higher wages and benefits.

Following the collapse of Youlou's regime – which labour had done much to bring about – the trade-union movement was centralised into one national federation, the Confédération Syndicale Congolaise (CSC). Progressively the Catholic union leaders, who resisted the centralisation, were deprived of whatever role they played in the National Assembly or the administration, and their union was forcibly merged with the CSC. Within the latter the top offices were allocated to leaders of the other former Congolese unions.

Since the revolution, organised labour has been tightly controlled by every regime in power in Brazzaville, though this has not prevented the eruption of periodic confrontations with the government over wages and conditions of work. In most instances the government has strongly retaliated against these manifestations of labour autonomy (demonstrations or strikes), by declaring the strikes illegal and contrary to proper Marxist-Leninist behaviour, dispersing them with units of the armed forces and imprisoning their leaders,[27] though ultimately (at a later date) satisfying many of the demands that had caused the upheaval. The unions are likewise alternating between pressures for greater radicalisation (and wider purges of lukewarm supporters of the revolution) and a preoccupation with the defence and expansion of their privileged class interests.

Youth

Since up to 60 per cent of Congo's population is below the age of sixteen, youth plays a vital political role in Congo. This is especially so in light of the general militancy and the high rates of unemployment among youth in the country's urban areas. Youth played a pivotal role in the disturbances that brought about the collapse of the Youlou regime in 1963, and, until its bloody confrontation with Colonel Ngouabi's armed forces in 1968, very much dictated the pace of political radicalisation in Congo.

Following the rise to power of Ngouabi, the unruly and highly autonomous JMNR formations were disbanded. Some elements were dispersed, others integrated into the armed forces (where they later constituted a leftist threat to Ngouabi), while the rump was restructured under the very close control of Ngouabi as the Union de la Jeunesse

Socialiste Congolaise (UJSC). It has been observed that despite the fettering of youth to the party and regime, Ngouabi has often acted as if youth and the UJSC has been his main constituency. The UJSC has remained the regime's main challenge and irritant from the Left, constantly prodding for a further radicalisation in Congo, though Ngouabi was able to keep it from linking up with student unions, playing off one against the other. Yhombi-Opango was less successful, however, since he had always been the reactionary *bête noire* of youth, accused both of counter-revolutionary tendencies and of 'non-Socialist' personal tastes.

RELIGION AND EDUCATION

Religion

Slightly more than half the Congolese population is animist, the rest being Christian or professing a number of Messianic or syncretic faiths. Of the Christian population two-thirds are Catholic. Less than 1 per cent is Moslem, nearly all these being alien urban Africans. The indigenous faiths include Matsouanism, Lassyism and Kimbanguism. The Catholic Missionary effort was initiated by the Portuguese at Laongo in 1663, though it was not until around 1880 that a serious effort was mounted. The Protestant effort is of much more recent vintage (around 1909), though it was crowned with considerable success. Many of the Protestant missions have been staffed by Scandinavians using local dialects (rather than French), both in their schools and in evangelical work.

Following Youlou's overthrow in 1963, a serious rift developed between the more militant successor regime of Massemba-Debat and the Church. The Catholic union leaders – at the forefront of the union youth demonstrations that led to Youlou's collapse – were harassed, forced abroad or arrested, and their unions dissolved. In 1965 evangelical activities were sharply curtailed when all mission schools were nationalised, sparking an exodus of missionary teaching staff from the country.[28] Simultaneously a Congolese was consecrated Archbishop of Brazzaville. In contrast, the Protestant missionaries had fewer difficulties in adjusting to the new ideology in Brazzaville, were better tolerated by the regime and gained converts from among the Catholic elites.

Relations between the government and the Catholic Church took a sudden plunge downwards in 1977, when, after Ngouabi's assassination, Cardinal Emile Biayende was kidnapped by Ngouabi's relations and murdered on the doubtful grounds of his having being involved in the conspiracy. Colonel Yhombi-Opango attempted to soothe the situation.

Education

Congo's educational system is one of Africa's most developed and encompasses nearly 80 per·cent of the country's children of primary-school age. There are regional disparties between the south (which is heavily serviced with schools) and the centre and north, where schooling drops off, and between primary schooling (six to sixteen years of age), where compulsory universal attendance is aimed at, and secondary schooling, which encompasses less than 20 per cent of children aged between sixteen and twenty. Higher education is provided locally through the Université de Brazzaville, created in 1973 following the nationalisation and expansion of an existing regional centre for higher education servicing francophone equatorial Africa, and abroad. The local university has some 2600 students, with roughly an equal number of students abroad, in both Eastern and Western institutions. Provisional figures for the student population in the 1977–8 school year are:

	Schools	Pupils
Primary	1,051	452,000
Secondary	85	93,000
Technical	36	5,500
University	1	2,600

Since 1965 all missionary schools are nationalised, though missions have been allowed to retain control over schools training priests and other religious staff. Students are highly politicised and militant, and have provided a continuous pressure upon all governments for the radicalisation of society. Their union, the Union Générale des Élèves et Étudiants Congolaise was founded in 1965 out of a merger of several student groups in order to mobilise support behind the revolutionary regime. It has as often as not called for strikes, demonstrations and resistance to the government (as in 1968, 1971, 1973, and so on) on the grounds that the government has been too docile with expatriate interests and lacking in revolutionary fervour. The regime, in cracking sharply at these manifestations of opposition, has tended to accuse the students of 'Leftist infantilism' and the like.

THE ECONOMY

The Congolese economy is characterised by a weak agricultural sector unable to feed both itself and the large urban masses, a largely extractive productive sector until recently under expatriate control, and a steadily growing bureaucracy and inefficient State sector consuming ever-larger percentages of the national budget.[29] Investment capital has practically dried up with the declaration of a People's Republic, and the crassly exploitative approach of existing foreign combines (rushing to amortise investments prior to anticipated nationalisation) has led to poor conservation policies (in the timber sector), little reinvestment in the economy, and high rates of capital repatriation.

TABLE 8.2 The Congo: major exports, 1973–6 (millions of SDRs)[a]

	1973	1974	1975	1976
Petroleum	35·1	133·7	108·8	112·4
Potash	11·8	20·8	28·2	20·5
Timber	31·5	31·3	27·5	23·4
Sugar	5·0	10·3	5·1	4·3
Other	19·1	20·0	13·6	15·4

[a] Special Drawing Rights (SDRs) issued by the International Monetary Fund are substitutes for gold in international payments.

With the sole exception of 1974, when unanticipated windfall profits from oil exports were not matched by massive imports, Congo's balance of trade has been in deficit (see Table 8.2 and 8.3, though budgets have usually been in equilibrium (see Table 8.4). A small State sector had been erected during Massemba-Debat's presidency, but the most profitable industries were left in expatriate hands, and foreign development capital (both private and public) was constantly sought after from all nations and given preferential terms.[30] Even Ngouabi, despite the radicalisation of rhetoric under his aegis, tolerated such a dual posture. As *West Africa* commented on the occasion of his assassination, he 'established the appearance of a socialist order, led by the PCT, but left the running of the economy to French expatriate capital and proprietors'.[31] Such inconsistencies between a thoroughly neocolonial economy and a political system with all the outward trappings and rhetoric of a Marxist state are part of the Congolese paradox.[32] Whether or not this reflects the development in Brazzaville of 'a culture of the word . . . in which

TABLE 8.3 The Congo: imports/exports, 1963–76 (CFA francs million)

	Imports	Exports	Balance of trade	Exports as % of imports
1963	15,269	10,295	− 4,974	67·4
1964	16,006	11,702	− 4,304	73·1
1965	15,974	11,518	− 4,456	72·1
1966	17,188	10,659	− 6,529	62·0
1967	20,239	11,730	− 8,509	57·9
1968	20,614	12,189	− 8,425	59·1
1969	20,292	11,383	− 8,909	56·1
1970	15,910	8,564	− 7,346	53·8
1971	21,910	10,960	− 10,950	50·0
1972	22,608	13,211	− 9,397	58·4
1973	27,730	19,614	− 8,116	70·7
1974	59,189	63,511	+ 4,322	107·3
1975	69,050	49,470	− 19,580	71·6
1976	78,560	50,469	− 28,091	64·2

TABLE 8.4: The Congo: budgets, 1960–78

Year	CFA francs thousand million
1960	4·9
1961	6·4
1962	8·0
1963	8·7
1964	9·2
1965	10·5
1966	12·1
1967	13·2
1968	13·2
1969	15·9
1970	18·1
1971	19·5
1972	21·8
1973	24·7
1974	43·8
1975	70·0
1976	52·4
1977	52·0
1978	61·4

spoken words seem all powerful',[33] irrespective of deeds, or the dichotomy between the desirable and the achievable, it was only in 1974 that Congolese socialism was able to forge ahead. For until then, despite official rhetoric about 'the experiment which will be set down in the history of political parties of the world',[34] the State sector – the 'motor' of the revolution – was so minute as to be irrelevant,[35] and Congolese socialism more an article of faith than reality.

The radicalisation of the revolution became possible through the unanticipated quadrupling of oil profits in 1974 – and the prospects of continued fiscal windfalls. In the bout of nationalisation that followed, a large number of enterprises were taken over, including banking, insurance and petroleum-distribution concerns, though the most profitable sectors were still left in expatriate hands. The euphoria of 1974 was dashed within a year – and an ambitious development plan, budget and import splurge were wrecked – when difficulties hit both Congo's phosphate industry and its petroleum industry, the chief sources of the country's riches. The former was to close down in 1977, when it was abandoned after disastrous floodings of the mines, while the latter brought in reduced earnings and the threat of very fast depletion of resources.[36]

Not only have these developments foreclosed the socialist option: it has also left Brazzaville saddled with some sixty-odd State enterprises that, as of May 1978, owed the Treasury 11,000 million CFA francs in back taxes and customs duties[37] and not only could not be expected to cover their debts but also were perennially in the red owing to mismanagement bordering on the criminal.[38] A good example is provided by the Sugar industry, nationalised in 1970, which should have been producing annual net profits of 2000 million CFA, but was instead bringing in deficits of 1,000 million CFA per year.[39] The assumption of power by Yhombi-Opango brought about a de-emphasisation in radical rhetoric and a cooling off of the revolutionary phase. Yhombi-Opango went out of his way to reassure France of Congo's goodwill, and French private capital of its need to become 'involved in the development of this country which certain foreigners regard as their second homeland'.[40] The problem of the spiralling deficits of the State sector and corruption at their top has been handled in a highly capitalist way: through the edict that all ministers report monthly to the PCT with income graphs of all industries and department branches under their authority.[41]

FOREIGN AFFAIRS

The guiding principle of Congo's foreign relations is ideological militancy and support for Third World and Eastern causes coupled with acute pragmatism and sensitivity to the core interests of France and the EEC upon whom she still relies economically. With the overthrow of the arch-conservative and xenophobic regime of Youlou, Congo's relations dramatically expanded to include most countries of the world. Close relations were established especially with the USSR (which helped to build a Party school) and Cuba[42] (which trained a section of Congo's paramilitary forces), as well as with China and North Korea.

Relations with other countries suffered accordingly. In 1967 Congo broke off relations with Taiwan, South Vietnam and South Korea, and in 1965 a crisis with the United States led to the withdrawal of the US Embassy. Later that year Congo broke with the United Kingdom (over Rhodesia's UDI), and in 1972, reflecting growing Arab influence in the continent, with Israel. Simultaneously with this diplomatic reorientation, constant efforts have been made to avoid unduly antagonising France or public and private risk capital. Over 8000 French citizens remain in Congo, active in all spheres of the economy, and, ideological differences notwithstanding, Franco-Congolese relations are close and likely to remain so – short of a decision by Congo to forgo all French aid. Policy pronouncements or UN speeches may denounce 'international capitalism' or neocolonialism but rarely attack France by name. And, though diplomatic relations with the United States were severed in 1965 (after the United States had complained of the constant harassment of its staff by youth militants), American 'capitalists and financiers' could still obtain visas for trips to Brazzaville.[43] (Relations were restored in 1977 by Yhombi-Opango.)

Relations with other countries in the Union Douanière et Économique de l'Afrique Centrale (Cameroun, Gabon, Chad and the Central African Empire) have been good, and, despite a great deal of friction and animosity during 1963–7, likewise with Zaire. Close relations exist in particular with Angola, which has in the past received arms and material through Pointe Noire.

BIOGRAPHIES

Colonel Denis Sassou N'Guesso, President of the People's Republic of the Congo, Minister of Defence, Chairman of the Political Bureau and

President of the Central Committee of the PCT.

No biographical data are available at the time of going to press.

Colonel Louis Sylvain Goma, Prime Minister of the People's Republic of the Congo. Born in Pointe Noire on 28 June 1941 and passed out of France's St Cyr, Goma was appointed commander of the Engineer Corps in 1966. Colonel Ngouabi's faithful ally since then, Goma was appointed Chief of Staff after Ngouabi's coup d'état in August 1968. He joined the government in 1970, first as Secretary of State for Defence, and later as Minister of Public Works and Transport. A year later he also assumed duties for Civil Aviation and became a member of the PCT Political Bureau. Promoted to Major in 1973, Goma's dedication to the Revolution and loyalty to Ngoubai brought about his appointment to the Revolutionary General Staff in December 1975 (when the Party organs were dissolved) and, also as Ngouabi's Prime Minister. After Ngouabi's assassination he retained the premiership, membership of the PCT Political Bureau and the post of the First Vice-President of the Comité Militaire du Parti. Following the purge of Yhombi-Opango on 8 February 1979, Goma lost the Premiership to N'Guesso, though, the former was retained in the interim cabinet as Minister of Planning. He again became Prime Minister on 4 April 1979, after the extraordinary congress of the PCT.

BASIC FACTS ABOUT THE CONGO

Official name: People's Republic of the Congo (Republique Populaire du Congo).

Area: 342,000 sq. km. (130,000 sq. miles).

Population (1975 est.): 1,320,000, increasing at 2·4 per cent per annum.

Population density (1975 est.): 3·8 per sq. km.

Population age distribution: 42 per cent of the population is below the age of 15.

Population distribution (1974): 33 per cent urban; 67 per cent rural.

Official language: French.

Membership of the PCT: 1423.

Administrative division: nine districts and the capital district Brazzaville.

Ethnic distribution: 77 ethnic groups, falling into some 15 cultural groupings, the largest of which are the Kongo (45 per cent of the population), Téké (20 per cent), Kouyou-Mbochi (15 per cent) and Sangha (7 per cent).

Population of major towns (1974 est.): Brazzaville, 302,000; Pointe Noire, 141,740; Kayes, 38,000; Loubomo, 28,000.

Main natural resources: limestone, petroleum, potassium, timber, iron.

Foreign trade (1976) in millions of CFA francs: imports, 78,560; exports, 50,469; balance of Trade, − 28,091; Coverage imports/exports, 64·2 per cent.

Currency: the CFA franc (pegged at 0·02 French franc).

Main trading partners: France, FRG, Netherlands, Benelux, USA.

State budget (1977): 61,404 million CFA francs.

Per capita income (1972): $200.

Per capita GNP (1974 World Bank est.): $390.

Gross domestic product (1971): primary sector, 13 per cent; secondary sector, 24 per cent; tertiary sector, 53 per cent.

Rail network: 517 km., the most important sections of which connect Brazzaville with Pointe Noire on the Atlantic coast.

Road network: 4500 miles of roads and 3770 miles of trails and tracks with only 350 km. of paved roads, mostly in the southern section of the country. Riverain transport is of paramount importance in Congo.

Education (1977): education level 49 per cent, with over 450,000 schoolchildren attending primary schools.

Universities: 1, with 2700 students (1977).

Foreign relations: diplomatic relations with over 46 countries; 18 diplomatic missions residing in Brazzaville; member of the UN, OAU, the French Community, and the UDEAC.

NOTES

1. For instance, the gorge of the Kouilou River has been tapped for hydroelectric power.
2. At Hollé. The extensive mines, developed with French capital, were disastrously flooded in 1976 and subsequently abandoned as uneconomical.
3. See especially M. Sinda, *Le Messianisme Congolaise* (1971); E. Andersson, *Messianic Popular Movements in the Lower Congo* (New York: W. S. Heinman, 1958); J. M. Janzen, 'Kongo Religious Renewal: Iconoclastic and Iconorthostic', *Canadian Journal of African Studies*, Spring 1971.
4. Including two coups (1963, 1968), several mercenary assaults from abroad (including one in 1978) and around fifteen commando assaults, plots and attempted putsches, culminating in the assassination of President Ngouabi in 1977.
5. J. A. Ballard, 'Four Equatorial States', in G. Carter (ed.), *National Unity and Regionalism in Eight African States* (1966); F. Constantin, 'Foulbert Youlou 1917–1972', *Revue Française d'Études Politiques Africaines*, June

1972; 'Brazzaville: Ten Years of Revolution', *West Africa*, 13 and 20 Aug 1973.

6. See J. M. Wagret, *Histoire et Sociologie Politiques de la République du Congo-Brazzaville* (1964); R. Devauges, *Le Chomage à Brazzaville* (1959).

7. S. Amin and C. Coquery-Vidrovitch, *Histoire Économique du Congo 1880–1968* (1969); C. Coquery-Vidrovitch, *Le Congo au Temps du Grandes Compagnies Concessionaires* (1974); P. P. Rey, *Colonialisme, Neocolonialisme et Transition au Capitalisme* (1971).

8. Indeed, Youlou proposed to turn over the north to the Central African Republic as part of his dream to revive the precolonial southern Bakongo empire on both sides of the Congo River.

9. E. Terray, 'Les Révolutions Congolaise et Dahoméenne', *Revue Française de Science Politique*, Oct 1964.

10. For biographical outlines, see V. Thompson and R. Adloff, *Historical Dictionary of the People's Republic of the Congo* (1974).

11. S. Decalo, 'Revolutionary Rhetoric and Army Cliques in Congo/Brazzaville', in *Coups and Army Rule in Africa* (1977); P. Decraene, 'Huit Années d'Histoire Congolaise, ou l'Irresistible Ascension des Militaires à Brazzaville', *Revue Française de Sciences Politiques Africaines*, Dec 1974; 'Brazzaville Socialism is Mostly Talk', *New York Times*, 25 Oct 1969; and J. M. Lee, 'Clan Loyalities and Socialist Doctrine in the People's Republic of the Congo', *World Today*, Jan 1971, pp. 40–6.

12. *Le Monde*, 26 Mar 1970.

13. P. Bonnafé, 'Une Classe d'Age Politique: la JMNR de la République du Congo-Brazzaville', *Cahiers d'Études Africaines*, III, no. 13 (1968) 327–67.

14. M. Ngouabi, *Vers la Construction d'une Société Socialiste en Afrique* (1975).

15. 'Congo', in *Africa Contemporary Record, 1976–77* (1977).

16. *West Africa*, 9 Apr 1973. See also the issue for 13 Feb 1971.

17. 'Congo', in *Africa Contemporary Record, 1976–77*, p. B497.

18. At the 20 Nov 1976 PCT congress, Ngouabi stated that 'corruption and embezzlement have reached disquieting proportions' (ibid., p. B493), while on 4 Apr 1977 *West Africa* noted that 'corruption in the PCT and state enterprises [is] throttling all progress'. Even before the expansion of the State sector, the civil service had expanded tremendously, from 3300 employees in 1960 to 21,000 in 1972, a 636 per cent increase. See *West Africa*, 19 Apr 1976.

19. *Le Monde*, 18 Dec 1971, and *New York Times*, 17 July 1972.

20. *West Africa*, 17 Nov 1975. See also S. Decalo, 'Ideological Rhetoric and Scientific Socialism in Two Peoples' Republics: Benin and Congo/B', in C. Rosberg and T. Callaghy (eds), *African Socialism in Subsaharan Africa* (Berkeley, Calif.: Institute of International Studies, 1979).

21. 'Congo', in *Africa Contemporary Record, 1975–76* (1976) p. B472.

22. See *Jeune Afrique*, 11 Mar 1972; *Afrique Nouvelle*, 8 Dec 1971; and *Africa Research Bulletin*, Dec 1971.

23. See A. H. House, 'Brazzaville: Revolution or Rhetoric?', *Africa Report*, Apr 1971.

24. 'Congo: Plus ça Change . . .', *Africa*, no. 78 (Feb 1978).

25. The latter was Congo's third. See 'Les Élections du 24 Juin et la Nouvelle Constitution', *Afrique Contemporaine*, no. 68 (July–Aug 1973), and

'Assassinat de Chef de l'État et Mise en Place de Nouvelles Institutions', *Afrique Contemporaine*, no. 91 (May–June 1977).
26. See the section on labour in Thompson and Adloff, *Historical Dictionary of the People's Republic of the Congo* (1974).
27. Several of whom are members of the PCT Central Committee and whose participation in a strike (such as that of March 1976) is regarded as treasonous behaviour.
28. In 1973 total religious staff in Congo was 227 priests in nineteen missions. For the Catholic Church in Congo, see especially S. Makosso, 'L'Église Catholique et l'État au Congo', *Afrique Contemporaine*, Nov–Dec 1976.
29. See 'Congo/Brazzaville', in International Monetary Fund, *Surveys of African Economics*, vol. I (Washington, DC: 1968) pp. 228–73, and 'République Populaire du Congo', in the latest annual edition of *Europe-Outremer*.
30. See, for example, *Le Monde*, 26 Mar 1970.
31. *West Africa*, 28 Mar 1977.
32. 'Congo Finds it Can't Exist on Marxism', *Los Angeles Times*, 20 July 1977.
33. P. Erny, 'Parole et Travail Chez les Jeunes d'Afrique Centrale', *Project*, Sep–Oct 1966.
34. *Le Moniteur Africain du Commerce et de l'Industrie*, 10 Aug 1972.
35. See Decalo, in Rosberg, *African Socialism*.
36. 'Congo', in *Africa Contemporary Record, 1976–77*, p. B497.
37. *Marchés Tropicaux et Méditerranéens*, 5 May 1978.
38. *West Africa*, 2 Jan 1978. In the Nov 1976 speech, Ngouabi noted that 'corruption and embezzlement have reached disquieting proportions' in the parastatal sector, including when it had been administered by the military, previously referred to as 'a sink of corruption'.
39. *Le Monde*, 30 Apr 1975.
40. *Africa Research Bulletin*, Economic Series, May 1977. See also *West Africa*, 9 May 1977.
41. 'Self-criticism in Congo', *West Africa*, 14 Nov 1977.
42. There are currently an estimated 300 Cuban military advisers and 150 civilian technicians in Brazzaville (*West Africa*, 2 Jan 1978).
43. Interview at the Congolese Mission to the UN Apr 1972.

BIBLIOGRAPHY

Amin, S. and Coquery-Vidrovitch, C., *Histoire Économique du Congo, 1880–1968* (Paris: Éditions Anthropos, 1969).
Andersson, E., *Messianic Popular Movements in the Lower Congo* (New York: W. S. Heinmann, 1958).
Area Handbook for the People's Republic of the Congo (Washington, DC: US Government Printing Office, 1973).
'Assassinat de Chef de l'État et Mise en place de Nouvelles Institutions', *Afrique Contemporaine*, no. 91 (May–June 1977).
Balandier, G., *Sociologie des Brazzaville Noires* (Paris: Librairie Colin, 1955).
Ballard, J. A., 'Four Equatorial States', in G. Carter (ed.), *National Unity and*

Regionalism in Eight African States (Ithaca, NY: Cornell University Press, 1966).

Bertrand, H., *Le Congo: Formation Sociale et Mode de Developpement Economique* (Paris: Maspero, 1975).

'Bilan Économique du Congo-Brazzaville', *Europe—France Outremer*, XLIV, no. 455 (Dec 1967) 35–60.

Bonnafé, P., 'Une Classe d'Age Politique: la JMNR de la République du Congo-Brazzaville', *Cahiers d'Études Africaines*, III, no. 13 (1968) 327–67.

'Brazzaville: Sept Ans après les 'Trois Glorieuses', *Afrique-Asie*, no. 21 (30 Aug 1970) 31–46.

'Brazzaville Socialism is Mostly Talk', *New York Times*, 25 Oct 1969.

'Brazzaville: Ten Years of Revolution', *West Africa*, 13 Aug 1973, p. 1103; 20 Aug 1973, p. 1160–1.

Comte, G., 'Le Congo-Brazzaville en Proie à la Revolution', *Le Monde*, 26 Mar 1970 and 2 Apr 1970.

——, 'Congo/B L'Embarras Française', *Revue Française d'Études Politiques Africaines*, June 1970, pp. 11–14.

'Congo: After Diawara', *Africa Confidential*, 27 Apr 1973.

'Congo Finds it Can't Exist on Marxism', *Los Angeles Times*, 20 July 1977.

'Congo: Plus ça Change . . .', *Africa*, no. 78 (Feb 1978) 54–5.

'Congo-Brazza: An V de la Revolution', *Jeune Afrique*, 28 July 1968.

'Congo', in *Africa Contemporary Record* (London, Rex Collings, annual).

'Congo/Brazzaville', in International Monetary Fund, *Surveys of African Economies*, vol. I (Washington, DC: 1968) pp. 228–73.

'Congo/B: Une "Revolution" Inquiéte et Permanente', *Revue Française d'Études Politiques Africaines*, Dec 1969, pp. 13–16.

Constantin, F., 'Foulbert Youlou 1917–1972', *Revue Française d'Études Politiques Africaines*, June 1972.

Coquery-Vidrovitch, C., *Le Congo au Temps des Grandes Companies Concessionnaires 1898–1930* (Paris: Mouton, 1972).

Croce-Spinelli, M., *Les Enfants de Poto-Poto* (Paris: B. Grasset, 1967).

Decalo, S., 'Revolutionary Rhetoric and Army Cliques in Congo/Brazzaville', in *Coups and Army Rule in Africa*, (New Haven, Conn.: Yale University Press, 1976) pp. 123–72.

——, 'Ideological Rhetoric and Scientific Socialism in Two Peoples' Republics: Benin and Congo/B', in C. Rosberg and T. Callaghy (eds), *African Socialism in Subsaharan Africa* (Berkeley, Calif.: Institute of International Studies, 1979).

Decraene, P., 'Huit Années d'Histoire Congolaise', *Revue Française d'Études Politiques Africaines*, Dec 1974, pp. 61–80.

Devauges, R., *Le Chômage à Brazzaville: Étude Sociologique* (Paris: Office de la Recherche Scientifique et Technique Outre Mer, 1959).

Dubula, S., 'The Congo/B Way to Socialism', *African Communist*, no. 67 (1976) pp. 43–55.

'Les Élections du 24 Juin et la Nouvelle Constitution', *Afrique Contemporaine*, no. 68 (July–Aug 1973).

Emy, P., 'Parole et Travail Chez les Jeunes d'Afrique Centrale', *Project*, Sep–Oct 1966.

Gauze, R., *The Politics of Congo-Brazzaville* (Stanford, Calif.: Hoover Institution Press, 1974).

Guerivière, J., 'Socialisme Scientifique contre Gauche Anarchiste', *Revue Française d'Etudes politiques Africaines*, Mar 1973, pp. 21–3.

House, A. H., 'Brazzaville: Revolution or Rhetoric?', *Africa Report*, Apr 1971, pp. 18–21.

Janzen, J. M., 'Kongo Religious Renewal: Iconoclastic and Iconorsthic', *Canadian Journal of African Studies*, Spring 1971.

Lacroix, J. L., 'Evolution, de l'Économie et Transformations des Structures au Congo depuis 1960', *Revue Française d'Études Politiques Africaines*, Oct 1970, pp. 48–68.

Lee, J. M., 'Clan Loyalties and Socialist Doctrines in the P. R. of the Congo', *World Today*, Jan 1971, pp. 40–6.

Makosso, S., 'L'Église Catholique et l'État au Congo', *Afrique Contemporaine*, Nov–Dec 1976.

Mberuba, J. M., *La Phase Révolutionnaire au Congo-Brazzaville apres la Chute du Youlou*, Mémoire DES (Sci. pol.) (Paris, 1973).

Ngouabi, M., *Rectifions Notre Style de Travail* (Brazzaville: Éditions du Comité Central du PCT, 1974).

——, *Vers la Construction d'une Société Socialiste en Afrique* (Paris: Presence Africaine, 1975).

Obenga, T., *La Cuvette Congolaise, les Hommes et les Structures* (Paris: Présence Africaine, 1976).

La République du Congo, Notes et Études Documentaires, no. 2732 (Le Documentation Française, 17 Dec 1970).

Rey, P., *Colonialisme, Neo-colonialisme et Transition au Capitalisme: Exemple de la Comilog, Congo/B* (Paris: Mespero, 1971).

'Self-criticism in Congo', *West Africa*, 14 Nov 1977.

Shundeyev, V., 'The New Way in Congo People's Republic', *African Communist* no. 59 (1974) pp. 86–96.

Sinda, M., *Le Messianisme Congolais* (Paris: Payot, 1972).

Sirren, P., 'Les Industries de Brazzaville', *Cahiers d'Outre Mer*, no. 99 (July–Sep. 1972) 277–306.

Teillac, J., and Robert, H., 'Le Congo: Est-il Socialiste?' *Le Monde Diplomatique*, Apr 1973.

Terray, E., 'Les Révolutions Congolaise et Dahoméenne de 1963, Essai d'Interpretation', *Revue Française de Science Politique*, XIV, no. 5 (Oct 1964) pp. 917–42.

Thomas, L. V., 'Le Socialisme Congolais', *Revue Française d'Études Politique Africaines*, Nov 1966.

Thompson, V. and Adloff, R., *Historical Dictionary of the People's Republic of the Congo* (Metuchen, NJ: Scarecrow Press, 1975).

Wagret, J. M., *Histoire et Sociologie Politiques de la République du Congo-Brazzaville* (Paris: Pichon and Durand-Auzias, 1963).

Woungly-Massaga, *La Révolution au Congo, Contribution à l'Étude des Problemes Politiques d'Afrique Centrale* (Paris: Maspero, 1974).

Glossary

assimilado	African negro registered as a Portuguese citizen (Angola)
kulak	rich peasant
mestiço	person of mixed European and negro ancestry (Angola)
okruz	district (Bulgaria).
qu.	See Table 7.1, notes
Realpolitik	politics which deal solely in terms of national interests and the realities of the situation, being neither doctrinaire nor idealistic and not concerned with ethics.
shi	urban municipality
xian	county (China)
xiang	township (China)
yuan renminbi	Chinese currency unit
zhen	market town (China)

Index